Disclaimer

This book contains numerous stories and examples that are based on real people and situations that the author has dealt with during his career. To protect the privacy of individuals, all names and other potentially identifying information, including numbers, have been changed. However, the nature of the descriptions remains true to the actual occurrences.

The tax code includes many quirks and nuances. This book offers general information for a variety of taxpayers and situations, is not all-inclusive, and might not apply to your specific situation. Tax laws and interpretations of those laws can change at any time. Any tax advice contained in this book is not intended or written to be used, and cannot be used, for the purpose of avoiding penalties under the Internal Revenue Code or for promoting, marketing, or recommending to another party any matters addressed herein. The information contained herein is not a substitute for legal, tax, investment, or other professional advice specific to your situation; nor should it be construed as advice or relied upon in such a manner. Always consult a Certified Public Accountant (CPA), attorney, or other professional tax advisor before implementing any tax strategy or making other significant financial decisions. The author shall not be liable for any loss or damages that may arise from reliance on information contained in this book and disclaims any accuracy of the text or misuse or misunderstanding on the part of any reader; nor is the author liable for the positions taken by the reader in particular situations.

The Foundation

The tax code is extremely complex. It is notoriously long and downright unpleasant to read. Most people would rather pretend it doesn't exist. Completely ignoring it or thwarting it, however, can lead to financial ruin. Even casual ignorance of it can lead to significantly fewer dollars in your bank account. It doesn't have to be that way.

The full focus and purpose of this book is to help you pull your head out of the sand and face the reality that taxes have a major impact on your life. More importantly, the goal of this book is to help you realize that *you can have a significant impact on your taxes.*

Part I is the essential foundation for achieving that goal. If you do nothing more with this book than read and understand the chapters of Part I, you will be so much further ahead in your efforts to minimize your taxes than the majority of the population.

I have made these foundational principles simple, straightforward, and easy to understand. If you study the five chapters of this first part you will never regret it. Then, as you move on to the rest of the book, you will be fully equipped to seize the valuable strategies it has to offer.

The Tax Code Demystified

Knowledge Is Power

I often remember a conversation I had with an acquaintance. He was telling me about the "smart" things he had done to reduce his taxes. His business had been successful that year, so in December he purchased several pieces of equipment that he didn't really need in order to offset his income. With a mischievous grin, he said, "It's a deduction, right?"

Right—it is a deduction (although that too is questionable). But as I spoke with him, it became clear that he thought a deduction of $3,000 meant he would pay $3,000 less in taxes. He thought he had just stiffed the government and gotten that equipment for free (because he spent $3,000 but saved $3,000 in taxes by doing so). He didn't understand how a deduction actually works. In reality, he saved about $900 in taxes. But because he spent $3,000 on equipment he didn't need, he ended up wasting $2,100. Most people dislike paying taxes, but you have to *really* hate giving the government money in order to waste $2,100 just to keep them from getting $900!

In reality, this man did not intend to waste the $2,100; he just misunderstood the meaning of the word "deduction." I see this type of misunderstanding far too often; when people fail to grasp the true effects of a particular tax strategy on their return, they often end up making costly mistakes. This chapter will help solidify your understanding of the main components of your own tax return and the key terminology that is involved. That understanding will then help you recognize to what extent different strategies will (or won't) help you reduce your taxes—helping you avoid similarly costly mistakes.

The Tax Code—Boiled Down

In actuality, the tax code is nothing more than one gigantic algebraic formula. While that image may scare you, it is meant to give you comfort in knowing that there is really no mystery or secret involved in determining your taxes. Once you understand the formula and where each number in the formula comes from, determining the amount of taxes that you owe is simply a matter of putting those numbers into the formula and voilà, out comes the answer! It is as simple as that.

The real secret within the tax code (and the great news) is that *you* control the numbers that go into the formula. Even better, there are many opportunities for you to decide *where* you want to place the numbers into the formula. Taking control of the numbers in your tax return and consciously placing them in the most advantageous places within the formula give you genuine power over your taxes and are the key ingredients of great tax planning.

⏪ **Example** In an algebraic formula, the placement of numbers can have a dramatic effect on the outcome of the formula. For example: (2 + 3 + 8) x 12 = 156, whereas (2 + 3) x 12 + 8 = 68. The placement of the + 8 in the first formula resulted in a solution more than two times greater than in the second one. There are many opportunities in the tax code to move the "eights" around in order to affect the final outcome of the taxes that you owe.

Tax Insight is devoted to unraveling the mystery in the tax code, teaching you the formula, and helping you understand where your opportunities for controlling that formula lie. Learning and understanding these opportunities is where you gain control of your tax destiny. To gain that control you must first understand the key pieces of the formula. In its simplest form the tax formula looks something like this:

⏪ **The Tax Formula** {[Income – (Adjustments + Deductions + Exemptions)] x Tax Rates} – Credits + Additional Taxes – Payments = Taxes Due or Refund.

In this master formula, each of the terms is a category (for example, "Credits") made up of many subcategories (child care credit, foreign tax credit, earned income credit, and so on). The value for each category term in the master formula is calculated from a separate formula that combines the contributions of the subcategories. And each subcategory number is in turn derived from its own set of formulas and rules.

The plan of this book is to drill down from the level of the simple master formula to the deeper levels of the subcategory formulas. In the subsequent chapters of this section we explore each of the components of the master tax formula as it relates to your tax return. In subsequent sections, we dive into the nitty-gritty of each subcategory, again in relation to the appropriate parts of your tax return. Every part of this book aims to help you reap a more plentiful harvest from your tax planning efforts.

The Key Components of the Tax Formula

You have surely heard the lingo of the tax aficionado: AGI, deductions, credits, exemptions, brackets, marginal rates, effective rates, above-the-line, below-the-line, itemized, phase-outs, etc. You probably recognize these words and phrases, but do you understand what they mean? Do you know which of these are affecting you, how they are affecting you, or which can help you? Do you know how one component affects another? Is it possible to claim a deduction or credit and have it make no difference—or, worse, actually increase your taxes? These are important questions, and understanding the answers to them, can be critical in your tax planning efforts.

For tax planning purposes, the tax formula given above as a simple equation gets re-expressed as a sequence of arithmetic operations done on the key components of the formula (which include key subtotals such as AGI and AMT):

+	Income
−	Deductions (Adjustments to Income)
=	Adjusted Gross Income (AGI)
−	Deductions (Standard or Itemized)
−	Exemptions
=	Taxable Income
×	Tax Rates
=	Income Tax (or AMT)
−	Credits (non-refundable)
=	Cannot equal less than $0 at this point
+	Other Taxes
−	Credits (refundable)
−	Payments
=	Taxes Due or Refund

The first two pages of the federal tax return, called Form 1040, are an expanded version of this tax formula. All the other schedules and forms in a tax return are used to create the numbers that you plug into the first two pages of the return, which in turn are entered into the formula that determines your tax. In fact, when you look at Form 1040 (Figure 1-1), you will notice that the IRS has organized the lines of the return into successive sections that are divided and labeled in a way that resembles the formula above.

Form **1040** Department of the Treasury—Internal Revenue Service (99) **U.S. Individual Income Tax Return** 20XX		OMB No. 1545-0074	IRS Use Only—Do not write or staple in this space.

For the year Jan. 1–Dec. 31, 20xx, or other tax year beginning , 20xx, ending , 20 | See separate instructions.

Your first name and initial	Last name	Your social security number
If a joint return, spouse's first name and initial	Last name	Spouse's social security number

Home address (number and street). If you have a P.O. box, see instructions. — Apt. no. — ▲ Make sure the SSN(s) above and on line 6c are correct.

City, town or post office, state, and ZIP code. If you have a foreign address, also complete spaces below (see instructions).

Presidential Election Campaign
Check here if you, or your spouse if filing jointly, want $3 to go to this fund. Checking a box below will not change your tax or refund. ☐ You ☐ Spouse

Foreign country name	Foreign province/state/county	Foreign postal code

Filing Status
Check only one box.

1 ☐ Single
2 ☐ Married filing jointly (even if only one had income)
3 ☐ Married filing separately. Enter spouse's SSN above and full name here. ▶
4 ☐ Head of household (with qualifying person). (See instructions.) If the qualifying person is a child but not your dependent, enter this child's name here. ▶
5 ☐ Qualifying widow(er) with dependent child

Exemptions

6a ☐ Yourself. If someone can claim you as a dependent, **do not** check box 6a . . . . .
b ☐ Spouse . . . .

c Dependents: (1) First name Last name	(2) Dependent's social security number	(3) Dependent's relationship to you	(4) ✓ if child under age 17 qualifying for child tax credit (see instructions)

If more than four dependents, see instructions and check here ▶ ☐

d Total number of exemptions claimed . . . .

Boxes checked on 6a and 6b
No. of children on 6c who:
• lived with you
• did not live with you due to divorce or separation (see instructions)
Dependents on 6c not entered above
Add numbers on lines above ▶

Income
Attach Form(s) W-2 here. Also attach Forms W-2G and 1099-R if tax was withheld.
If you did not get a W-2, see instructions.
Enclose, but do not attach, any payment. Also, please use Form 1040-V.

7	Wages, salaries, tips, etc. Attach Form(s) W-2	7	
8a	**Taxable interest.** Attach Schedule B if required	8a	
b	Tax-exempt interest. **Do not** include on line 8a . .	8b		
9a	Ordinary dividends. Attach Schedule B if required	9a	
b	Qualified dividends	9b		
10	Taxable refunds, credits, or offsets of state and local income taxes . .	10	
11	Alimony received	11	
12	Business income or (loss). Attach Schedule C or C-EZ	12	
13	Capital gain or (loss). Attach Schedule D if required. If not required, check here ▶ ☐	13	
14	Other gains or (losses). Attach Form 4797	14	
15a	IRA distributions . 15a	b Taxable amount . .	15b	
16a	Pensions and annuities 16a	b Taxable amount . .	16b	
17	Rental real estate, royalties, partnerships, S corporations, trusts, etc. Attach Schedule E	17	
18	Farm income or (loss). Attach Schedule F	18	
19	Unemployment compensation	19	
20a	Social security benefits 20a	b Taxable amount . .	20b	
21	Other income. List type and amount	21	
22	Combine the amounts in the far right column for lines 7 through 21. This is your **total income** ▶	22	

Adjusted Gross Income

23	Reserved	23		
24	Certain business expenses of reservists, performing artists, and fee-basis government officials. Attach Form 2106 or 2106-EZ	24		
25	Health savings account deduction. Attach Form 8889 .	25		
26	Moving expenses. Attach Form 3903	26		
27	Deductible part of self-employment tax. Attach Schedule SE .	27		
28	Self-employed SEP, SIMPLE, and qualified plans .	28		
29	Self-employed health insurance deduction . .	29		
30	Penalty on early withdrawal of savings	30		
31a	Alimony paid b Recipient's SSN ▶	31a		
32	IRA deduction	32		
33	Student loan interest deduction	33		
34	Reserved	34		
35	Domestic production activities deduction. Attach Form 8903	35		
36	Add lines 23 through 35		36	
37	Subtract line 36 from line 22. This is your **adjusted gross income** . . . ▶		37	

For Disclosure, Privacy Act, and Paperwork Reduction Act Notice, see separate instructions. — Cat. No. 11320B — Form **1040** (20xx)

Figure I-Ia. Form 1040 (first page)

Form 1040 (20xx)   Page **2**

Tax and Credits	38	Amount from line 37 (adjusted gross income)	**38**	
	39a	Check { ☐ **You** were born before January 2, 1948, ☐ Blind. } **Total boxes** if: ☐ **Spouse** was born before January 2, 1948, ☐ Blind. } **checked ▶ 39a**		
Standard Deduction for—	b	If your spouse itemizes on a separate return or you were a dual-status alien, check here ▶ 39b☐		
• People who check any box on line 39a or 39b or who can be claimed as a dependent, see instructions.	40	**Itemized deductions** (from Schedule A) **or** your **standard deduction** (see left margin) . . .	**40**	
	41	Subtract line 40 from line 38	**41**	
	42	**Exemptions.** Multiply $3,800 by the number on line 6d	**42**	
	43	**Taxable income.** Subtract line 42 from line 41. If line 42 is more than line 41, enter -0- . .	**43**	
	44	**Tax** (see instructions). Check if any from: **a** ☐ Form(s) 8814 **b** ☐ Form 4972 **c** ☐ 962 election	**44**	
• All others:	45	**Alternative minimum tax** (see instructions). Attach Form 6251	**45**	
Single or Married filing separately, $5,950	46	Add lines 44 and 45 . . . . ▶	**46**	
	47	Foreign tax credit. Attach Form 1116 if required	**47**		
Married filing jointly or Qualifying widow(er), $11,900	48	Credit for child and dependent care expenses. Attach Form 2441	**48**		
	49	Education credits from Form 8863, line 19	**49**		
	50	Retirement savings contributions credit. Attach Form 8880	**50**		
Head of household, $8,700	51	Child tax credit. Attach Schedule 8812, if required . . .	**51**		
	52	Residential energy credit. Attach Form 5695	**52**		
	53	Other credits from Form: **a** ☐ 3800 **b** ☐ 8801 **c** ☐	**53**		
	54	Add lines 47 through 53. These are your **total credits**	**54**	
	55	Subtract line 54 from line 46. If line 54 is more than line 46, enter -0- . . . . . ▶	**55**	
Other Taxes	56	Self-employment tax. Attach Schedule SE	**56**	
	57	Unreported social security and Medicare tax from Form: **a** ☐ 4137 **b** ☐ 8919	**57**	
	58	Additional tax on IRAs, other qualified retirement plans, etc. Attach Form 5329 if required	**58**	
	59a	Household employment taxes from Schedule H	**59a**	
	b	First-time homebuyer credit repayment. Attach Form 5405 if required	**59b**	
	60	Other taxes. Enter code(s) from instructions _____	**60**	
	61	Add lines 55 through 60. This is your **total tax** . . . . ▶	**61**	
Payments	62	Federal income tax withheld from Forms W-2 and 1099 .	**62**		
	63	2012 estimated tax payments and amount applied from 2011 return	**63**		
If you have a qualifying child, attach Schedule EIC.	64a	**Earned income credit (EIC)**	**64a**		
	b	Nontaxable combat pay election	**64b**			
	65	Additional child tax credit. Attach Schedule 8812 . . .	**65**		
	66	American opportunity credit from Form 8863, line 8 . . .	**66**		
	67	Reserved	**67**		
	68	Amount paid with request for extension to file	**68**		
	69	Excess social security and tier 1 RRTA tax withheld . . .	**69**		
	70	Credit for federal tax on fuels. Attach Form 4136	**70**		
	71	Credits from Form: **a** ☐ 2439 **b** ☐ Reserved **c** ☐ 8801 **d** ☐ 8885	**71**		
	72	Add lines 62, 63, 64a, and 65 through 71. These are your **total payments** . . . . ▶	**72**	
Refund	73	If line 72 is more than line 61, subtract line 61 from line 72. This is the amount you **overpaid**	**73**	
	74a	Amount of line 73 you want **refunded to you.** If Form 8888 is attached, check here . ▶ ☐	**74a**	
Direct deposit? ▶ **See instructions.**	b	Routing number		▶ **c** Type: ☐ Checking ☐ Savings	
▶	d	Account number			
	75	Amount of line 73 you want **applied to your 2013 estimated tax ▶**	**75**		
Amount You Owe	76	**Amount you owe.** Subtract line 72 from line 61. For details on how to pay, see instructions ▶	**76**	
	77	Estimated tax penalty (see instructions)	**77**		
Third Party Designee	Do you want to allow another person to discuss this return with the IRS (see instructions)? ☐ **Yes.** Complete below. ☐ **No**			
	Designee's name ▶	Phone no. ▶	Personal identification number (PIN) ▶	
Sign Here **Joint return? See instructions.** **Keep a copy for your records.**	Under penalties of perjury, I declare that I have examined this return and accompanying schedules and statements, and to the best of my knowledge and belief, they are true, correct, and complete. Declaration of preparer (other than taxpayer) is based on all information of which preparer has any knowledge.			
	Your signature Date Your occupation		Daytime phone number	
	▶ Spouse's signature. If a joint return, **both** must sign. Date Spouse's occupation		If the IRS sent you an Identity Protection PIN, enter it here (see inst.)	
Paid Preparer Use Only	Print/Type preparer's name Preparer's signature	Date	Check ☐ if self-employed PTIN	
	Firm's name ▶		Firm's EIN ▶	
	Firm's address ▶		Phone no.	

Form **1040** (20xx)

Figure 1-1b. Form 1040 (second page)

Next, we delve into a deeper understanding of the makeup of these key components. In doing so, you will begin to understand how each piece of the formula flows together and how the pieces affect one another. Once you have a solid understanding of each component and its effect on the formula, you will be better prepared to apply the strategies found in the other sections of this book.

Key Components Defined

A Better Understanding

Now that you are familiar with the tax formula, it is important that you understand how each of the key components works, and how each will affect your tax. This chapter will give you a deeper understanding of the following components:

- Income
- Deductions (Adjustments to Income) and AGI
- Deductions (Standard or Itemized)
- Exemptions
- Taxable Income
- Income Tax, Tax Brackets, and Marginal Rates vs. Effective Rates
- The Alternative Minimum Tax (AMT)
- Credits (Non-Refundable)
- Other Taxes
- Credits (Refundable)

Income

My client, Jim, called me on the phone one day and said he would be making about $200,000 more that year than in the previous year. He wanted to know how much he should save for taxes. My answer was, "Somewhere between 0 and 50%." Now, in reading my response you might think that Jim needed another tax advisor. But what he really needed was to tell me how he was earning that extra income. The tax consequences really could have been any-where in that range. Once I knew the source of that income, I was able to tell him how much to save.

Taxable income includes nearly all income, from whatever source it is derived. Other than a few types of income that are specifically excluded in the tax code, all other types of income are taxable. However, not all income is equal in the eyes of the law. Some types of income receive beneficial tax rates, some have punitive tax rates, some are not taxed, and some are taxed only in cer-tain circumstances. This varying treatment of how different income sources are taxed is just one reason why a few people love tax planning and the rest avoid it like a plague. Nothing is simple or straightforward in the tax code ... *nothing.*

Total gross income is the first key component of the tax formula. Nearly all sources of income (taxable and non-taxable) are reported on your tax return, and all of the taxable sources are added together to arrive at your total gross income. Here is a list of the categories of income sources, each of which has a unique method of taxation:

- Ordinary income
- Tax-exempt income (no tax)
- Preferred income (lower than normal tax rates)
- Deferred income (eventually taxed, but not currently)
- Potentially or partially taxed income (including Social Security)
- Penalized income (higher than normal tax rates)
- Earned and unearned income
- Passive income

Each of these types of income is analyzed in Chapter 3. For now, you should focus on three important points. First, nearly every source of income (or increase in wealth) is taxable. There are *very* few exceptions to this rule, and even those exceptions do not apply 100% of the time. The purpose of the tax code is to enable the government to take your money. Exceptions and exemptions are counterproductive to the very purpose of the code.

Second, the tax code is used to influence, punish, reward, and guide your decisions. This is the reason that there are so many different ways that income sources are taxed.

Third, it is to your advantage to learn how each type of income is taxed and then use that knowledge to adjust your income sources over time to reduce your taxes. Ultrawealthy individuals often pay taxes at a lower rate than middle-class individuals because they have shifted their sources of income to those that are taxed lightly or not taxed at all. Over time you can do the same.

Deductions (Adjustments to Income) and AGI

AGI is an incredibly important acronym. It stands for *Adjusted Gross Income*. You'll find it on the last line of the first page of Form 1040 (see Figure 1-1). It is arguably the most important line on your tax return. It can significantly affect the amount of tax you owe. It can also affect your ability to get loans, tuition assistance, and other types of financial support. Your AGI has a far-reaching effect on your financial life.

Remember where adjustments to income enter into the tax formula:

+ Income

– Deductions (Adjustments to Income)

= Adjusted Gross Income (AGI)

To understand AGI, you must first understand the meaning of the word "deduction." A deduction is an expense the government allows you to subtract from your income before you are taxed. It reduces your *taxable* income to an amount that is lower than your total income.

⮑ **Example**   Ted has a total income of $80,000 from taxable sources. However, he contributed $5,000 to his IRA account, paid $4,500 in alimony, and paid $500 in student loan interest. Because each of these expenses is considered deductible in the tax code, Ted has a total of $10,000 in deductions ($5,000 + 4,500 + 500 = $10,000). Thus Ted's taxable income will be $10,000 less than his actual income, or $70,000 ($80,000 – 10,000 = $70,000).

Deductions come in two varieties. They can be considered **"above-the-line"** or **"below-the-line"** deductions. "The line" refers to the bottom line of the first page of the tax return—your AGI. Above-the-line deductions (or adjustments to income) are subtracted from your total income, directly reducing that income when you arrive at AGI.

AGI is a very important number because it determines your eligibility to utilize below-the-line deductions and credits (discussed in the next section). The tax code limits the availability of many deductions and credits to those who have lower- or middle-income levels. (These limits are referred to as phase-outs.) If your AGI is too high, you can lose the ability to use a deduction or credit. For this reason, above-the-line deductions have a very important place in your tax planning. Some examples of above-the-line deductions include:

- Retirement plan contributions
- Student loan interest
- Tuition and fees
- Health savings account contributions
- Self-employed health insurance premiums
- Educator expenses
- Moving expenses
- Alimony
- Self-employment taxes
- Penalties from early withdrawals from savings

Understanding the portion of the tax formula that determines your AGI may be the most important thing that you can do to reduce your total tax liability.

Deductions (Standard or Itemized)

Once you have calculated your AGI it is time to turn to page 2 of your tax return (see Figure 1-1b) in order to complete the remaining items in the tax formula. The next piece of the tax return contains the below-the-line deductions. Here is the formula to this point:

$$
\begin{aligned}
+ \quad & \text{Income} \\
- \quad & \text{Deductions (Adjustments to Income)} \\
= \quad & \text{Adjusted Gross Income (AGI)} \\
\hline
- \quad & \text{Deductions (Standard } \underline{\text{or}} \text{ Itemized)}
\end{aligned}
$$

Just as with the above-the-line deductions, below-the-line deductions reduce your total taxable income. However, your ability to claim the below-the-line deductions may be limited or eliminated by your AGI.

When determining your below-the-line deductions you are given two options. The first option is to use the standard deduction. The standard deduction is a fixed dollar amount, adjusted for inflation by the IRS each year, that a taxpayer can claim regardless of his or her actual expenses. It is not based on any real deductible expenses incurred during the year. Rather, it is based on your filing status (single, married filing jointly, head of household, etc.). You can always choose to claim the standard deduction, regardless of what your true itemized deductions add up to (except for special rules applying to those who are married and filing separately).

As an alternative to the standard deduction, you may add together all of your *actual* deductible expenses, known as "itemized" deductions. If the sum of itemized deductions is higher than the standard deduction, you will usually achieve a better tax result by itemizing.

Expenses eligible to be claimed as itemized deductions are familiar to most taxpayers. Some of the more common ones are:

- Medical expenses
- Mortgage interest (and certain other interest)
- State income and sales taxes
- Property taxes
- Charitable contributions
- Employee expenses (not reimbursed)
- Investment expenses
- Tax preparation fees

Nearly all of the itemized deductions have limitations placed on them based on your AGI. For example, you only can deduct medical expenses that are greater than 10% of your AGI (or greater than 7.5% if you are over age 65 and not subject to the Alternative Minimum Tax). The list of reductions and limitations on itemized deductions is long, but each can serve to reduce or eliminate the benefit of the deductible expenses.

It is also important to understand that itemized deductions will do you no good if they do not add up to more than the Standard Deduction (after they have been reduced by the AGI limitations). It is not uncommon for a client to have a sudden increase in his itemized deductions, such as a large medical expense or a new mortgage, and then be confused because it did not make a difference in his taxes or even show up on his tax return. All of the deductions must be subjected to their AGI limitations *and then* still add up to more than the Standard Deduction in order to be of any benefit to your taxes. Don't be caught spending money on "deductible" expenses, only to realize that you won't be able to deduct them. (In contrast, the usefulness of above-the-line deductions is not affected by the standard deduction.)

Deductions cannot reduce your taxable income below zero. Put another way, if all of your deductions add up to more than your taxable income, any additional deductions will do you no good. The benefits of those deductions are lost when you have no corresponding taxable income to reduce.

Exemptions

Generally, each taxpayer is allowed to reduce his or her taxable income by an additional amount known as an exemption. An exemption is a fixed dollar amount, adjusted for inflation, that a taxpayer can claim as a reduction to his or her taxable income in addition to the standard or itemized deductions. Here is a look at the placement of exemptions in the tax formula:

$$
\begin{array}{rl}
+ & \text{Income} \\
- & \text{Deductions (Adjustments to Income)} \\
\hline
= & \text{Adjusted Gross Income (AGI)} \\
- & \text{Deductions (Standard } \underline{or} \text{ Itemized)} \\
- & \text{Exemptions}
\end{array}
$$

The theoretical reasoning for the exemption is to protect a minimal amount of income from taxes, approximately the amount that is needed to cover the most basic of life's necessities, such as food. In addition to claiming a personal exemption, each person is also allowed to claim an additional exemption for every individual who qualifies as a dependent, since the costs of those basic necessities increase with each dependent.

⌐ **Example**   Mike and Julie are married and have three young children who qualify as their dependents. Mike and Julie can claim five exemptions on their tax return (one for Mike, one for Julie, and one for each of their three dependent children). If the individual exemption amount happened to be $4,000 in a given year, Mike and Julie could claim $20,000 in exemptions as a reduction to their taxable income for that year (5 exemptions x $4,000 each = $20,000).

These exemptions help to reduce taxable income further. Beginning in 2013, exemptions are reduced or eliminated for taxpayers with a high AGI. The rules regarding personal and dependency exemptions and specific dollar amounts are discussed in detail in Chapter 4.

Taxable Income

Once you have determined the proper amounts to report for AGI, deductions, and exemptions, you are able to complete the most significant portion of the tax formula:

+	Income
−	Deductions (Adjustments to Income)
=	Adjusted Gross Income (AGI)
−	Deductions (Standard or Itemized)
−	Exemptions
=	Taxable Income

After reducing your total income by claiming all allowable adjustments, deductions, and exemptions, you arrive at your taxable income. Taxable income is the amount of your income that is actually subjected to the income tax. It is also the figure that determines your marginal tax bracket (the tax rate at which your next dollar of income is taxed).

Income Tax, Tax Brackets, and Marginal Rates vs. Effective Tax Rates

The next step in the tax formula is to determine your initial income tax liability, based on the rates in the income tax brackets:

+	Income
−	Deductions (Adjustments to Income)
=	Adjusted Gross Income (AGI)
−	Deductions (Standard or Itemized)
−	Exemptions
=	Taxable Income
×	Tax Rates
=	Income Tax (or AMT)

Our income tax system is progressive, which means that as your taxable income increases, the increased amounts are taxed at increasing rates. Your total income is broken into pieces and each group, or segment of that income, is taxed at a different rate. For the sake of simplicity, let's imagine that the tax bracket tables look like this:

Imaginary Tax Table	
Taxable Income	Tax rate
$1–$20,000	10%
$20,001–$50,000	20%
$50,001–$100,000	30%

In this scenario, if Mary had a *taxable* income of $60,000 during the year, she would have an income tax obligation of $11,000. This is so because the first $20,000 of her taxable income is taxed at a rate of 10%, or a $2,000 tax ($20,000 x 10% = $2,000). The next $30,000 of her taxable income (the income between $20,001 and $50,000) will be taxed at a 20% rate, or a $6,000 tax ($30,000 x 20% = $6,000). The remaining $10,000 of her taxable income (the amount over $50,000) will be taxed at a rate of 30%, or a $3,000 tax. Adding each of those taxes together ($2,000 + $6,000 + $3,000) brings us to a total tax of $11,000.

This illustration brings us to another important distinction: the difference between marginal and effective tax rates. When you hear a person say something like, "I am in the 25% tax bracket," what they are referring to is their *marginal* tax rate. Your marginal rate is the amount of tax that you pay on your last dollar earned. In the illustration above, Mary's marginal tax rate is 30%, because that is the rate that she paid on her last portion of income. Had she stopped earning money $10,000 sooner, she would have had a lower marginal rate (20%).

On the other hand, Mary's *effective* tax rate is 18.33% (as compared to her marginal tax rate of 30%). The effective tax rate is the average rate that you pay on *all* of your income combined. While Mary paid 30% on the last part of her income, she also paid 10% on a different portion of it and 20% on another part of it. When taken as a whole, her effective rate would be 18.33% ($11,000 tax/$60,000 taxable income = 18.33%).

Note There is one more way to look at the true tax rate that Mary paid. Marginal and effective tax rates are both based on *taxable* income. Mary actually had a *gross* income of $88,000, but $10,000 of that income came from non-taxable sources and she had $18,000 in deductions and exemptions ($88,000 gross income – $10,000 non-taxable income – $18,000 deductions and exemptions = $60,000 taxable income). If you look at the amount of tax that Mary paid as a percentage of her gross income, it would be only 12.5% ($11,000 tax $88,000 gross income = 12.5%). So, Mary's marginal tax rate is 30%, her effective tax rate is 18.33% and her tax as a percentage of her gross income is 12.5%.

I received a call from a client one day who was trying to decide whether to accept a promotion at work (and the increased income that would come with it). He knew from our previous conversations that he was on the cusp of entering the next tax bracket—a 10% jump from his current one. He was worried that earning extra money because of the promotion would suddenly push him into a new tax bracket and he would be stuck paying 10% more on *all* of his taxable income.

This, of course, was not the case. If it were, the increased taxes from the higher tax bracket would effectively cancel out his raise or possibly make him worse off than before. What he did not understand was that only the *new* income would be subject to the higher tax rates. I have found this to be a very common misconception.

The Alternative Minimum Tax (AMT)

Up to this point in the chapter, I imagine everything has been fairly straight-forward. You have been able to follow and understand the terminology, prin-ciples, and formulas that determine how much tax you must pay. Don't get caught thinking anything in the tax code is straightforward, though! Remember, nothing is simple or straightforward in the tax code . . . *nothing*.

A prime example of complication in the tax code is the Alternative Minimum Tax (AMT). Once you have completed the first portion of the tax formula and have computed your total income tax, the government reserves the right to determine that the income tax you owe is not high enough. To ensure that your tax is at least as high as it "should" be, you may be required to recalculate your tax using a different (or alternative) formula. This alternative formula calculates the tax that you would owe if they were to take away some of your deductions, add in some of your tax-exempt income, and then calculate a tax based on a new (higher) set of tax brackets.

Once you have completed the second formula, you then compare your new tax figure with the original income tax. If the alternative tax is higher than the original tax, you must pay the additional amount. This new, higher tax is appropriately named the *Alternative Minimum* Tax. You see, there is a minimum amount you *should* pay, in their eyes, and so you are not allowed to use the standard rules if it results in a tax that is too low.

The AMT is becoming an increasingly important area of tax planning. It is affecting more and more people each year because the income levels that it applies to are not linked to inflation. Many people who are far from "rich" are finding out the hard way that the AMT is a part of their tax formula. It can have a significant financial impact on people with relatively modest incomes. You will find a more in-depth discussion of the AMT and the strategies available to reduce it in Part 7 of this book.

Credits (Non-Refundable)

Now we have arrived at the good stuff. Credits are the biggest, juiciest berries on the bush. If they are available to you (determined by your AGI), they can bring a lot of "bang for your buck." Here is how non-refundable credits fit into the tax formula:

+	Income
−	Deductions (Adjustments to Income)
=	Adjusted Gross Income (AGI)
−	Deductions (Standard <u>or</u> Itemized)
−	Exemptions
=	Taxable Income
×	Tax Rates
=	Income Tax (or AMT)
−	Credits (Non-Refundable)
=	Cannot equal less than $0 at this point

It is important to understand the difference between a *credit* and a *deduction*: they are not one and the same. In fact, they are dramatically different. Deductions reduce your *taxable income*. That means that your tax savings from a deduction is equal to your *marginal* tax rate multiplied by the amount of the deduction.

↪ **Example** If your marginal tax rate is 15%, you will pay $15 in taxes for every additional $100 you earn (until you reach the next tax bracket). Conversely, for every $100 you have in deductions, you will save $15 in taxes. Deductions reduce your taxes proportionate to your tax bracket—so the higher your tax bracket is, the more valuable deductions can be.

Credits, on the other hand, reduce your *taxes* (not taxable income) directly. For every $100 you have in credits, you will save $100 in taxes. Credits reduce your taxes *dollar for dollar*, whereas deductions reduce your taxes only by the percentage of your marginal tax rate. This gives credits a very important role in your tax formula.

The first credits available on the tax return are non-refundable. In other words, these credits can reduce your tax to $0, but no less (they can't create a refund greater than the amount of tax you have paid or withheld—hence the term *non-refundable*). Even though they cannot create a surplus refund, reducing your tax to $0 is still really good. Some of the more common non-refundable credits are:

- Child Tax Credit
- Child and Dependent Care Credit
- Education Credits
- Residential Energy Credits
- Elderly and Disabled Credits
- Foreign Tax Credit
- Retirement Savings Contribution Credit
- Adoption Credit
- Prior Year AMT Credit
- General Business Credits

Understanding which of these credits apply to your situation can make a significant difference in the taxes that you owe.

Other Taxes

In addition to the regular income tax and the Alternative Minimum Tax, there are a few other taxes that enter the picture in the next portion of the formula:

+	Income
−	Deductions (Adjustments to Income)
=	Adjusted Gross Income (AGI)
−	Deductions (Standard <u>or</u> Itemized)
−	Exemptions
=	Taxable Income
×	Tax Rates
=	Income Tax (or AMT)
−	Credits (Non-Refundable)
=	Cannot equal less than $0 at this point
+	Other Taxes

For some people the "other" group of taxes can be more significant than the income tax and AMT. Two factors contribute to this. The first is that these "other" taxes are determined without regard to adjustments, deductions, exemptions, or credits. Therefore, you can't reduce these additional taxes through traditional methods. Second, these additional taxes do not count toward minimum tax calculation to reduce the gap between the regular and minimum tax. The "other" taxes are in addition to the regular tax and the AMT.

A good illustration of this is in the tax return of a client I'll call Bob. Bob has an above-average income. He also has a lot of personal expenses that qualify as deductions. In fact, by the time you subtract all of his deductions from his income, Bob has *zero taxable income*—no tax!

Unfortunately for Bob, however, most of his income comes from owning a business. Even though he has no income tax liability, he is on the hook for an "other" tax—the self-employment tax. The self-employment tax is calculated separately from income taxes, without regard to personal adjustments, deductions, exemptions, or credits. It is a flat 15.3% tax of his net business income. As a result, he pays several thousand dollars in taxes each year that he wouldn't have owed if his income had come from another source, such as from investments.

Included in the group of "other" taxes are:

- Self-employment tax
- Penalties for early withdrawal of retirement funds
- Taxes on tips
- Taxes on household employees (such as a maid or nanny)
- Repayment of the homebuyer credit

Just when you think you have made it safely through the tax maze and are aware of what you owe, these other taxes can jump out and get you. This is an area of the tax return where careful planning can make a big difference for business owners.

Credits (Refundable)

In the world of taxes, it doesn't get any better than this. If the "other taxes" section of Form 1040 were to be named the "devil of the tax return," refundable credits would be the "guardian angel," ready to save you in the end. If you qualify for these special credits, they will be the best part of your tax return. Here they are, near the end of the calculation:

+	Income
−	Deductions (Adjustments to Income)
=	Adjusted Gross Income (AGI)
−	Deductions (Standard or Itemized)
−	Exemptions
=	Taxable Income
×	Tax Rates
=	Income Tax (or AMT)
−	Credits (Non-Refundable)
=	Cannot equal less than $0 at this point
+	Other Taxes
−	Credits (Refundable)

There are two reasons why the refundable credits play such an angelic role. First, these credits come after the "other taxes" section on the tax return. This means that, unlike the non-refundable credits, these credits can reduce your entire tax bill, *including* penalties and the self-employment tax. Second, these credits are refundable. What this really means is that even if your tax bill is zero, these credits can take your tax bill into negative territory. In other words, these credits can make the government owe *you* money. Even if you haven't paid one dime in taxes, you could get a "refund." These credits are treated the same as if they were "payments" that you had made.

⇨ **Example**   After taking into account all of Nancy's income, adjustments, deductions, exemptions, and non-refundable credits, her tax liability is $0. During the year she had $500 withheld from her paycheck. Nancy also qualifies for $1,000 of Earned Income Credit (a refundable credit). Under normal circumstances, if she owed no taxes she would get a refund of the $500 that was withheld from her paycheck. However, because the Earned Income Credit is refundable, she will also receive an additional $1,000 "refund" because of the credit, for a total refund of $1,500—even though she paid only $500 in taxes during the year!

I'm not sure that "refund" is the appropriate word for this scenario, but whatever you call it, this is a great tax break for those who qualify. The most common refundable credits are:

- Earned Income Credit
- Additional Child Tax Credit

- American Opportunity Credit
- Adoption Expenses
- Health Coverage Tax Credit

In addition to the credits listed above, there are a few other refundable credits available for taxes that you were required to pay but should not have been. These are:

- Excess Social Security Tax Withheld
- Tax on Fuels (for off-road use)
- Minimum Tax

The old adage of "save the best for last" definitely applies here. The best part of the tax formula comes at the end in the form of refundable credits.

The Calculation Is Complete

As you can see, each section of the tax return plays an integral part in the formula that determines your tax. Understanding each part is the foundation of successful tax planning. The final piece of the formula is to subtract any payments that you have made, which will give you the final determination of whether you owe the government money or they owe you. Here is one last look at the complete formula:

+	Income
−	Deductions (Adjustments to Income)
=	Adjusted Gross Income (AGI)
−	Deductions (Standard <u>or</u> Itemized)
−	Exemptions
=	Taxable Income
×	Tax Rates
=	Income Tax (or AMT)
−	Credits (Non-Refundable)
=	Cannot equal less than76.5 pt $0 at this point
+	Other Taxes
−	Credits (Refundable)
−	Payments
=	Taxes Due <u>or</u> Refund

No longer need you be confused by all of the lingo and jargon of the tax world. No longer should you be intimidated by the complexity of the code. With this solid foundation under your belt, you are more prepared to move forward and take control of one of the biggest and most complex expenses in your life.

⧉ **Note** Be sure to read the remaining chapters in Part 1 before going on to the rest of this book in order to gain a deeper understanding of the different types of income, the effects of filing status, the role of dependency exemptions, and some of ways that the tax code is rigged against you. Once you have a firm grasp of the information presented in Part 1, the remaining chapters and appendices of the book will help you discover strategies you can use within each section of the tax return, as well as recognize what value they may have in your individual circumstances. You will be ready to recognize and harvest the juiciest berries on your unique taxberry bush.

Income

Not All Income Is Created Equal

It seems like politicians never tire of discussing whether the rich pay their fair share of taxes. In the 2012 election, there was much discussion in the political arena about the fact that Warren Buffett (one of the wealthiest people in the world) pays taxes at a lower marginal rate than his secretary. "How can a man who is worth billions and earns millions every year have a lower tax rate than his middle-class secretary?" they would say. "What tricks do his accountants and attorneys use to get his taxes so low? What secrets do they know?"

In reality, there is *no* secret involved in how he reduced his tax rates. The key to his tax prowess lay in the very open and obvious parts of the tax code that are related to income. Warren Buffett does not have lower tax rates because of complex schemes involving hidden deductions, credits, and off-shore accounts. He has reduced his tax rate by shifting his *sources* of income to those given preferential treatment in the tax code.

The great news is that his "secrets" to lower tax rates are available to everyone. Even better, through conscious effort you too can shift your income to these preferred sources—lowering your overall tax rate every step of the way. To do so, you must first gain an understanding of each type of income and how each is taxed. Then you will be ready to carefully plan a way to get your effective tax rate as low as possible.

Here again is the list of the categories of income sources (from Chapter 2), each of which has a unique method of taxation:

- Ordinary income
- Tax-exempt income (no tax)
- Preferred income (lower than normal tax rates)

- Deferred income (eventually taxed, but not currently)
- Potentially or partially taxed income (including Social Security)
- Penalized income (higher than normal tax rates)
- Earned and unearned income
- Passive income

The remainder of this chapter is dedicated to a close-up look at each income source.

Ordinary Income

Ordinary income is the catch-all term for any income source that does not have special tax rates or tax treatments. Most income falls into this category and is taxed at "ordinary" income tax rates—those rates found in the income tax tables (the tax brackets that you are familiar with). The most common sources of ordinary income are:

- Salaries, wages, and tips
- Interest (not from state or municipal bonds)
- Dividends (non-qualified)
- State tax refunds
- Business income
- Capital gains (short-term)
- IRA distributions, pensions, and annuities
- Rental income
- S-corporation and partnership income
- Unemployment benefits
- Alimony
- Royalties

The highest tax rates that you pay will be on income that comes from these sources (other than those income sources that are penalized). In fact, some of these ordinary income sources fall into a special category known as "earned" income (explained in detail at the end of this chapter), which have employment taxes placed on them in addition to ordinary income taxes. It probably goes without saying that as you reduce the percentage of your income that is derived from these "ordinary" sources, the better your financial picture will be.

Tax-Exempt Income (No Tax)

As you might guess, the list of income sources that the government does *not* tax is very short. However, a few types of income do escape the levy of Uncle Sam. Usually these tax-exempt income sources are the best types of income to have when it comes to minimizing your tax bill. Not only are these types of income tax-free, but they also have no direct effect on your AGI (which means that they don't have an effect on most of your deductions, your credits, or your marginal tax rates). The most common sources of tax-exempt income are:

- Tax-exempt interest (state and municipal bonds)
- Roth IRA distributions (within certain guidelines)
- Employing your own children (within limits)
- Workers' compensation
- Certain insurance proceeds
- Some lawsuit proceeds

It is not in the government's best interest to allow *any* type of income to be tax-free. So, of course, there are exceptions in the law wherein each of these income sources can be taxed. For example, portions of your tax-exempt interest can be pulled into the Alternative Minimum Tax calculation. Insurance proceeds can be taxed at times. Workers' compensation payments that reduce your Social Security benefit are considered Social Security income for tax purposes and can thus be taxed indirectly. If you withdraw money from your Roth IRA at the wrong time, you are hit with a penalty tax, and so on. You really have to hand it to lawmakers—they will get you any way they can, even finding ways to tax your *tax-free* income.

Preferred Income (Lower Than Normal Tax Rates)

Those who write the tax laws often use the code as an opportunity to encourage (by taxing less) or discourage (by taxing more) certain behaviors. It is the preferred way to motivate the populace to do (or not do) certain things without blatantly taking away our freedom to choose. Examples of this would be the punitive taxes that are placed on tobacco products (discouraging behavior) or the deductions that come from saving for retirement (encouraging behavior).

One behavior that is encouraged and rewarded by the tax code is investing in business. If you are willing to put money at risk in order to start a business (or invest in an existing one) you are rewarded by the tax laws for doing so. The reward comes in the form of significantly lower taxes on income derived from such an investment. In this way the lawmakers encourage people to put their money at risk in order to grow the economy and bring innovation. As an aside, it is these sources of income (business investments) that are the "secrets" behind Warren Buffett's lower tax rates.

In Chapter 2, I wrote about a client who told me that he would be earning $200,000 more income in the current year than in previous years. He wanted to know how much money he should set aside for the taxes on that income and I told him it would be somewhere between 0 and 50%, depending on the source of the income. I was relieved for him when I found out that the extra $200,000 was from the sale of a business that he had owned for many years. Selling a business is a great source of income from a tax perspective, because the bulk of such income is taxed at special rates—rates that are less than half of the rate that he would have been taxed if the income had simply come from the profits of operating that same business. This special type of income is called "capital gains" income.

Capital gains occur when you sell something for a greater price than you paid for it. The most common source of capital gains income is from investments. Capital gains income has its own special set of tax rates that apply if you have owned the asset for more than one year (known as *long-term* gains). *Short-term* gains (when you owned the item one year or less) are taxed at ordinary income rates. Long-term capital gains income is taxed at a significantly lower rate than ordinary income. Lawmakers talk a lot about increasing these rates as a way to increase tax revenue, but at least for now long-term capital gains remain a great source of low-tax income. Some common sources of long-term capital gains are:

- Stock or bond sales
- Mutual fund ownership
- Sale of a business
- Sale of a home (sometimes)

Another type of income that is given preferential treatment is "qualified dividends." Generally, dividends are taxed at ordinary income tax rates. However, if you receive dividends from preferred companies and hold the stock for a specified time period, you can then receive a preferred tax rate on that income. This special tax treatment for qualified dividends is to encourage long-term investments in domestic companies. The tax rate on qualified dividends is equal to the long-term capital gains rate. Long-term Capital Gains taxation is discussed in greater depth in Chapter 11.

Deferred Income (Eventually Taxed, but Not Currently)

A story will help me describe the principle of deferred income. Jenny, an artist, earned between $30,000 and $40,000 each year selling her artwork to local retailers. One year she was faced with a "good" problem: a national whole-saler discovered her work and bought her entire collection for $200,000—just in time to distribute it for the Christmas season. Though the unexpected income was exciting for Jenny, she feared the looming tax consequences of being thrust into a much higher tax bracket from the sale. With this new income she would be making a lot less money per item sold, from an after-tax perspective, because she would be in a higher bracket.

As she put her mind to work on this problem she came up with a creative solution to reduce her tax bill—or to at least delay it: she would wait until January to cash the wholesaler's check. That way the money would not show up as income until the following year, giving her a lot more time to figure out how to reduce her taxes, or at least more time to pay them.

There was only one problem with Jenny's idea—it wouldn't work. Many peo-ple have tried to do exactly as Jenny had planned, but the IRS does not allow the postponement of tax payments based solely upon the timing of cashing a check. *However,* the strategy of delaying (or deferring) income *is* allowed when done the right way. In fact, tax deferral is a principal technique that tax writers use as a means to encourage desired behaviors. Some of the opportunities that *are* available for deferral of taxable income include:

- Earned income diverted (contributed) into tax-qualified retirement accounts (such as IRAs, 401(k)s, etc.)

- Gains on investments within tax-qualified retirement, education, and health savings accounts

- Gains on investments within annuities, life insurance products, and pensions

- Exchanges of investment properties, such as selling a rental house and buying another with the proceeds

- Livestock reproduction and farming (deferred until sold, or tax-free when you use it personally)

There are two main benefits derived from income deferral. First, it allows the income to remain invested (whereas part of it would have otherwise gone to taxes), leaving more money available for additional growth. Second, deferral provides an opportunity to lower the rate at which your income is taxed, assuming that your future marginal tax rates are lower (when you use the money) than your current rates (when you earned the money).

You should consider some potentially negative factors when deferring income. First, when you defer income you are usually agreeing to rules that govern that deferral. This means that you must use the money only in certain ways or at certain times, as stipulated in the tax code (such as for education, or after reaching retirement age). If you act contrary to these rules you are penalized with extra taxes (discussed in the "Penalized Income" section below).

Second, in the case of some tax-deferred accounts, growth in the account is taxed at *ordinary* income tax rates (instead of the capital gains rates normally associated with investments) when the money is withdrawn—bringing the potential for a much higher tax rate on the growth of the investments if they were not in a deferred account. Third, the deferral can backfire on you if the tax laws change and the rates increase during the deferral period—causing you to pay higher taxes than you would had you not deferred the income.

Tax deferral is one of the most commonly used tax planning strategies. Understanding the rules that govern the different types of deferrals will help you determine whether a particular strategy is right for you.

Potentially or Partially Taxed Income (Including Social Security)

On one occasion I was asked to analyze an elderly couple's tax situation. The wife was considering going to work part-time to supplement their lifestyle. They were concerned that they would be losing most of what she earned to new taxes, due to the special rules that determine the taxation of Social Security income. It turned out that their fears were justified.

Social Security income falls into the "potentially or partially taxed" category. This category refers to income sources that are taxed only when certain conditions are met. The amount of tax levied on these "potentially or partially taxed" income sources is variable. The tax is determined by a formula that takes into account your total income (including tax-free sources), the deductions you have claimed, and the amount of each type of income you have received. The formula then dictates whether the income will be taxed, and to what extent. Common "potentially or partially taxed" income sources are:

- Social Security benefits
- State tax refunds
- Sale of a home

Of these income sources, Social Security income is of particular interest because it affects so many people and because it is a particularly nasty kind of "potential or partial" tax. Once your total income rises above a certain (minimal) level, part of your Social Security income can start to be taxed—with a maximum of 85% of it being taxed when your total income reaches certain levels. The nastiest part of this tax is that you are *double*-taxed on the new income. You are charged income and payroll taxes on every new dollar earned *and* you're also taxed on a new part of your Social Security income that would not have been taxed otherwise.

The irony of this is that Social Security income theoretically comes from the taxes that you paid throughout your working career—you are being taxed on the taxes that you previously paid (even though you didn't get a deduction when you paid them). Social Security Income taxation is covered in much greater detail in Chapter 7.

Penalized Income (Higher Than Normal Tax Rates)

When it comes to using the tax code as a means to manipulate behavior, there are certain behaviors that are clearly discouraged by lawmakers. In regard to income, the most common behavior that is discouraged by tax writers is using money contributed to tax-qualified accounts for reasons outside their intended purpose. Examples of this would include withdrawing money from an IRA or 401(k) before you are 59½ years old or using money in a Health Savings Account (HSA) for over-the-counter medicine. If you don't use these special accounts in the way that the government deems acceptable, the tax code will punish you. Not only will you pay ordinary taxes on that income, but you will also pay an additional penalty tax. Some of the most common forms of penalized income include:

- Not withdrawing a minimum amount of money from tax-qualified retirement accounts after you reach the age of 70 ½ (**50% penalty**).

- Withdrawing funds from a tax-qualified retirement account before the requirements for age are met (**10% penalty**).

- Contributing more than is allowed to a tax-qualified retirement account. This penalty continues each year until the extra funds are withdrawn (**6% penalty**).

- Withdrawing funds from an education savings account for uses other than those specified in the code (**10% penalty**).

- Using money in an HSA account for items that are not allowed (**20% penalty**).

When deciding to establish a tax-qualified account, it is very important to first understand all of the rules that govern the account so that you don't find yourself unknowingly crossing a line and owing a stiff penalty.

Earned and Unearned Income

Another important distinction between sources of income is whether the income is "earned" or "unearned." In simple terms, earned income is received as a result of your own efforts, not from the efforts of others. If you are employed by a business, all of your income from that employment is considered "earned" income because you receive it for the service that you provide the company. If you own a business with employees and you also work in the business, some of your income is earned and some may be unearned, because some of the income can be attributed to your own efforts and some of it comes from the efforts of others. On the other hand, if you have ownership in a business in which you don't work (such as owning the stock of a company in your investment account) and you receive income from that business (such as dividends), that income is *un*earned because you did not perform any personal service to receive the income.

This distinction between earned and unearned income is very important because it can significantly affect the amount of taxes you owe. Earned income is a type of ordinary income (taxed at the highest rates). On top of the ordinary income taxes, earned income is also subject to employment taxes (Social Security, Medicare, Unemployment, etc.). These additional taxes add a significant burden to the income that you "earn," making it potentially the most costly income that you receive.

For business owners, the distinction between earned and unearned income can also be a factor in determining which type of business entity is chosen for the operation of the business (such as a corporation, a sole proprietorship, or a partnership). The proper entity choice may enable some of the profits from the business to be considered "unearned," resulting in a lower tax on that income.

The distinction between earned and unearned income is often the largest factor in determining a person's overall tax burden. It is a key place to focus when planning the way that you will earn (or un-earn ☺) your living.

Passive Income

Two sources of income fall into the "passive" category. The first is income received from rental activities and the second is income originating from a business in which you have ownership but do not "materially" participate (meaning you don't really have any role in the operation of the business—only an ownership interest).

The importance of passive income is mainly in how the designation affects the treatment of losses. If you lose money in a business you can generally subtract those losses from other sources of income. However, if the business loss came from a passive source, you cannot offset other non-passive income with those losses—meaning the losses do you no good from a tax perspective (in the current year).

⇨ **Example** Shane has several sources of income. He is a computer programmer at a software company, he is trying his hand at a multilevel marketing business selling nutrition supplements, and he has an investment in a partnership where he contributed startup money but does not participate in the operations of the company. In the current year Shane earned an $80,000 salary from the software company, lost money in the nutrition business (spent $2,000 more than he made), and the partnership he invested in lost money as well (his portion of the loss was $5,000). On his tax return Shane can subtract the $2,000 loss in the nutrition business from his salary, reducing his total gross income to $78,000 ($80,000 salary – $2,000 business loss = $78,000). However, he cannot subtract the $5,000 loss in the partnership from his gross income because that income (or loss) is passive and can be subtracted only from other passive income (neither the salary nor nutrition business is passive). Even though there was a real loss of money in the partnership business, it will not help reduce Shane's tax bill in that year.

This description gives you the basic concept of the limitations that are placed on passive income and the tax consequences of those limitations. Of course, there are exceptions to these rules (and exceptions to the exceptions). However, the key difference to remember is that passive losses can benefit your taxes in the current year only if you have other passive income to use them against.

Unleash the Power of Warren Buffet's "Secret"

Now that you have an understanding of the various ways that income is taxed you are armed with great power in your personal tax planning. The great secret of wealthy taxpayers is conscious control of their sources of income. You can put a lot of effort into learning and implementing the myriad deductions and credits that are available—and by all means, you should. *However*, the reality is that in order to claim a deduction or credit, you must *spend money*. Worse yet, the money that you spend will *always* be more than the tax savings that you receive. Deductions and credits are great, but they should be used only for things that you would have spent money on *regardless* of the tax consequences.

On the other hand, changing your sources of income can dramatically reduce your tax burden without spending one dime. You could literally owe between $0 and $587 in taxes for $1,000 of income, depending on its source. Multiply that effect by all of the thousands of dollars of income you earn and you quickly conclude that using differences in taxation to your advantage will make a significant difference in your wealth over time.

↪ **Example**   It is not just the Buffet types who know and take advantage of this "secret." Lawmakers who write the tax code know exactly what they are doing and personally take advantage of these different strategies as well.

Of course, I am not suggesting that you quit your highly taxed job today and try to live off of municipal bond interest in order to be tax-free. What I am suggesting is that you craft a personal strategy that builds tax-free and low-tax sources of income over time. Then, as those sources of income grow, you can wean yourself from the highly taxed sources of income. As you make these shifts in your income streams you will free yourself from the significant burden that the tax code places on our less informed citizens.

Dependents and Filing Status

Backstage Directors in Your Individual Tax Formula

A chess board and a checkers board are identical. Both are made up of 64 tessellated squares that alternate between two colors. You can use the same board for either game. Other than the similarity of the game board, however, the two games are very different. They are governed by different rules that control how the pieces move and where they can go. While the rules of the game are usually unseen during play, their existence is continuously felt and the entire outcome of the game is based on them.

In a tax return a similar scenario exists. There are two components of the return that act as an ever-present influence over the remaining rules that govern the tax formula. The first component is the determination of who qualifies as a "dependent" of a taxpayer. The second governing component is for what filing status a taxpayer qualifies. These two determinations will exert their influence throughout the tax formula, much like the rules of a game or an unseen director managing a play from behind the curtain. They have a significant and continuous effect on the final outcome of the tax return, determining the deductions, credits, exemptions, taxable income, and tax tables that you will use for your return.

Dependents

Whether you can claim an individual as a dependent on your tax return has a far-reaching effect on the amount of tax you will pay. The qualification of a dependent can change your deductions and credits. It will determine the number of exemptions that you can claim. It can even affect the filing status that you claim. There is no portion of the tax return (other than income) that is not influenced by the claiming of a dependent.

For the most part, whether or not you can claim a person as a dependent is determined by the rules that govern the dependency exemption. Even when considering a deduction or a credit, whether or not a person qualifies as a dependent will be based on the exemption rules. For that reason we will focus on the dependency exemption.

Dependency Exemptions

As a reminder, exemptions are a specific amount of income that is exempt (or free) from tax. This dollar amount changes every year, based on inflation. The exemption is subtracted from a taxpayer's income, in addition to other deductions, in order to arrive at "taxable income."

Each taxpayer is generally allowed one exemption for him- or herself (assuming the taxpayer is not another person's dependent), one for his or her spouse (if married), and an additional exemption for each person who qualifies as his or her dependent. As an example, if a married couple has one dependent child they would be allowed to claim three exemptions (one for each spouse and one more for the child). If the exemption amount for a particular year were $4,000, that couple would be allowed to claim $12,000 in exemptions (3 exemptions x $4,000 per exemption = $12,000). Thus, $12,000 of their income would be free of tax.

Exemption Phase-out

Beginning in 2013, the dependency exemption phase-out rules have been revived from a decade earlier. Under the phase-out, the total amount of exemptions that a taxpayer can claim is reduced once his or her taxable income reaches a certain level.

Once a person's taxable income has crossed the applicable threshold, that individual's exemptions are reduced by 2% for every $2,500 (or portion thereof) that the income exceeds the threshold. This means that in a year where the exemption is worth $4,000, $80 is subtracted ($4,000 x 2% = $80) for *each* exemption for which a person otherwise qualifies, for every $2,500 by which their income exceeds the threshold. In fact, if that individual's income is $122,501 (or more) above the threshold, the exemptions are completely eliminated.

↪ **Example** Trisha and Stan claim five exemptions on their tax return—one for each of them, two for their children, and one more for Trisha's father, who lives with them. In a year in which exemptions were valued at $4,000, ordinarily these five exemptions would allow them to claim $20,000 less taxable income ($4,000 per exemption x 5 exemptions = $20,000). However, Trisha and Stan have $380,000 in taxable income, which is above the threshold and thus triggers the phase-out of their exemptions. As a married couple filing jointly, their threshold is $300,000, which puts them $80,000 over in taxable income. That $80,000 reduces their exemptions by 64% ($80,000 ÷ $2,500 increments = 32 increments over the threshold. Each increment reduces the exemption by 2%, so 32 increments x 2% = 64%), or $12,800 (64% x $20,000 of exemptions = $12,800). Because of this they can only claim $7,200 in exemptions ($20,000 − $12,480 = $7,200).

It is also worth noting that this method of reducing exemptions is very disproportionate in its consequences for various circumstances. For example, if the exemption dollar amount for a given year were $4,000, the phase-out would trigger an $80 reduction for *each* exemption for every $2,500 that taxable income exceeded the threshold. For an individual claiming one exemption, $2,500 of additional income would reduce the exemption by $80. But a taxpayer with five exemptions would suffer a $400 reduction in exemptions for the same $2,500 of increased income ($80 per exemption x 5 exemptions). Because of this, the taxpayer with more dependents to care for is the one hit with a significantly larger increase in tax!

The exemption dollar amount for 2013 is $3,900 per exemption. The thresholds that trigger these exemption phase-outs are shown in Table 4-1. The income levels at which the exemptions are completely eliminated are shown in Table 4-2.

Table 4-1. Taxable Income Thresholds Which Trigger Phase-outs for 2013

Single	Married Filing Jointly	Head of Household	Married Filing Separately
$250,000	$300,000	$275,000	$150,000

Table 4-2. Taxable Income Levels at Which Exemptions Are Eliminated for 2013

Single	Married Filing Jointly	Head of Household	Married Filing Separately
$327,501	$422,501	$397,501	$272,501

Qualifying as a Dependent

There are three classifications of individuals who can qualify as a dependent, each with its own set of rules. The three classifications are:

- Qualifying Child
- Qualifying Relative
- Qualifying Non-Relative

In order to be a **Qualifying Child**, the individual must meet the following requirements:

- The child must be a **close relative** (son, daughter, stepson/daughter, brother, sister, stepbrother/sister, or a descendent of any of those individuals). Children who are adopted, placed with the taxpayer for adoption, or placed with the taxpayer as a foster child meet this test for qualification.

- The child must meet an **age limit** test (must be younger than the taxpayer, younger age 19—or 24 if a full-time student—or be totally and permanently disabled).

- The child must meet **residency and filing status** requirements [must have the same principal residence more than half of the year and not file a joint return (unless solely to claim a refund—meaning zero tax liability)].

- The child must *not* have provided for more than half of his or her own **support**. (The taxpayer need not have provided half of the child's support.)

⌐ **Note**   A child born any time during the year qualifies as having lived with the taxpayer during the entire year, even if born on December 31st.

In order to be a **Qualifying Relative**, the individual must meet the following requirements:

- The individual must be **a relative** (children, grandchildren, stepchildren, parents, grandparents, brothers, sisters, aunts, uncles, nieces, nephews, and in-laws). (Foster parents and cousins fall under the non-relative rules.)

- The taxpayer must have **provided** for **more than half** of the person's **support**. Support means providing for the actual expenses incurred for the individual. (If no one person has contributed more the 50% of the support, a group of taxpayers who together have provided more than 50% can decide which person can claim the exemption. An example of this might be three children combining to equally cover the living expenses of an aged parent.)

- The person being claimed as a dependent must not have an annual gross income greater than the exemption amount for that particular tax year. Tax-free income is not included in the calculation (scholarships, tax-exempt interest, and possibly Social Security).

- The person must be a U.S. citizen, or a resident of the United States, Canada, or Mexico.

- The person being claimed must not file a joint return (unless solely to claim a refund—meaning zero tax liability).

 Note   In the case of a divorced couple, the parent who has actual custody of a child for more than half of the year will generally be the one to claim the exemption. This is determined by the amount of time that the parent has the child, not by the divorce decree. It does not matter whether the parent provided more than half of the child's support. If the parents have exactly equal custody, the parent with the higher AGI will receive the exemption.

In order to be a **Qualifying Non-Relative**, the individual must meet all of the requirements for a Qualifying Relative, except:

- The person must live with the taxpayer for the *entire* year, not just 50%. (In addition, the taxpayer's relationship with the dependent must not violate local law.)

If a person qualifies as your dependent, it will be a great benefit to you in the final result of the taxes you will owe. If you have a person who is not clearly a dependent, but could possibly be one, it is worth spending the time to understand what rules need to be met so that he or she qualifies.

Filing Status

While the declaration of your filing status is a simple check-box at the beginning of your tax return, it has far-reaching effects into several key parts of the tax formula. Your filing status governs the limits of eligibility for many above-the-line deductions and credits. It determines the point at which Social

Security income is taxed. Your filing status also determines the dollar value of the Standard Deduction that you are allowed to claim. Finally, your filing status also determines which set of tax brackets (or tables) you are subject to, which in turn determines your tax, and can dramatically affect the amount of tax you will owe.

There are four sets of tax tables. Two of these tables apply to married individuals and two apply (generally) to singles. The main reason for the differences in filing status is to reduce the penalty that would be assessed on a married couple for combining their income, and to attempt to reflect the reality of combined expenses with that combined income.

☞ **Example**   Cynthia and Robert each earn $45,000 per year in their respective jobs. As unmarried individuals, this income (minus the standard deduction and exemption) would place them in the 15% marginal tax bracket. However, if Cynthia and Robert married each other and there were not in an alternate tax bracket, their combined income of $90,000 would subject a significant portion of their income to the 25% tax bracket. The various tax brackets that relate to differing filing statuses are an effort to minimize such a discriminating penalty against a couple who is married over one who is not. (However, the marriage penalty still exists in many instances—just not to the degree that it would if there were not separate filing statuses.)

Each of the four tables corresponds to a particular filing status. There is one additional filing status that is intended to ease the transition from married to single for those whose spouse has died but who still care for a dependent. This final filing status allows a single widow(er) to use the tax tables of married couples for two years.

The filing status that you select will have an effect on several parts of your tax formula. It will determine how much you can claim for various deductions and credits, as well as your effective tax rate. While each one of the five statuses is governed by strict rules that you must meet in order to claim a particular status, it is good to understand those rules and the implications of each status, because if you meet the qualifications of more than one filing status, you may choose which one to use. The following is a list of the five filing status options:

- Single (S)
- Married Filing Jointly (MFJ)
- Married Filing Separately (MFS)
- Head of Household (HofH)
- Qualifying Widow(er) with dependent child (QW)

Your marital status is determined on the last day of the year. Even if you get married on December 31st, you are considered married for the *entire* year for tax purposes. The same is true if a divorce becomes final on the last day of the year—the individuals are considered single for the entire year. The following is an explanation of the qualifications that determine which filing status applies to you:

- **Single (S)**—This is the default status, meaning that if none of the other statuses apply to you, you must file as single. Conversely, you *cannot* file as single if you are married. This status generally applies to you if you have never been married or if you are legally separated or divorced (and not married to someone else) on the last day of the year. However, some singles will qualify for the better tax brackets that belong to the Head of Household or Qualifying Widow(er) statuses, described below.

- **Married Filing Jointly (MFJ)**—If you are married on the last day of the year you must either file jointly or separately. Filing jointly means that the tax return takes all of the income and deductions of a couple and combines them together as if it were all from one individual instead of from two (you are allowed to file jointly even if only one spouse has income). Joint filing also means that both spouses are fully responsible for the taxes owed on the return, no matter which spouse's income or withholdings led to the liability. You may not claim this status if you are legally separated or have received a final divorce decree.

- **Married Filing Separately (MFS)**—This is the other option for those who are married. It is very rare that filing MFS would result in paying fewer taxes. Lawmakers have gone to great lengths to ensure that people do not file separately for the sole purpose of thwarting the tax code and reducing their taxes. To this end, the tax brackets and phase-outs associated with MFS are fairly punitive.

  Under most circumstances, the only time it is better to file separately is if one spouse believes that the other is not being honest with his or her tax return or if one spouse owes a lot of money that the IRS is trying to collect and the other is due a refund. In addition, it may also be a good choice to use the MFS status if spouses are truly separated. On rare occasions the MFS status can result in lower taxes for a couple, so to be safe you could try running the numbers both ways, but it will take significantly longer to do (and cost more if you use a tax preparer), with little chance of a better result.

- **Head of Household (HofH)**—The Head of Household status will result in lower taxes for those individuals who qualify to claim it because it grants a higher standard deduction and has more generous tax brackets associated with it than those that are available to the Single and MFS statuses. In order to qualify a person must be single, legally separated, or be married but living apart from his or her spouse during the last six months of the tax year. The individual must also maintain a home that is the principal residence for more than half of the year for one of the following:

  - A dependent son or daughter (legally adopted children, stepchildren, and descendants all qualify as a son or daughter). This filing status applies even if the individual has waived his or her right to the child's dependency exemption.

  - The individual's father or mother. (In this case only, the parent does not have to live with the individual, so long as the individual maintains a home (contributing over half the cost of upkeep) for the parent (including a nursing home).

  - A dependent relative (must live with the taxpayer). This includes parents, grandparents, brothers, sisters, aunts, uncles, nephews, nieces, stepparents, and parents-in-law (but does *not* include cousins, foster parents, or unrelated dependents).

- **Qualified Widow (Surviving Spouse) with Dependent (QW)**—This is a special filing status that is granted to those who would have qualified as married had the spouse not passed away. In the year that the spouse dies the widow(er) is allowed to file MFJ, even though he or she is not technically married on the last day of the year. Then, for the following two years the surviving spouse is allowed to claim the QW status (as long as he or she does not remarry), which essentially grants the same standard deduction and tax tables as those used by MFJ couples.

  In order to qualify for the QW status, though, the surviving spouse must also maintain a household that is the principal residence for a dependent son, daughter or stepchild by blood or adoption (and qualify to claim the exemption for that child).

Use the Rules to Your Advantage

When the game board is placed before you, a choice to play chess or checkers must be made. When a significant amount of your money is on the line, you would be wise to choose the game whose rules favor your skills the best. Once you choose the game, the rules govern from that point forward.

In this same way, once a filing status is chosen and dependents are determined, the rules governing these components will take over and govern everything else that happens in your personal tax return. It would be wise to understand the implications of those rules, in order to put yourself in the best possible position for the game.

The Tax Code Is Rigged

It Enforces, Enhances, and Enshrines the Wealth Gap—but It Can Be Beat

For centuries, economists and social scientists have recognized that people's actions, no matter how well thought through, have unintended and un-anticipated consequences. At times the unintended consequence is minimal, such as the temperature in a freezer getting temporarily warmer when you place a new item inside of it. At other times the unintended consequence is so significant that instead of bringing a solution to a problem, it actually makes it worse.

⮕ **Example**   Mack and Jessica were at a dinner party with several other couples. During the meal, Mack noticed that Jessica had a piece of food on her cheek. Hoping to help her remove the food before others noticed, Mack tried to signal to Jessica that she needed to wipe her face. However, he did it in such a way that all of the other people at the table saw him and then looked at Jessica to see what the matter was. In trying to save her embarrassment and take care of the problem before others noticed, he actually drew attention to it—the opposite of what he intended to do.

The phenomenon I am describing is known as the *Law of Unintended Consequences*. It is fascinating to learn about it and become aware of the innu-merable examples of its occurrence in everyday life. Perhaps nowhere is its existence more apparent than in the acts of government, where continuous efforts are made to control people and the world around them, with limited ability to foresee all of the consequences that will result.

Unintended consequences are pervasive in the tax code. There are dozens of examples. In my mind, the most damaging and misunderstood of these unintended consequences in the tax code is found in the attempts to tailor the tax code to help the poor and extract more from the rich.

📖 **Note** It can be argued that these consequences are not unintended, but rather they are intentionally placed in the tax code to benefit the rich. In calling them "unintended" I am giving Congress the benefit of the doubt. When the purposes of individual provisions of the tax code are explained, especially at the time they are voted on in Congress, the noblest reasons are given for each law—often based on bringing benefits to the lower and middle class while disallowing these benefits for the rich. Based on these stated reasons, the resulting consequences could only be seen as unintended. However, many people believe that ulterior motives are at work.

Though they may have short-term benefits to those with lower incomes, the very attempts to help those in the lower and middle classes through tax incentives have the *opposite* effect when those individuals are trying to climb into a higher economic class. At the same time, those same tax rules end up working to the benefit of the truly rich.

These Three Things

This "greatest" of the unintended tax consequences is caused by the combination of three factors of the tax code. Together these three factors form a potent formula to prevent upward movement in economic status:

- Unequal treatment of income (certain types of income being taxed at higher rates than others)

- Progressive tax rates (increasingly higher rates with higher income)

- Phase-outs of deductions and credits (reducing or eliminating tax benefits for those with higher incomes)

While the first of the three factors is not directly intended to help the poor and middle class (its intent is to spur business investment and job growth), the full focus and purpose of the second and third factors is to reduce the tax burden on those with lower incomes and increase it on those with higher incomes—to help the poor and tax the rich. However, the way the tax code is written actually brings about a totally different result.

The problem lies in the fact that our primary taxing system is an *income* tax, not a *wealth* tax. Because of that, when we place a higher burden on the "rich" we are actually placing the burden on a higher income. The more your income increases, the greater the burden you bear. The reality, though, is that the truly "rich," or wealthy, may not have (or need) a high employment income—they can live off of their wealth. What the tax code actually does is make it very hard to accumulate wealth, or move from one economic class to the next. Once you have accumulated wealth, the tax code does not exact any great burden on you—in fact its burden is lifted. It is in getting to that point where the real weight of our tax code is felt. In other words, our tax code is written in a perfect way to keep the lower and middle classes down.

➢ **Illustration**   Imagine a three-story building. Each story represents a level of wealth: the ground floor is for the poor, the second floor is for the middle-class, and the third floor is for the rich. Each of the floors has an opening between it and the next floor so that a person has the opportunity to move up from the first to the second and, finally, to the third floor. To move from one floor to the next, however, that person must build a stairway out of blocks to climb up to the next floor.

On the first floor the government provides several blocks to the poor, free of charge, to help them get started building their staircase. Once a person begins to create additional blocks beyond those that the government offered, however, the government begins to take back the person's blocks and give them to others in need. The more blocks a person creates on his or her own, the more blocks the government takes away. In fact, the government will even begin to taking away the person's own blocks once all of the original government blocks have been removed. The person is left working furiously to accumulate blocks at a faster rate than the government takes them away until he or she manages to reach the third floor (if ever).

Once he or she reaches the third floor, however, the rules for that individual change. Once on the third floor it no longer matters if the blocks in your staircase are removed because you are already on the third floor—you don't need them anymore. In fact, when you are sufficiently rich you can structure your income sources in such a way that they are significantly protected from the government's ability to take them away, allowing you to maintain your status on the top floor, unscathed by the government's attack on earned income (the blocks).

This imaginary scenario is a demonstration of what truly happens to people as they encounter the three potent factors of the tax code. Though phase-outs and progressive tax rates may protect the poor and middle class, it is true only as long as the individuals are content to stay poor or middle-class. As soon as they begin to make enough money to *move* from poor to middle class or from the middle class to rich, those phase-outs and tax rates will kick in and make it very difficult for them to accumulate enough wealth to climb to the next higher class. On the other hand, the different ways in which income sources are taxed works to protect the wealthy from losing their status.

To help you visualize the dramatic effects that these three factors working together can have on a person who is trying to get ahead, I want to walk you through some illustrative specific numbers.

First, assume that the cost of living for a family of four is $100,000 per year. Second, $50,000 of the family's income is not taxable, due to deductions, exemptions, and credits. Third, all of the income that remains after taxes and living expenses will be put toward savings in order to accumulate wealth. Fourth, we will assume that a family is wealthy once it accumulates $3,000,000 in savings. At that point the family could cover its $100,000 in living expenses by living off of the interest from a tax-free municipal bond earning 3.5% and allowing some of the interest to compound in order to keep up with inflation.

Next, I will apply each of the three factors to this family's situation, one at a time, in order to see how long it will take them to become wealthy under each circumstance. As the illustration progresses, the compounding effect of this trio will become obvious—as will the reality that the tax code is written very effectively to penalize wealth accumulation.

We'll start with a baseline scenario in which none of the three factors exist. In this scenario a family earns $300,000 per year; has $50,000 in deductions, exemptions, and credits; and spends $100,000 in living expenses. For the baseline, we will assume that there is a 15% flat tax on all types of income and at all income levels. In this scenario the family is left with $162,500 to put toward savings. At this savings rate it would take 19 years for the family to arrive at the goal of $3,000,000. This baseline scenario is illustrated below.

	Income	Deductions	Taxable	Taxes	Living Expenses	Savings	Years
1	$300,000	$50,000	$250,000	$37,500	$100,000	$162,500	19

For the second scenario we'll introduce the first of the three factors: the tax rate is increased by an extra 15% (for a total of 30%), based on the fact that the source of the $300,000 of income is considered "earned" income (which is subject to Medicare and Social Security taxes, or payroll taxes). In this second scenario it would take 24 years to achieve the goal, as illustrated in line 2 below.

	Income	Deductions	Taxable	Taxes	Living Expenses	Savings	Years
1	$300,000	$50,000	$250,000	$37,500	$100,000	$162,500	19
2	$300,000	$50,000	$250,000	$75,000	$100,000	$125,000	24

Now, in the third scenario we will introduce the progressive tax system, or tax rates that get higher as your taxable income increases. For this illustration we will assume that the family's tax rate at their income level is 33%, making an effective tax rate of 20% (because the tax is progressive), bringing the total tax (including payroll taxes) to 35%. As you can see on line 3 below, it will now take 27 years for them to achieve their goal of $3,000,000 in savings.

	Income	Deductions	Taxable	Taxes	Living Expenses	Savings	Years
1	$300,000	$50,000	$250,000	$37,500	$100,000	$162,500	19
2	$300,000	$50,000	$250,000	$75,000	$100,000	$125,000	24
3	$300,000	$50,000	$250,000	*$87,500*	$100,000	*$112,500*	27

For the fourth scenario we will also include phase-outs on their deductions and credits. We will assume that at an income level of $300,000 the family has 80% of its deductions and credits phased out, allowing only $10,000 in deductions instead of the $50,000 that would have been allowed without the phase-outs. In addition, having fewer deductions increases the taxable income, which in turn increases the amount of income taxed in the highest bracket, bumping the family's effective tax rate up to 39%. As this third factor compounds with the previous two, it will take the family 35 years to achieve its goal—nearly twice as long as it would have taken in the original scenario and very difficult to achieve by the time the parents reach a normal retirement age (they would need to be earning this high income from an early age).

	Income	Deductions	Taxable	Taxes	Living Expenses	Savings	Years
1	$300,000	$50,000	$250,000	$37,500	$100,000	$162,500	19
2	$300,000	$50,000	$250,000	$75,000	$100,000	$125,000	24
3	$300,000	$50,000	$250,000	*$87,500*	$100,000	$112,500	27
4	$300,000	*$10,000*	*$290,000*	*$113,000*	$100,000	*$87,000*	35

Now, let's compare this unfortunate family with a family who has already achieved $3,000,000 of wealth. Because the already-wealthy family has no need for earned income (the members have invested their $3,000,000 in tax-free bonds and are able to cover all of their living expenses from the interest, paying $0 tax), it is not subjected to progressive tax rates or higher rates on earned income. What is more, the family also has $50,000 in deductions that are going unused because its income is from tax-free sources. The members could go out and earn an additional $50,000 without paying any additional income tax because the income would be offset by those unused deductions. They could then put the full $50,000 to work building their wealth even further (virtually free of the burden of taxes). See how the incomes of the two families compare below.

	Income	Deductions	Taxable	Taxes	Living Expenses	Savings	Years
1	$300,000	$50,000	$250,000	$37,500	$100,000	$162,500	19
2	$300,000	$50,000	$250,000	$75,000	$100,000	$125,000	24
3	$300,000	$50,000	$250,000	*$87,500*	$100,000	*$112,500*	27
4	$300,000	*$10,000*	*$290,000*	*$113,000*	$100,000	*$87,000*	35
5	$105,000	$50,000	$ 0	$ 0	$100,000	—	—

As you can see from this illustration, these three potent factors in the tax code (progressive tax rates, phase-outs, and differences in how income sources are taxed) work together to make it extremely difficult to move from one economic status to a higher one (in this case from middle-class to rich). In similar fashion, those who are trying to move from poor to middle class have many tax credits pulled out from under them, making their progress up the economic ladder difficult as well (as you will see illustrated in the example below about a client named Maggie). The very tools that are used in the tax code to ease the burden on low- and middle-income earners and increase it on high incomes benefit the lower and middle classes only if the individuals stay put. If they attempt to improve their situation they are faced with very stiff headwinds that, for most, won't ever be overcome.

Phase-Outs: The Devil in Disguise

In Chapter 3 you learned about how different income sources are taxed at different rates, and in Chapter 2 you learned about the progressive structure of the tax code, meaning tax rates become increasingly higher as taxable income increases. However, the third factor in the rigging of the tax code is phase-outs, and it merits a thorough discussion to ensure that you fully understand how they work and their implications.

When Congress creates a tax deduction or credit, it usually limits its availability to a certain group of people (usually to those within a certain range of income). Congress most commonly accomplishes this through a technique known as phase-outs. Though the intent of these phase-outs is clear (and perhaps justifiable), the unintended consequences can sometimes be unbelievable.

⇝ **Example**   Suppose that Congress creates a new credit called the "Gas Purchase Assistance Credit (GPAC)." The purpose of this credit is to help low-income workers afford the increasing cost of gas for their vehicles. The credit gives a $1,000 tax refund for the first $2,000 of fuel purchased during the year. However, to keep wealthy individuals from also claiming this credit, Congress stipulates that the GPAC credit be available only to those individuals with an Adjusted Gross Income (AGI) below $35,000. This limitation is called a phase-out.

Phase-outs come in three varieties, differing in how quickly or dramatically the phase-out occurs. One variety is an absolute cutoff, as in the preceding example. With the GPAC credit, if your AGI were $34,999 you could receive up to $1,000 in tax credits. If it were $1 higher, you would get nothing. This type of phase-out does not make a lot of sense, is not really equitable, and leads to a great temptation for dishonesty for those who are near the threshold of the cutoff. There is a lot of incentive to fudge the numbers in order to get the credit—$1 more in reported income could cost you $1,000 in taxes. Nevertheless, this type of phase-out is found in several places in the tax code. An awareness of these types of "cutoff" phase-outs in your tax planning can make for a dramatic difference in your taxes.

The second type of phase-out offers more of a smooth transition between receiving and not receiving the benefits of the deduction or credit. If the GPAC example were written to be this type of phase-out, it would reduce the benefit over a range of incomes, such as reducing the available credit by $1 for every $5 of AGI over $35,000. In this way the credit would get smaller and smaller until it disappeared completely at an AGI level of $40,000. This type of phase-out does a much better job at meeting its intended purpose by not making such a dramatic distinction between taxpayers whose incomes may differ by only a few dollars.

The third and least common type of phase-out is a tiered or stepped version. It has distinct cutoff points, but those cutoffs remove only a portion of the deduction or credit available. The GPAC credit under this type of phase-out might look like this: $1,000 credit available for an AGI below $35,000, $500 available for an AGI below $37,500, and $0 available for an AGI above $40,000.

Why does all of this matter?

It matters because, if you are not aware of phase-outs, they can easily take you by surprise on your tax return and they often come with a powerful punch. They must be watched very closely as you engage in tax planning, because they can have a far more significant effect on your taxes than you would experience by simply entering into a new marginal tax bracket. Every year I find instances where the effective tax rate on a client's marginal income is 80% or more, due to the compounding effects of phase-outs.

☞ **Example** I have prepared the tax return for Maggie and her husband for several years. Each year things are pretty much the same—a little W-2 income, a side business, and a rental. Each year they have about the same income and receive a similar refund. However, this year was different. While their income did not really change, their tax bill shot up by nearly $6,000! I was really surprised (as were they), until I looked into the details. What I found was that they had crossed a particularly important (and unpleasant) phase-out limit. Their rental income had increased only a little (about $1,000), but that increase pushed their allowable rental income $854 over the phase-out limit for the Earned Income Credit. That $854 cost them an additional $5,751 in taxes because of the lost credit. In essence they were being charged a 673% tax on the $854! This is a real-life example of the dramatic effects that fixed-dollar phase-out limits can have on the tax liabilities of individuals.

As you can see, being caught unaware of the phase-outs that affect you can really hurt. Had Maggie and her husband engaged in tax planning with me during the year they could have forgone the extra income and saved a great deal of money in the process, not to mention having a happier renter (by receiving lower rents or nice improvements). Phase-outs are ever looming and you must be actively aware of them to fend off the damage that they could inflict.

It is important to understand that phase-outs affect people at nearly all income levels, not just those who have a high income. In fact, at times they can have their most dramatic effect on low-income individuals.

☞ **Example** Becky's husband, Mike, died at an early age, leaving her to care for their daughter on her own. Becky receives Social Security survivor benefits of $18,000 per year, but must supplement that income with other work to pay the bills. Last year her income from employment came to $25,000, giving her a total of $43,000. In an effort to get into a better financial position, Becky found a way to do some extra work from home this year, earning an additional $3,000. However, because Becky's income fell within the ranges of two phase-outs (Social Security taxation and Earned Income Credit), she will not be able to keep very much of that additional $3,000. In fact, even though she is in the 15% marginal tax bracket, the phase-outs actually create an effective tax of 58% on that additional income. Once you also account for payroll taxes on that income, Becky will actually keep only 44% of the $3,000, or $1,320!

This same scenario plays out again and again throughout the tax code. Phase-outs can begin negatively affecting a taxpayer with an income as low as $8,000, and will continue to wreak havoc on his or her income all the way up to $450,000. Littered throughout that range of income are numerous opportunities for the tax code to extract extremely high effective rates of tax on additional income—much higher than the tax brackets would lead you to believe. While the phase-outs are intended to reduce the tax benefits available to the rich, they actually extract their greatest toll on the poor and middle class who are trying to break out of their current financial status.

Making this worse still, these phase-outs often take effect on taxpayers at the same time as their marginal tax rates have increased, giving a solid one–two punch. So, not only do they lose the benefits of their deductions and credits, but they are also paying a higher marginal tax rate on their income. It is not uncommon for me to see a person's effective marginal tax rates be 80% or greater as he or she crosses over the thresholds of these phase-outs.

Turn It on Its Head

We need to significantly change and simplify the tax code in order to fully overcome these obstacles. However, the only power that most of us have to bring a complete restructuring to pass is through our educated vote. In the meantime, there are still things that you can do to make the best of the situation that we've be given.

Understanding how these three factors work together to keep people down is the key to knowing how to overcome them. The wealthy don't pay very much in taxes (relative to their wealth and income) because they understand these three factors well, and have adjusted their incomes accordingly. They have shifted their income sources to those that are taxed at lower rates or are not taxed at all. They have also adjusted their income needs downward so that their taxable income for the year does not put them into higher tax brackets or subject them to phase-outs.

As you build your wealth you can do the same things, in order for that wealth to accumulate more quickly. Be vigilantly aware of the phase-outs that go into effect in the range of income that is near your current AGI. Use that to your advantage as you work to time your income and deductions in a way that will keep you from being affected by those phase-outs. Also, be aware of the income brackets and how close you are to crossing into a higher (or lower) bracket. Finally, as quickly as you can, begin shifting your sources of income to those that are subject to lower or no taxation.

As you come to understand these factors it will be more clear to you how and when to implement the strategies that are contained in the remainder of this book. You will be able to effectively plan and structure your financial life in such a way as to take maximum advantage of the tax code, helping you build wealth instead of giving it up to the IRS.

Ordinary Income

OK, I admit that a title like "Ordinary Income" is not exactly an attention-getter. I didn't make up the term, so don't blame me for being boring. However, I can *guarantee* that the extremely high taxes that you will pay on your "ordinary" income will get your attention and cause more than a little bit of excitement in your soul.

No income is taxed at a higher rate than ordinary income—especially the subcategory of ordinary income known as "earned" income. Worse yet, no other type of income is more common. Ordinary income is what all of us ordinary folks earn—but it's not the kind of income that the elite use to fund their fortunes and their lifestyles.

Ordinary income is extraordinarily taxed, and it is only through unordinary means that you can avoid an excessive tax liability. That awareness and avoidance is what Part II is all about.

Employment Income

The Most Highly Taxed Income of All

Employment income, known as earned income in the tax code, is taxed at a higher overall rate than any other income, except for sources of income that have penalties attached to them. It is unfortunate (though by design) that this is the case, since employment income (salaries, wages, and tips) is by far the most common type of income that exists. Individuals and families struggling to make ends meet and trying to get ahead are the ones hit the hardest by this part of the tax code.

Income that comes from employment is subject to the ordinary income tax tables. Employment income is also subject to payroll taxes, including the taxes for Medicare, Social Security, and Unemployment (in addition to state taxes in many places). I sometimes hear people state that they paid no taxes because their income was not high enough or their deductions were sufficient to create no taxable income. What they are usually forgetting, though, is that they did pay payroll taxes—they just weren't conscious of them because the taxes are taken out of their paychecks before they ever see the money. In fact, the payroll taxes are *regressive*, meaning they have a greater effect on those with low incomes than on those with higher incomes. Most of the payroll taxes actually phase out at higher income levels.

The reality is, though, that most people must be employed in order to survive. You can do two things to improve your situation if you currently depend on employment income. First, do all that you can to begin shifting your income to other sources over time, so that eventually you will not need this kind of income, allowing you to retire on income that is taxed favorably or not taxed at all. Even if you are not ready to retire you will have shifted your sources of income to those which allow you to keep more of what you earn. In other words, save as much money as you can and invest it in the types of income-generating investments that receive favorable tax treatment. Second, while you are employed, be sure to take advantage of any opportunity that you have to reduce the taxability of that income and therefore your overall tax bill. There are three main strategies to accomplish this:

- Claim employee business expenses.
- Deduct insurance premiums pre-tax.
- Defer or postpone income.

As you reduce your taxes you will in turn be able to save more money and deliberately put it to work in ways that will increase your non-earned–income sources so that eventually you will not have to be employed to meet your needs.

Claim Employee Business Expenses

Luke phoned me one day after a referral from another client, hoping that I could help him reduce his taxes. As we talked, I realized that his only source of income was from his employment as a salesperson and that he had very few deductions. Generally, the combination of those facts means there is not a lot that I can do to help.

However, Luke did have one thing working for him. As part of his efforts as a salesperson he incurred lots of expenses traveling and entertaining clients, for which his employer did not provide reimbursement. Together we estimated what those expenses would add up to for an entire year, which we figured was around $8,000. At that point I knew we had a good chance of saving Luke up to $2,850 in taxes by employing one of the strategies below.

If you are required to spend personal money for work–related expenditures, there are three ways to reduce the burden of those expenses:

- Get a full reimbursement from your employer.
- Get a full reimbursement, but have your pay reduced by an equal amount.
- Claim the expenses as a Miscellaneous Itemized Deduction.

This may seem obvious, but the first and best choice is to have your employer reimburse you for those expenses. If you track the expenses properly and turn the receipts in to your employer, the business will be able to reimburse you for those expenses free of tax. If Luke's company were willing to do this (it wasn't), it would have saved him the full $8,000 and not affected his taxes.

If your employer will not reimburse the expenses, the next best thing is to ask the employer if the company would reimburse the expenses and reduce your income by the same amount. That way the employer is not out any additional money. In fact, doing so would actually reduce your taxes *and* the employer's taxes. You would not pay income tax or payroll taxes on the reimbursed amount and the employer would pay fewer payroll taxes as well. It is a little more cumbersome for the employer to adjust your pay, but if it is done only once or twice a year it could be worthwhile for both parties.

⇨ **Example**   Luke had $8,000 in expenses for his work, which his employer would not reimburse. Luke asked his employer if the company would reduce his commissions by the amount of the reimbursement, which it agreed to do. Because of this arrangement the employer saved $612 in payroll taxes (7.65% employer payroll tax × $8,000 = $612) and Luke saved $2,852 [(7.65% employee payroll tax + 28% marginal income tax rate = 35.65% total tax rate) × $8,000 = $2,852]. This is a win–win, saving money for both Luke and his employer.

If your employer is stubborn and will not reimburse you, even though it would save the company money, then your third option is to claim the expenses as a *Miscellaneous Itemized Deduction*. This strategy is the least effective, but can still be worthwhile. Although you are not able to reduce your *payroll* taxes by claiming this type of deduction, you may be able to reduce the taxable income on which your *income* taxes are calculated.

Unreimbursed employee expenses are claimed as part of itemized deductions on Schedule A. They fall into a category of itemized deductions that are known as Miscellaneous Itemized Deductions, which are limited (or phased out) by your overall income. Only the portion of miscellaneous deductions that is greater than 2% of Adjusted Gross Income (AGI) can be used toward the total itemized deductions that you can claim. In addition, all of your itemized deductions must add up to more than the standard deduction in order to be of benefit.

⇨ **Example**   Luke has an AGI of $125,000. Only the portion of miscellaneous deductions greater than $2,500 (2% limitation × $125,000 AGI = $2,500) can be used as an itemized deduction. If the only miscellaneous deductions that Luke had were his unreimbursed expenses, he could claim $5,500 of those expenses ($8,000 expenses − $2,500 limitation − $5,500) as an itemized deduction. If Luke is eligible for a standard deduction of $6,000 he would need an additional $500 of itemized deductions before there would be any advantage to itemizing deductions. As an example, if Luke had given $1,500 to charity he would have a total benefit of $1,000 in deductions greater than the standard deduction [($1,500 charity + $5,500 miscellaneous = $7,000 itemized) − $6,000 standard deduction = $1,000 overall additional benefit from itemized deductions].Luke is in the 28% marginal tax bracket, so his tax savings generated from itemizing his deductions is $280 ($1,000 more deductions than the standard deduction × 28% = $280).

When compared to the previous example, in which his tax savings were $2,850 from being reimbursed in lieu of commissions, you can see that itemizing unreimbursed expenses may not be as favorable. In reality, the benefit of itemizing unreimbursed expenses can vary, anywhere from $0 in benefit up to an amount that is equal to that from the reimbursement method. The level of benefit will depend upon how many other itemized deductions and miscellaneous deductions you already have.

⇨ **Example**   If Luke had $2,500 in miscellaneous deductions other than his unreimbursed expenses and $6,000 in other itemized deductions (such as charitable contributions), then every dollar claimed as an unreimbursed expense would benefit him. He would have already surpassed the 2% limitation on miscellaneous deductions, as well as the $6,000 standard deduction with his total itemized deduction. Since both of those limitations have been passed, every additional dollar claimed as an unreimbursed employee expense would reduce his taxes at his marginal tax rate.

If you are required to spend personal money for things that you do in your role as an employee, it could definitely be worth tracking those expenses and utilizing one of the three previously mentioned methods to reduce the expenses or reduce your taxes. If you plan to do this, it is also important to understand which expenses are OK to claim and what stipulations are placed upon those claims.

🖉 **Note**   The IRS is currently scrutinizing this strategy. Their initial stance is that if an employee's income is substantially the same, whether or not the expenses are claimed, then the reimbursements should be counted as wages. If they hold strong to this position and it stands up in the courts then a variation of this strategy will need to be used in order for it to continue to be viable.

Expenses That Can Be Claimed and How to Claim Them

In general, you can claim any expense that you personally pay for (and for which you are not reimbursed) that would be considered ordinary and necessary for your job. That would be any expense that is common and accepted in your trade or profession and is helpful and appropriate for your business. The expense does not have to be required to be considered "necessary." While a list of possible expenses would be very large, these are several very common ones:

- Transportation
- Business meals
- Business entertainment
- Safety equipment
- Small tools
- Supplies
- Uniforms (required by the employer, but not suitable for ordinary wear)
- Protective clothing (e.g., hard hats, safety shoes, glasses)
- Physical exams (required by the employer)
- Subscriptions to professional journals
- The expenses incurred in seeking employment (in your *present* occupation)
- Business use of your home
- Certain Education Expenses

It is also worth noting that there are several expenses that you are not allowed to claim. Some of the more common ones are:

- Personal meals (no business purpose)
- Personal entertainment (no business purpose)
- Commuting (to and from home and work)
- Club membership dues (even if there is a business purpose)
- Travel (personal time on a trip, or business travel for employment away from home lasting more than one year)

Claiming most of these expenses is straightforward. If you incurred the expense for a legitimate and ordinary business purpose and you were not reimbursed, you can count it as a miscellaneous deduction. A few of these expenses, however, have special rules attached to them. These rules determine whether an expense can be claimed, and how much of the expense is eligible.

For example, to claim a meal as a business expense there are rules about whom the meal is with, as well as what is done before, during, and after the meal. If those rules are met, there are other rules that apply to how expensive the meal can be and how much of it is deductible (usually 50%). The expenses with special rules also come with an additional form (or forms) that must be filled out (principally Form 2106). These special expenses include:

- Transportation
- Business meals
- Business entertainment
- Business use of the home
- Tools and equipment that are depreciated

Part 4 of this book, "Business Income and Deductions," has a chapter devoted to explaining each of these expenses with special rules. If any of these expenses apply to you, be sure to study the applicable chapters to fully understand the rules and how to use these deductions to your greatest advantage.

Deduct Insurance Premiums Pre-Tax

Another way to reduce the taxation of employment income is by deducting health insurance premiums from pre-tax income. This is done by contacting the person in charge of payroll and asking for your portions of the premium to be treated that way. The employer has to establish a Section 125 plan for this to be possible, but it is very easy to do and almost all employers already have.

Deducting premiums from your paycheck saves you *and* the employer money. This is because the deduction counts for both payroll and income taxes.

⇨ **Example** Tina's employer makes her pay $250 per month from her paycheck to cover a portion of her health insurance premiums. If Tina's marginal tax rate is 25% and she elects to have those premiums taken out of her paycheck pre-tax, she will save $980 in taxes [(7.65% employee payroll tax + 25% marginal income tax rate = 32.65% total tax rate) × $3,000 = $980]. In addition to her savings, the employer will also save $230 because the company will not need to pay the employer portion of the payroll taxes on the $3,000 (7.65% employer payroll tax × $3,000 = $230).

If you deduct premiums from your paycheck pre-tax you cannot also claim the health insurance premiums as a part of your medical expenses when you itemize your deductions. Even so, taking the premiums out pre-tax will almost always be a better choice. This is true for a few reasons. First, the paycheck option reduces income and payroll taxes, whereas itemized deductions only reduce income taxes.

Second, the medical expense deduction is subject to a phase-out—you can deduct only those expenses that are greater than 10% of AGI. In 2013–2016 the phase-out is 7.5% of AGI for those who are 65 years old and older, unless they are subject to the Alternative Minimum Tax, which would bring the threshold up to 10% as well. Beginning in and in 2017 it is 10% for all taxpayers (due to the new health insurance law, the Affordable Care Act.) For this reason, part or all of the premium may not really be deductible. (The itemized deduction rules are discussed in greater detail in Part 6 of this book. This is just a quick overview to put the pre-tax deductions in context.)

The third reason that pre-tax deductions are better than itemized deductions is that your total itemized deductions might not be greater than the standard deduction, and thus the overall advantage of those deductions could be diminished or even nullified.

Defer or Postpone Income

One more way to reduce your taxable income is through deferral and postponement. The most common way to do this is through employer-sponsored retirement plans or through Individual Retirement Accounts (IRAs).

To defer means to put off to a later time. There are several ways that the government has allowed for the legal deferral of income, meaning that you don't have to count income that you have earned in the current year until a future year when you actually access that income. As long as the income is kept in an approved way—and you don't access it—you don't have to include it in your taxable income for the year.

⇨ **Example**   Luisa earns $30,000 per year as an administrative assistant. Her employer offers a 401(k) retirement plan, to which Luisa contributes (defers) $5,000 of her income per year. For income tax purposes, it is as if Luisa earned only $25,000 ($30,000 income − $5,000 deferred = $25,000).

There can be significant benefits from deferring income. First, the full amount of income is available for investment (not just the amount left over after tax). Second, deferring income has the potential of lowering your marginal tax rates, since you have a lower taxable income. Third, deferring income could also mean you will not be subject to certain phase-outs of deductions and credits, lowering your taxes even further. Finally, income deferral will reduce your AGI, which in turn reduces all of the Itemized Deduction thresholds (such as the 10% for medical deductions and 2% for miscellaneous discussions discussed earlier in this chapter).

⇨ **Example**   By deferring $5,000 in income, Luisa increases her refund by $1,400, or 28% of the $5,000 deferred, even though her $30,000 income places her in the 15% tax bracket (15% of 5,000 is $750). This dramatic change in her tax happens because her marginal tax rate is reduced to 10% *and* she has less of a phase-out of the Earned Income Credit because of her reduced AGI. The compounding effect of a lower AGI (because of all of the factors that are governed by that number) resulted in nearly double the benefit from the deduction that the marginal tax rates would have had on their own.

As you can see, tax deferral can have substantial effects on the taxes an individual will have to pay. Numerous ways to defer income are available and are delineated throughout the remainder of the book. Many of them are found in Part 3 under the chapters devoted to retirement savings strategies. The important take-home message for you at this point is this: Understand how deferral works and the ways in which it will affect your taxes.

Retirement Income

Even During the Golden Years the IRS Is Still After Your Gold

People find numerous ways to pay for their expenses in retirement. Some live off of savings. Some have pensions. Many depend on Social Security, and others work "till they drop," so to speak. For most people, the strategy is to use a combination of these.

Because of the great variety of income sources in retirement, nearly every form of taxation comes into play in retirement tax planning. There is the taxation for ordinary income, tax-exempt income, preferred income, deferred income, potentially and partially taxed income, etc. Each of these income sources, as you know, comes with its own set of rules that govern how it is taxed.

Many of these sources of income are covered in other chapters of this book. However, there are three common types of retirement income that have unique rules attached to them, which are the focus of this chapter. These unique rules create the need for special tax planning and awareness. The three income sources that are governed by these special rules are:

- Social Security income
- Pensions and annuities
- Retirement accounts and Required Minimum Distributions

It is critical to understand these rules as you plan for your retirement, so that you can be aware of the significant effect that taxes can have on your income during those "golden" years.

Social Security Income

Once you begin receiving Social Security benefits you will need to pay close attention to a new wrinkle this creates in your tax formula. When your total income exceeds a threshold, the income you receive from Social Security begins to be taxed. As your income increases over that threshold, the amount of Social Security income that is taxed also increases until a maximum of 85% of your Social Security income is taxed. The way that the formula is set up actually creates a multiplying effect on your tax, meaning your total tax will increase more rapidly than your marginal tax rates would suggest.

The formula that calculates the amount of Social Security income subject to tax creates some important tax planning issues. The good news is that by understanding the formula for Social Security taxation you will be able to structure your income properly to avoid as much of this additional taxation as possible.

If the income that you receive from Social Security were sufficient to maintain a desirable lifestyle, this additional tax would likely not be a concern. In nearly all cases, the government taxes Social Security income only if you are also drawing income from other sources. However, for many people, the paltry amount of income that Social Security provides is just not enough. For this reason, many choose to supplement their Social Security through other sources, be it drawing money from their savings and retirement accounts or finding employment. Even those who do not need extra income can be affected as they are forced to withdraw money from their retirement accounts when they are older than 70½ and the tax code requires minimum distributions. Whatever the case may be, if you have sources of income that are in addition to your Social Security income, you must pay special attention to the tax consequences that come from that additional income.

The taxation of Social Security income occurs in a stair-step fashion through a fairly complicated formula. The first step in the formula is calculating something called "provisional income." Knowing how provisional income is calculated is the key to understanding how to plan for and manage this tax. Provisional income is determined by adding tax-free interest income, deductions taken for student loan interest, deductions taken for tuition expenses, and one half of your Social Security income to your Adjusted Gross Income (AGI), as seen in Table 7-1.

Table 7-1. Provisional Income Calculation

	Actual Occurrence	Initial AGI Calculation	Provisional Income
Ordinary Income	$27,000	$27,000	$27,000
Tax-Free Interest Income	$2,000	$ —	$2,000
Social Security Income	$16,000	$ —	$8,000
Total Income	$45,000	$27,000	$37,000
Student Loan Interest	$(500)	$(500)	$ —
Tuition Expenses	$(1,500)	$(1,500)	$ —
Adjusted Gross Income (AGI)	$43,000	$25,000	$37,000

Provisional income is calculated by adding four additional numbers into the initial calculation for AGI.

If your provisional income is above the applicable threshold, the next part of the formula kicks in and a portion of your Social Security income becomes subject to tax. The first threshold that triggers taxation is when provisional income reaches $32,000 for those who are married and filing jointly (MFJ), or $25,000 for all other taxpayers. (There are special rules for those who file separately [MFS] but lived together during the year.) If your provisional income is above the threshold, then every dollar of provisional income over that threshold results in $0.50 of Social Security income becoming subjected to tax.

⇒ **Example**   Assume that Table 7-1 represents the income and deductions of Mitch and Liz. Their provisional income calculation came to $32,000. This means that their provisional income is above the first threshold ($37,000 provisional income – $32,000 threshold = $5,000). Because they are $5,000 over the threshold, $2,500 of their Social Security income will be subject to taxes and will be an increase to their final AGI.

Table 7-2 illustrates how the inclusion of Social Security income occurs, as described in the previous example.

Table 7-2. Social Security Income Subjected to Taxation Calculation

	Initial AGI Calculation	Provisional Income	Final AGI Calculation
Ordinary Income	$27,000	$27,000	$27,000
Tax-Free Interest Income	$ —	$2,000	$ —
Social Security Income	$ —	$8,000	$2,500
Total Income	$27,000	$37,000	$29,500
Student Loan Interest	$(500)	$ —	$(500)
Tuition Expenses	$(1,500)	$ —	$(1,500)
Adjusted Gross Income (AGI)	$25,000	$37,000	$27,500

Because the provisional income is $5,000 above the initial threshold, $2,500 of the Social Security income (or one half of the amount over the threshold) becomes a part of AGI and is taxed.

There is also a second threshold in this stair-step formula. When provisional income reaches $44,000 (MFJ) or $34,000 (all others), every dollar of income above the second threshold causes $0.85 of Social Security income to be taxed (instead of $0.50), until a full 85% of your Social Security is included in taxable income. No more than 85% of Social Security income can be taxed.

⮑ **Example**   If the numbers in Tables 7-1 and 7-2 were actually for Mitch as a single taxpayer (no longer Mitch and Liz), the provisional income would be above both thresholds. The first threshold for a single tax payer is $25,000 and the second is $34,000. So, the $9,000 of provisional income between the first and second thresholds would have caused $4,500 of his Social Security income to be taxed (one half of the amount over the initial threshold), and the $3,000 of provisional income over the second threshold would have caused an additional $2,550 to be taxed (85% of the amount over the second threshold). Those two amounts combined would make a total of $7,050 of Mitch's Social Security income subject to tax, or 88.1% of the $8,000. However, no more than 85% of all Social Security income can be taxed, so the total amount of his Social Security income subject to tax would be reduced to $6,800 (85% max × $8,000 S.S income = $6,800), which is the actual amount that would be added into his AGI.

The most sinister part of this taxation formula is that once your income goes above the provisional-income threshold, each additional dollar you earn is essentially **taxed twice**. If, for example, you earn an extra dollar at work or in your savings, you will obviously pay income taxes on it. However, in addition to those taxes you will *also* pay income tax on $0.50 to $0.85 of Social Security income that you *wouldn't have paid* tax on *before* you earned that dollar.

↪ **Example**   Bill and Emily have a joint income of $48,000, placing them in the 15% tax bracket. Normally this marginal tax bracket would mean that each additional dollar of income that they earn would be taxed at 15%. However, because they are Social Security recipients, each additional dollar that Bill or Emily earns will effectively be taxed at a rate of 27.75%—*almost twice as much*—because each additional dollar of income also causes $0.85 of Social Security income to be newly taxed.

Knowing your provisional income allows you to make educated decisions about earning additional income. Understanding how this complicated formula works will help you be aware of the amount of additional gross income you need, in order to arrive at the true post-tax income that will be available to you for your retirement needs.

◯ **Tip**   Once a full 85% of your Social Security income is being taxed the issue is off of the table. At that point it is no longer necessary to calculate the effects that additional income will have on the taxation of your Social Security. For example, a single individual with a $70,000 AGI has already been taxed to the maximum amount on his Social Security income. Any additional income will be taxed only at the applicable rates for that new income. For this reason, you need to consider the taxation of Social Security income only if you are within (or close to) the range of provisional income where there are incremental, disproportionate effects on your tax.

Understanding the formulas that affect the taxation of Social Security income is important not only to those who currently receive Social Security benefits. *Before* reaching retirement you should carefully consider the effects of this tax on your retirement income as you make plans for the amount and sources of income that you will need to meet your needs.

✦ **Caution**   Be aware that if you are in the range of provisional income where more Social Security dollars are being taxed with each additional dollar earned, the effectiveness of many tax reduction strategies (such as income from tax-exempt interest, qualified dividends, and long-term capital gains) is diminished. Because a dollar from *any* income source causes an additional dollar from Social Security to be taxed, even "tax-free" income is essentially being taxed.

Table 7-3 summarizes the levels of provisional income that trigger taxation of Social Security income and the amount of that income that can be taxed at those thresholds.

Table 7-3. Social Security Taxation Provisional Income Thresholds and Amounts Taxed

	Married Filing Jointly	MFS and Living with Spouse	Single and All Others
50%	$32,000–$44,000	—	$25,000–$34,000
85%	$44,000+	$1+	$34,000+

Pensions and Annuities

Pensions and annuities are essentially the same thing. Both provide a pre-determined income stream to an individual for a set amount of time. The duration of the income stream can be for a fixed number of years or it can be for the life of the recipient, no matter how long he or she lives. (In some cases it continues for the life of the individual *and* his or her spouse.) The main difference between a pension and an annuity is that a pension is generally provided by an employer and an annuity is usually set up by an individual on his own.

The income stream from a pension or an annuity is partially taxable. The portion of that income that represents investments the individual made is tax-free. Many employers require employees to contribute to the pension from their paychecks. As this portion of the money comes back during the pension's payout years, it is free from tax and considered a return of principal, not income. The same is the case for all of the money contributed by an individual to an annuity.

The portion that represents the growth of the account, or the payments made by the employer, is taxable to the individual at ordinary income tax rates. Note that even the growth of the account is taxed at ordinary rates, *not* at capital gains rates as would normally be the case for investment gains. Although a benefit of an annuity is the deferral of tax during growth years, the higher taxation of that growth at ordinary rates may lessen the benefits of the deferral.

The amount of income that is considered tax-free vs. taxable is determined by the expected duration of the income. For example, if an annuity is fixed as an income stream for 10 years, no matter how long the individual lives, and the total investment made into the annuity was $50,000, then $5,000 per year will be considered a tax-free return of investment and any amounts of income from the annuity that are greater than $5,000 during the year will be considered taxable income ($50,000 total investment/10 years = $5,000 per year return of principal).

If an annuity or pension will be paid over a person's lifetime, instead of a fixed number of years, then IRS life expectancy tables are used to estimate the duration of the payments.

⮑ **Example**   Sarah is 62 years old and has just retired. She has begun receiving income from her annuity and has chosen to receive the payments for the length of her life, not for any fixed number of years. The annuity income will be $1,000 per month ($12,000 per year). If the IRS tables placed her expected years of life at 25 years, then the total expected payments from the annuity would be $300,000 ($12,000 per year × 25 years = $300,000). Sarah's total investment in the annuity was $120,000. Based on this information, 40% of Sarah's annuity income would be considered a tax-free return of principal ($120,000 total investment/$300,000 total expected income = 40%). From Sarah's total annuity income of $12,000, $7,200 would be taxable and $4,800 would be tax-free (40% tax free × $12,000 = $4,800).

If a person lives longer than the IRS's expected lifetime, then all of the annuity income received after that point would be taxable, since the entire invested principal had been previously accounted for in tax-free income. It is important to understand how the taxation of pensions and annuities works so that you are able to plan properly for the after-tax income you will need in retirement.

Retirement Accounts (the Non-Roth Variety) and Required Minimum Distributions

Most people have at least a little money in a government-regulated (qualified) retirement plan by the time they retire. These plans feature tax deductibility when putting money in (most of them) and tax deferral while the money remains in the account (meaning that the growth of the investments is not taxed as long as it remains in the account). There are numerous versions of these plans, but some of the most common types of these retirement accounts are:

- 401(k) plans
- 403(b) plans
- 457 (b) plans
- Individual Retirement Account (IRA)
- Simplified Employee Pension (SEP) IRA plans
- Salary Reduction Simplified Employee Pension) (SARSEP) plans
- Savings Incentive Match Plan for Employees (SIMPLE) IRA plans
- Profit-sharing plans

When you remove money from a qualified retirement account it is generally taxed at *ordinary* income rates. This is the case even if some of the funds in the account have come from the growth of the investments (which would normally be taxed at the lower capital gains rates). This fact is a significant downside to using such accounts, which must be weighed against the benefits of the account before investing in one.

Because of the tax consequences of withdrawing funds from qualified accounts, many people prefer to leave the funds in the account for as long as possible to allow them to continue to grow with tax deferral. However, the government wants to ensure that it gets its money at some point (none of the money in the account has ever been taxed), so the tax code requires that an individual begin taking a minimum amount out of the account each year once he or she is 70½ years old. This mandatory withdrawal (and taxation) of the account's funds is called a Required Minimum Distribution (RMD).

Note   If an individual is still employed when he or she is 70½, the requirement to withdraw money from an employer-sponsored plan is postponed until the person retires. However, this is not the case for IRAs or for employer plans where the individual is a 5% or more owner in the business; in these two cases the RMDs must be taken even if the individual is still employed.

Caution   While it may seem tempting to just ignore this rule and not take any distributions, do not give into that temptation. Congress anticipated that many would be so inclined and has imposed one of the stiffest penalties in the entire tax code failing to take an RMD. The IRS requires investment companies to report to them the value of your qualified accounts each year and if you do not take an RMD sufficient to cover the minimum requirement you will be *fined 50%* of the amount that you should have taken!

Tip   A request for waiver of this penalty can be made on Form 5329 (with a letter of explanation attached) if it can be shown that the shortfall was due to a reasonable error and that reasonable steps are being taken to remedy the shortfall. Just know that "I forgot" probably won't qualify as reasonable if it is the sole reason given.

There are a set of formulas and tables that determine the amount that you must take out each year. In essence, the formulas and tables seek to estimate your anticipated lifespan and divide up the account over that lifespan so that the last dollar will be withdrawn in the last year of your expected life. Each year your expected lifespan is recalculated based on your current age, and the amount that you are required to take out of the account changes accordingly. The amount that you are required to withdraw is a predetermined percentage of the value of each of your qualified accounts on the last day of the previous year.

↩ **Example** Karen will be 75 years old on the last day of the current year. On the last day of the previous year the value of Karen's qualified account was $100,000. According to the IRS tables, at age 75 Karen must withdraw at least 4.367% of that year-end value from her qualified account during the current year, or $4,367. (Actually, the IRS guidelines instruct Karen to divide the account balance by her expected life span [found in the tables], which at age 75 is 22.9 years. This works out to be the same number as shown in the calculation above, only presented in a different way.)

For the year that a taxpayer turns 70½ the withdrawal must be made no later than April 1 of the following year. For all subsequent years the RMD must be taken no later than December 31 of the current year. Withdrawing the amount later than the deadline will result in the 50% penalty mentioned previously. The three IRS tables that govern RMD distributions (showing the distribution factors based on the person's age) are reproduced in the Appendix of this book, and can also be found in the IRS *Publication 590*, as well as on the IRS website.

The calculation to determine the RMD must be made separately for each qualified account that the individual owns. However, once the calculation is made, the full RMD for all IRA accounts may be taken from one IRA, as is also the case with 403(b) accounts. This is not the case, though, with other types of qualified accounts, such as 401(k)s and 457(b)s. These types of accounts require a separate distribution from each account.

📖 **Note** This chapter focuses only on the issues related to withdrawals from non-Roth qualified accounts. For a discussion on the benefits of *contributing* to a retirement account, see the retirement strategies chapters found in Part 3 of this book.

Are there any ways to reduce this tax burden?

In recent years there has been one way available to avoid the tax effects of an RMD. In the past Congress had allowed the direct transfer of an RMD to charitable organizations. (It doesn't work to take the money out and then give it to charity—it must be a direct transfer.)

Making a direct charitable contribution of your RMD could have several benefits. This is because such a transfer keeps the RMD from becoming a part of your AGI. The subsequent reduction in AGI can have a positive effect on the amount of Social Security income that is taxed, help you avoid the Medicare surcharge that was enacted as part of the Affordable Care Act, and possibly keep your AGI below key phase-outs of deductions and credits. None of these benefits is available using the normal itemized deduction for charitable contributions, which only reduces your taxable income (and that is only if all of your itemized deductions add up to more than the standard deduction).

🗒 **Note**   As of the publication deadline of this book, Congress has only authorized this tax break for 2013. This annual reauthorization has historically been done near the end of the year, so be sure to find out if it is available after 2013.

How do RMDs affect an individual who receives an IRA through an inheritance (a beneficiary IRA)?

There are three ways that an inherited IRA is dealt with, based on the relationship of the beneficiary to the deceased person and whether the deceased person had reached the age for RMDs prior to his or her death.

First, if the person inheriting the IRA is the spouse of the deceased individual, the beneficiary can choose to treat the IRA as his or her own by rolling it into another IRA or just changing the name on the account. By doing so, the IRA RMD calculations would be based on the *beneficiary's* age, not the age of the deceased. Alternatively, the spouse may elect to treat the IRA as any another beneficiary would.

For a beneficiary who is not a spouse (or a spouse who chooses this route) there are three possibilities. First, the beneficiary may withdraw the entire IRA and pay taxes on the withdrawal accordingly. Second, if the original owner had not reached 70½ by the time of death, the beneficiary will base the IRA distributions on his or her own age. Third, if the original owner was older than 70½ at the time of death, the beneficiary can take RMDs based on the *longer* of his or her own life expectancy, or the life expectancy (from the tables) of the deceased (had there been no death).

Caution   If the deceased IRA owner would have been required to take an RMD, that RMD *must* be taken in his or her behalf and sent to the estate *before* the IRA is transferred into the name of the beneficiary.

🗒 **Note**   There are other rules governing the distributions of IRAs for beneficiaries, such as what to do if the beneficiary is not an individual (such as a trust), or there are multiple beneficiaries, or the beneficiary dies and there is another beneficiary, etc. These issues are beyond the intended scope of this book and should be discussed with a competent tax professional.

Other Sources of Ordinary Income

Each with Its Own Quirks

In addition to employment income and retirement income, there are almost innumerable other sources of "ordinary" income. The purpose of this chapter is to address some of the more common sources of ordinary income that can catch a taxpayer unaware because of the special rules or misperceptions attached to them. The ordinary income sources covered in this chapter are:

- State tax refunds
- Alimony
- Debt forgiveness
- Gambling winnings
- Royalties
- Awards for legal damages
- Unemployment income
- Bartering (trading)

State Tax Refunds

State tax refunds fall into the "potentially taxed" category of income. The key to whether a refund is taxed is whether you claimed state taxes as an itemized deduction for the tax year that the refund belongs to. If you did not claim state taxes as a deduction, then you are not taxed on the refund. If you did claim the taxes as a deduction then you *may* have to pay tax on part or all of the refund, but not always.

The idea behind taxing state refunds is that if you used the taxes as a deduction, but overpaid the tax, then you claimed a deduction that was too large to begin with. If you get a refund, then the deduction should have been smaller to accurately reflect the state tax that you truly paid, so you need to add the refund amount (or a portion of it) back into your income for the current year so that you can be properly taxed on it. It would be more accurate if the tax code required that a refund be shown in the previous year through an amended return (so that the deduction is for the correct amount in that year), but because of the deluge of amended returns that this would cause, Congress has instead required it to be recognized in the year that you receive the refund.

This requirement would be simple if all you needed to do were to add the refund into your income for the year, but, since the words "simple" and "tax code" are diametrically opposed to each other, there are some extra steps you must go through to find out the proper amount of the refund to add into your income. Because of how the deduction for state taxes is determined, part or all of the refund could actually be tax-free.

When itemizing deductions you have a choice between claiming the state income tax that you paid during the year and claiming the sales taxes that you paid. Since you have a choice of deductions, the added value of choosing the state income tax deduction is really only the difference between the state income tax and the sales tax that you paid. If you choose to deduct state income taxes because they are $100 higher than the sales taxes were, then the added value that you gain from choosing the income tax deduction is $100.

⤶ **Example**   Fritz had the choice of claiming $500 in sales tax or $600 in state income taxes. Choosing to use the state income taxes as his deduction gives Fritz an additional benefit of $100 ($600 state income tax – $500 sales tax = $100 greater deduction by claiming the income tax).

When you receive a refund of your state income tax, it is because you paid more to the state than you really owed, which means that the deduction for state income taxes that you claimed was too high. (It's like paying $20 for a $15 item at a store and getting $5 back in change. You didn't really pay $20 for the item; you paid $15.) You must claim that extra amount paid (the refund or "change") as income, but only to the extent that it brought you a greater benefit on the previous year's taxes than you would have received if you had not claimed it.

⤳ **Example** In the previous example, Fritz received a refund of $200 from the state after filing his taxes. Fritz will need to claim $100 of that refund as income because that is the additional benefit that he received by claiming state taxes as a deduction. If he had originally only paid the $400 that he truly owed ($600 paid – $200 refund = $400 truly owed) then he would have claimed the $500 sales tax deduction instead of the income tax deduction, because the sales tax deduction would have been larger. So, the tax benefit that he received because of paying $200 more in state income tax than he really owed was $100, the amount that by which it was greater than the other deduction that he could have claimed. Even though he had a $200 refund, the amount deducted on the previous year's return was only $100 more than it would have been otherwise, so that is all that is included in this year's income.

There are other factors that go into this calculation as well. One of these is to take into account the standard deduction vs. the itemized deduction, and how much of an additional benefit there was from claiming the state tax deduction as compared to just using the standard deduction. Another factor is whether the taxpayer had taxable income after deductions, and how much it would have changed taking the refund into account.

The end goal in all of the factors that need to be considered is to determine what portion of the refund (or overpayment/over-deduction of state income tax) actually benefited the taxpayer. That portion, if any, is the amount added back into the current year's tax return as income, to make up for the reduction in taxable income from the previous year.

Alimony

Alimony is the payment of money by one ex-spouse for the support of the other ex-spouse. This payment is a deductible expense for the spouse who is paying it (as an above-the-line adjustment to income) and is recognized as taxable income for the spouse who is receiving it. For the alimony to be deductible/taxable, the following conditions must exist:

- The payments must be required by law, written in a divorce or separation agreement. If they are not legally required, then any payments made are considered a gift.

- The payments must be made in cash or cash equivalents, or made directly to another person or entity for the benefit of the spouse (such as paying the spouse's rent or utilities, etc.).

- The payments cannot extend beyond the death of the spouse receiving payments (such as to an heir or beneficiary).

- Payments cannot be made to members of the same household. (You can't pay a spouse from whom you are separated but still living with. This is to keep people from playing games with the tax system.)

- Payments must not be designated as anything other than alimony (such as child support).

- The spouses may not file a joint tax return (which would be silly anyway, because the income and expense would cancel each other out if they were on the same return).

Alimony and Child Support Tax Rules

Any portion of the alimony payment that is considered child support for minor children (as determined by the divorce decree or separation agreement), or is based upon a child's status, is not taxable/deductible. In addition, if the paying spouse does not pay the full required amount of alimony and child support during the year, the payments that are made count first toward the child support until the entire obligation to the child is fulfilled; then any additional amount remaining can be considered alimony.

↪ **Example**   Seth and Valery are divorced, and Valery has custody of their two minor children. The divorce decree stipulates that Seth must pay Valery $2,000 per month and designates $1,500 of that amount as child support ($18,000 per year) and $500 as alimony ($6,000 per year). During the year Seth paid the full $2,000 each month to Valery, until he lost his job on November 1. At that point Seth made no more payments to Valery for the remainder of the year. Of the $20,000 that he paid Valery ($2,000 per month × 10 months paid = $20,000), $18,000 will be considered child support and $2,000 will be alimony, even though the division of child support to alimony was really $15,000 and $5,000. This is because all of the child support must be met before any amount can be considered alimony for tax purposes. As a result, Seth can claim only $2,000 for alimony as a tax deduction and Valery needs to claim only $2,000 as income.

Debt Forgiveness

In general, if any personal debts are cancelled or forgiven, you must pay income tax on the amounts forgiven. The reasoning behind this is that if you purchase an item using debt, and then later the debt is forgiven, the money used to purchase the item is essentially income, since you don't have to pay it back but received the benefit of it.

If the item that you purchased with debt is repossessed you will need to pay taxes only on the difference between the debt owed and the market value of the item.

➾ **Example** Jack bought a new car for $40,000, using a loan to make the purchase. After two years Jack lost his job and stopped making payments on the car. When the car was repossessed he still owed $25,000 on the loan. The bank was able to sell the car for $20,000. Jack will owe taxes on $5,000 of debt cancellation income ($25,000 of debt cancelled – $20,000 value of repossessed car = $5,000 debt cancellation income).

While it is the general rule that cancelled debts lead to taxable "income," there are many exceptions to that rule. If one of the exceptions applies to you, then it would be good to seek professional guidance so that you do not end up paying more taxes than necessary. Some of the more common types of debt cancellation that have special guidelines include:

- Student loan debt
- Debt on your principal residence
- Debts cancelled in bankruptcy
- Debts cancelled when you are insolvent (insolvent means your liabilities exceed the fair market value of your assets)
- Business real estate debt
- Farm debt

One item from the preceding list merits a more detailed discussion in this book because of the large number of people it affects and because it has special rules affecting it at this time. The exception for non-taxation of debt cancellation income for personal residences is temporary, since it was enacted as part of the economic relief legislation during our last economic downturn. Typically debt relief on a house is considered taxable income. However, this temporary rule makes it non-taxable for any debt (up to $2,000,000) that is cancelled between 2007 and the end of 2013.

In order for the debt cancellation to be tax-free, the debt must have been used solely for the purchase, construction, or improvement of the taxpayer's principal residence. Any amount of debt that was used for other purposes and merely secured by the house would be taxable.

↪ **Example**   Alisha and Allen purchased a home five years ago for $300,000, making a down payment of $30,000 and securing a loan for the remaining $270,000. Three years after the purchase the home's appraised value had jumped to $420,000, while the loan principal balance had been paid down to $250,000. Alisha and Allen refinanced the home, securing a loan of $350,000. They used the additional loan funds to pay for a $60,000 remodel of their kitchen and bathrooms and used the remaining $40,000 from the loan to pay off credit card debt and take a vacation. Soon afterward, through tragic circumstances, they were not able to make the payments on the home and it was foreclosed. In a foreclosure sale the bank was able to get $300,000 for the home. This sale resulted in $50,000 of debt cancellation income ($350,000 debt − $300,000 sale price = $50,000 debt cancellation). Of the $50,000 of debt cancellation, $40,000 is taxable to Alisha and Allen ($40,000 of the loan refinancing was used for things other than the purchase, construction, or improvement of the home, which makes that portion of the debt forgiveness ineligible for the special exclusion from taxes).

At times you may be able to use more than one exclusion to reduce your taxes. For instance, in the preceding example, if Alisha and Allen were insolvent at the time of the foreclosure they could use the principal-residence exclusion for part of the debt forgiveness and the "insolvency" exclusion for the portion of the loan that they used for personal expenses.

🗎 **Note**   When you have had a debt cancelled for an item that fits into one of the "exception" categories, you may not need to recognize income on that debt forgiveness. However, if you still own the asset, you will have to reduce the cost basis of that item by the amount of debt that was forgiven—meaning the asset didn't really cost you as much as the original price because some of the debt was forgiven. For example, if you have $50,000 of debt forgiven on your residence that originally cost $250,000, it is now as if the house really only cost you $200,000 ($250,000 original cost − $50,000 non-taxable debt forgiveness = $200,000). The end result of this is that when you sell the asset in the future you may have a larger gain from the sale because of the "lower" original purchase price, increasing the taxable portion of the income from the sale.

Gambling Winnings and Losses

The way in which gambling winnings are taxed is unique. The laws governing gambling taxation are not favorable and actually seem to intentionally penalize those who receive this type of income.

Gambling winnings are fully taxable as ordinary income. In fact, *all* winnings are included in income, *not* net winnings (winnings minus losses). If you spend

$1,000 at a casino, and from that $1,000 win $200, the full $200 is included in income *even though you really lost $800!* ($200 won − $1,000 spent = $800 lost.) You may be able to deduct a portion of those losses, but because of the unique tax rules for this kind of income, many people end up being taxed on some or all of their "income," even when they had a net loss.

The most important rule regarding gambling income is that you can deduct losses only to the extent of your winnings. So, if you had $200 in winnings and $30,000 in losses, you can still deduct only $200 of those losses. Any losses that are greater than your winnings are, well . . . lost.

The next important rule is that the losses that you *are* allowed to deduct must be taken as an itemized deduction on Schedule A. You cannot simply net the loss against the income and claim no gambling income. You must still claim the winnings as income, and then take the itemized deduction.

This rule has two significant consequences. First, your Adjusted Gross Income (AGI) will be increased, possibly affecting your ability to claim other deductions and credits, and potentially affecting your marginal tax rates. Second, if all of your itemized deductions do not add up to be more than the standard deduction, the itemized gambling losses that you could have claimed are worthless to you because you do not have enough total itemized deductions to claim on your return.

⮑ **Example**   Luis loves to gamble, but his gaming isn't very successful. During the year Luis bet $40,000 on various gambling excursions. From those bets he actually won $10,000. Even so, Luis' total gambling experience for the year was a net loss of $30,000 ($10,000 in winnings − $40,000 in bets = $30,000 in net losses). Luis must claim $10,000 of income from gambling winnings on his tax return. Even though he had $30,000 in losses, the maximum deduction he could possibly take is $10,000 because the deduction for losses cannot be greater than the income he received. Worse yet, Luis doesn't have any other expenses that qualify as itemized deductions. Since the $10,000 in losses is less than the standard deduction available to Luis and his wife, he is not able to claim *any* of the losses. He has to claim $10,000 more income for the year, which is not offset by any of the losses, even though he really lost $30,000 during the year! If Luis were in the 25% tax bracket he would actually have to pay $2,500 in taxes on that "income," even though there wasn't any real net income at all.

As you can see, when you choose to gamble you may be risking even more money that you put on the betting table. In essence, when you make a bet you are also gambling with your tax bill—and the tax code has pretty good odds at getting its take.

🖺 **Note**   There is actually a way to get around some of these rules. To do so, you must qualify as a professional gambler. To qualify you must devote a significant amount of your time to gambling on a regular basis, depend on gambling winnings as a significant source of your income, and keep records in the same way that you would if you were running a business. If you qualify, you will report all of your winnings as income on Schedule C (for businesses) and all of your losses up to (but not greater than) your winnings. In addition, you could deduct other expenses, such as travel, lodging, and meals.

Caution   There is a significant downside to claiming the professional gambler designation. By doing so you are claiming gambling as your business, and as such you are required to pay self-employment taxes on your net income. This additional tax may eliminate the benefits of being able to claim losses (from expenses) in bad years.

Royalties

The tax code treats royalty income in two different ways, depending on the source of the royalty income. The key distinction is whether you perform work in order to receive the income, or if it is simply coming from an investment.

Royalties received from creative work, such as writing, music, art, or inventions are generally considered self-employment income (which means they are taxed at ordinary income rates *and* are subject to the self-employment tax). To receive this kind of income, you had to perform some kind of work. This kind of royalty income is reported on Schedule C (for business income), which allows for the deduction of expenses from the income. An example of an exception to this rule is if you are receiving royalties from a creative work that you did *not* create yourself, such as inherited royalties.

Other royalties, such as those from oil, gas, and mineral rights, are considered passive income and are reported on Schedule E (unless you own and operate a well or mine—then it would be employment income).

Just remember that the important factor is not what the income is called (such as "royalty") but what you had to do to receive that income. If you had to work to get it, then it is probably self-employment income, subject to self-employment tax and reported on Schedule C. If you did not perform any labor to receive a right to the income, then it is probably passive income and reported on Schedule E.

Awards for Legal Damages

There are three types of legal awards that are taxable as ordinary income. The first is any award for "punitive" damages (except for wrongful death damages in states where the only damages allowed are punitive). The second type of taxable legal damages are those awarded for a loss of personal reputation. Finally, any damages that are intended to replace lost income are taxable also.

Unemployment Income

Income from unemployment benefits is taxed as ordinary income. It is replacing the income that you would have had if you had remained employed, so it is taxable. However, you do not have to pay the payroll taxes on that income that you would have if you had been employed. Although there are no special rules or issues with this income, I have included this brief explanation because I am often asked whether unemployment income is taxable.

Bartering (Trading)

Bartering is making a trade with someone without exchanging money. I have often heard people talk about trading products or services with each other as a way to avoid taxes on the exchange. Though it may be hard for the government to track, the tax code is clear that such exchanges are taxable. If I provide tax preparation services for you in exchange for a weekend stay at your vacation home after the busy season, I should recognize income in my business at the value of the services or products that we have exchanged, as you should for the "rental" of your vacation home.

Tax-Free "Unordinary" Income from Non-Investment Sources

What Name Do We Give It?

There are several sources of income that don't fit nicely into a particular category, such as employment income, investment income, or business income. These sources don't really even fit into the "other ordinary income" category, in large part because these sources of income are often tax-free and don't come as a result of normal income-generating activities. Thus I group all of these sources into one chapter and called them "*un*ordinary" income. Included in this newly named category are:

- Workers' Compensation
- Disability income

- Gifts and inheritance

- Scholarships and grants

- Insurance proceeds

- Lawsuit proceeds

The first two items on the list, Workers' Compensation and Disability Income, are pretty simple. In nearly all cases the entire amount of income received from these sources is tax-free. The last four items on the list, however, have nuances and stipulations to the "tax-free" title that they bear, and so I focus on these four sources for the remainder of this chapter.

Gifts and Inheritance

When you receive a gift or an inheritance you do not need to worry about being taxed. If the value of a gift or inheritance is large enough to trigger a tax, the tax is levied on the giver (or the estate of the deceased) and not on the receiver. Each year I have clients call to find out how much they will owe on money that they have inherited. The answer is always the same—they owe nothing.

Caution   There is one important exception to this rule. If the administrator or trustee of an estate distributes the assets of the estate to the heirs *before* paying the IRS any gift or estate tax owed, the IRS does have the right to get the money back from the heirs. This is not a tax on the receiver as much as it is a recovery of money from the estate that belongs to the government and was improperly distributed.

However, taxes do eventually come into the picture for the receiver. When the person who received the gift or inheritance sells part, or all, of the gift, then the sale of the asset becomes subject to tax. There are interesting rules that govern the sale of gifted and inherited assets.

Gifts

When a person receives a gift, the asset generally retains the *giver's* cost basis. "Cost basis" in its most basic form is what a person paid for an item. Cost basis is what determines the taxable gain (or loss) on the sale of an asset—the difference between the cost and the sale price is the gain (or loss).

⇌ **Example**   Sylvester bought a work of art for $1,000 in celebration of his daughter's birth. His cost basis is $1,000. Later, Sylvester gave his daughter the artwork as a present when she turned 18. Even though the art is now worth much more than the original $1,000 that he paid for it, his daughter's cost basis for the art is still $1,000. If she were to sell it later for $10,000 she would have a $9,000 taxable gain on the sale of the art ($10,000 sale price – $1,000 cost basis = $9,000 taxable gain).

There is one important exception to this rule. If the fair market value (FMV) of the gift is *lower* than the cost basis at the time of the gift, a new set of rules kicks in when the asset is later sold. The rule that determines the gain or loss is based on the amount for which the asset was sold. If the asset was sold for less than the FMV at the date of the gift, the cost basis used to determine the loss is the FMV at the date of the gift. If the asset is sold for more than the original giver's cost basis, then the cost basis that determines the gain is the original giver's cost basis. If the asset is sold somewhere between the FMV at the date of the gift and the original giver's cost basis, then no gain or loss is recognized. Study Figure 9-1 for a visual illustration of this concept:

Asset is sold for a higher price than the giver's cost basis.	Use the cost basis to determine the gain.
Giver's Cost Basis	
Asset is sold for a price between the FMV and the cost basis.	No gain or loss.
FMV at time of the gift	
Asset is sold for a lower price than the FMV at the date of the gift.	Use the FMV to determine the loss.

Figure 9-1. The sale price, in comparison to the giver's cost basis and the FMV at the date of the gift, determines whether there is a gain or loss on the sale

⇌ **Example**   If the artwork that Sylvester had given his daughter was worth only $500 at the time of the gift, a new set of rules would kick in because the FMV is less than his $1,000 cost basis in the gift. If she later sold the art for $400 she would claim a loss of $100 ($400 sale price – $500 FMV when gifted = $100 loss). If, on the other hand, she sold the art for $1,500 she would have a $500 gain on the sale ($1,500 sale price – $1,000 cost basis of giver = $500 gain). Finally, if she sold the art for $700 there would be no gain or loss because the sale price was higher than the FMV but lower than the cost basis.

The holding period for the recipient of the gift (to determine whether the sale constitutes long- or short-term gains) is the same as the holding period of the giver. The only exception to this is if the FMV of the gift is lower than the giver's cost basis *and* the sale price is lower than the FMV was on the date of the gift, in which case the holding period starts on the date of the gift.

Inherited Assets

In general, the cost basis for an asset that you inherit is the FMV of that asset on the date that the decedent died. That basis could be higher or lower than the original owner's cost basis—whatever it is on the date of death is the new basis for the new owner.

In addition to the new cost basis, the new owner is also given an automatically assumed long-term holding period for the asset. Even if the decedent bought the asset a week before dying, and the new owner sold it a week after the decedent's death, the holding period is considered long-term and, as such, is given the benefit of long-term capital gains rates.

Caution   The rules governing the basis for inherited assets from people who died in 2010 were very different. If you inherited assets from an individual who died in 2010, be sure to check with the preparer of the estate return to ensure that you have the correct basis of those assets.

Note   Inherited assets are different than income from estate or trust. Income that is distributed from an estate or trust is taxable to the beneficiary as if it were his or her own income.

Scholarships and Grants

Scholarships, grants, and fellowships are tax-free to the extent that they pay for tuition, fees, books, and supplies. Amounts given for room and board *are* taxable and treated as income.

In addition, these funds cannot be given based on services that the student provides to the institution—in other words, they cannot be given in place of wages for services performed. Graduate assistants who receive a reduction in tuition are taxed on that reduction if it is their only compensation, but not if it is in addition to other taxable compensation (such as wages).

Finally, these benefits are tax-free only if the student is actively seeking a degree. There is no pretending that an employee is an eternal student in order to compensate him or her with tax-free income.

Insurance Proceeds

Most insurance proceeds are tax-free. The reason for this is that the money that comes from insurance is seen not as income, but as a replacement for something that was lost.

Life insurance proceeds are usually not taxable. In nearly all cases the money paid from an insurance policy goes to the beneficiary free of tax. However, there are two exceptions to this rule. The first exception is if the deceased person's estate (including the insurance) is large enough to be subject to the estate tax, in which case the insurance proceeds will be taxed as part of the estate (even worse than income tax). The second exception is if the life insurance policy owner is a business, and the business has deducted the insurance premiums as an expense, in which case the proceeds are considered income.

Tip There are two ways to keep the proceeds of your life insurance policy from being included in your estate. The first is to create an Irrevocable Life Insurance Trust (ILIT). You cannot be the trustee of the trust, but through the language of the trust and the choice of trustee you will be able to control the end results of where and how the insurance proceeds are distributed.

The second way to keep life insurance proceeds out of your estate is to have a person other than yourself be the owner. Once you do so you will no longer have control over important things relating to the insurance (such as naming beneficiaries and paying premiums), so there is some risk involved in this decision. However, if there is a person whom you can trust to be the owner and follow through on your wishes, this will allow you to get the insurance out of your estate. In addition, you can give the owner a gift of the money needed for the premiums without tax implications, as long as the amount is less than the annual gift tax exclusion for the year.

There are fairly complicated rules that come into play when you receive insurance proceeds for a damaged or destroyed asset that is a business asset, or that has been depreciated. If this occurs, it is worth taking your situation to a tax professional to ensure that you treat those insurance proceeds the proper way.

Lawsuit Proceeds

Court awards and damages received can be taxable or tax-free, depending on their nature. The best way to determine whether the money received is taxable is to consider what the proceeds are intended to replace. If the money is meant to replace income or wages then it is taxable (just as the income or wages would have been). Other taxable proceeds include punitive damages, attorney's fees, and damages related to a business or pension.

Proceeds awarded pursuant to a court hearing for a personal injury or sickness are not taxable. This would include damages for emotional distress that is a result of physical injury or illness. However, damages for emotional distress not caused by a physical injury or sickness—such as emotional distress caused by discrimination—*are* taxable.

Investment Income and Deductions

Interest, dividends, capital gains, long-term gains, short-term gains, original issue discounts, basis, dispositions, swaps, straddles, wash sales ... the list of terms associated with investment taxation goes on and on. Fortunately, the list of ways to reduce your tax bill through investments is fairly extensive as well. Part III is the largest section of the book and it is fully devoted to the ways that investment income is taxed and the deductions and strategies that can be used to reduce that tax.

Tax planning and investment planning should go hand in hand. There are a great many tax considerations that should be understood and remembered as you make investment choices. With that said, it is also important to not let the tail wag the dog, so to speak. Taxes are only one of many things to consider when making an investment. However, they are an important factor and can make a significant difference in the net growth and income that you derive from your investments. Study the chapters in Part III to prepare yourself for a great investment strategy.

Tax-Free Investment Income

Municipal Bonds, Roth Accounts, Your Residence, and Food

Very few sources of income are *not* taxed. In fact, I can't think of one that is *never* taxed. However, some sources of income can be tax-free, as long as you follow all of the rules. Depending on your marginal tax bracket, this tax-free treatment of certain income sources can equate to a significant increase in the true value of that income, in comparison to income from other sources.

☞ **Example**   Linda is the vice president of a large technology company and is paid a high salary. Her income places her in the 33% federal tax bracket, as well as in the highest tax bracket in her state of California, which is 9.3%—bringing her total marginal tax rate to 42.3%. Linda has invested most of her savings in California municipal bonds, which pay her an average of 5.25% in interest per year on her investment. Because the interest from these bonds is tax-free at both state and federal levels, the 5.25% that she is earning is actually the *after-tax* equivalent of earning 9.1% interest from a taxable source. She would have to find a taxable investment that pays more than 9.1% in order to end up with a greater *after-tax* income than she gets from the 5.25% municipal bonds, because so much of the taxable interest is eliminated by the tax (9.1% taxable interest earned − 42.3% tax on that interest = 5.25% left after tax).

As you can see from this example, finding sources of tax-free investment income can result in a significant difference in the after-tax benefit of that investment, especially for those in higher tax brackets. The way that a particular income source will be taxed must weigh heavily on the decision of where to invest your money.

Tax-free income sources can affect your overall tax burden in an additional way as well. Tax-free income sources are not included in the calculation of your Adjusted Gross Income (AGI). As you learned earlier in this book, a large number of deductions and credits are limited (phased out) by a high AGI. The tax-free income sources discussed in this chapter are not calculated into many of those phase-out formulas, which can lower your taxes even more.

This chapter focuses on four sources of tax-exempt "investment" income. Two of these sources are traditional investment options, while the other two may not be thought of in that way. The four investment sources discussed are:

- State and municipal bond interest
- Roth retirement accounts
- Home ownership
- Agriculture and livestock development

Each of these investments has special rules that must be followed. When those rules are broken, the tax-free income source becomes taxable. If you learn how each of these sources of income is developed and taxed, then you will be on your way to fewer taxes.

State and Municipal Bond Interest

The interest that is paid on state-issued bonds and municipal bonds (those bonds issued by local governments, municipalities, and their agencies) is tax-free at the federal level. The interest is also tax-free in most states for bonds issued within their own state (i.e., a California bond is tax-free in California, but a Virginia bond would not be tax-free in California).

As nice as this tax-free income may be, you must be certain to follow the governing rules. If you are not careful there are three things that could trigger a tax on this "tax-free" income:

- Capital gains tax
- Social Security
- The type of bond

Capital Gains Tax

Although the interest on municipal bonds is tax-free, any gains received from the sale of those bonds are subject to the capital gains tax. If, for example, you purchase a municipal bond for $1,000 and later sell it for $1,200, the interest that you earned while holding the bond would be tax-free, but the $200 gain *will be taxed*. In this way you can end up paying taxes on investments that you specifically chose to help you avoid taxes.

It is especially important to be aware of this factor when you purchase shares of a tax-free bond mutual fund. If the mutual fund manager sells bonds in the fund, a portion of the gains will be passed on to you at the end of the year. Even with funds that are geared toward minimizing such gains, neither you nor the manager can control the actions of the other owners in the fund. If those other investors withdraw their money (forcing the fund to sell some bonds) there will be capital gains (or losses) and a portion will be passed on to you.

The only way to ensure that you pay no tax on your investment is to buy individual bonds and hold them to maturity.

Social Security

Tax-free bond interest income is generally not included in the calculation of AGI. However, the formula that determines the amount of Social Security income subject to taxation *does* include this interest. Because of this, "tax-free" interest income can result in additional Social Security income being taxed, which really amounts to an indirect taxation of "tax-free" bond interest. This is an important factor to consider in retirement planning. For more information on this indirect taxation of tax-free interest, see the portion of Chapter 7 that covers Social Security taxation.

The Type of Bond

The tax-free status of municipal bonds has been a part of the tax code since 1913. However, it has been modified in the last few decades. Today several types of municipal bonds *are* taxable, or can be taxable, so take care to verify the type of the municipal bond you are planning to buy and how it will interact with your personal tax situation.

A prime example of this is a new type of municipal bond that was created in the wake of the global financial crisis, between 2009 and 2010, in an effort to stimulate the economy. These new bonds are referred to as Build America Bonds and had special federal subsidies attached to them to help the bond issuers and insurers. These municipal bonds offer a higher interest rate than their counterparts, but they are *taxable*. Don't make the mistake of buying this kind of municipal bond in hopes of earning tax-free interest. (However, you could buy these bonds in a tax-qualified account, such as an IRA, which would defer the tax on the interest until you withdraw funds from the account.)

Another instance in which "tax-free" bond interest can become taxable is found in a subset of municipal bonds known as "private activity" bonds. These are bonds that are sponsored by a government but are being used for a non-traditional government purpose, such as building a sports arena. If you are subject to the Alternative Minimum Tax (AMT), take extra care in choosing bonds (or bond funds) that do not include private activity bonds, because interest from those bonds is added to your income when the AMT is computed, potentially subjecting that interest to tax.

⌕ **Note**   In 1988 the U.S. Supreme Court ruled that the federal government is able to tax state and municipal bond interest (overturning a previous ruling from 1895 that made it unconstitutional to do so). Even so, Congress has continued to allow that interest to remain tax-free. In recent years, however, leaders in both political parties have indicated a willingness to begin taxing that income. It may be that the future lifespan of this prevalent tax strategy is limited.

Roth Retirement Accounts

Another source of tax-free income is found in Roth-qualified accounts. In a traditional qualified account—IRAs, 401(k)s, 403(b)s, and so on—you receive a tax deduction for the money that you contribute to the account, tax-deferred growth while the money remains in the account, and then you are taxed at ordinary income rates on any amount of money that you withdraw from the account. Roth-designated accounts work in the opposite way: you receive no tax benefit for contributing money to the account, but the growth in the account is not taxed while the money remains in the account and there is *no* tax on any money that you withdraw in the future (as long as you follow the rules). All income withdrawn from a Roth account is tax-free.

↪ **Example**   A Roth account gives Linda more tax-free investment options than any other investment account. Investments held within a Roth account can be of any type—bonds, stocks, mutual funds, and so on—and their growth is tax-free. For Roth accounts, the after-tax rate of return is a moot point because all types of investments are on an equal playing field in regard to taxes. So, Linda does not need to find a 9.1% interest rate in order to beat the after-tax income of her 5.25% municipal bond—anything greater than 5.25% would be sufficient because the municipal bond holds no tax advantage over any other investment when held within a Roth account.

The benefits of this tax-free income strategy could be tremendous if you expect your tax rates in retirement to be higher than they are in the current year, whether that is from a higher income in retirement or from higher tax rates that come in future years. I have many clients whose effective tax rate is currently very low but who can expect their rates to be higher in future years as their incomes increase and their deductions go away (homes paid off, children gone, etc.). A Roth contribution strategy for future income is clearly beneficial for these clients.

↪ **Example**   Sean and his wife Beth are 30 years old. Because of their large number of deductions and credits, their effective tax rate is close to 0%. As they observe the ever-increasing life spans of people as well as the increasing eligibility age for Social Security, they don't anticipate entering into full retirement until they are 70. At their current income levels they are each able to make a $5,500 contribution to a Traditional IRA or a Roth IRA, for a total of $11,000. If we anticipate an average growth rate of 7% on their investment over the next 40 years (when they reach age 70) and a marginal tax rate of 25% in their retirement, the difference between a Traditional IRA contribution and a Roth IRA contribution is dramatic. The after-tax value of the Traditional IRA money after 40 years would be around $124,000. The value of the Roth IRA would be nearly $165,000. That is 33% more after-tax income available to them by choosing the Roth IRA, all else being equal.

Another benefit of Roth-based plans is that you are not required to withdraw the money at any certain time in the future. You can let the money stay in the account and grow tax-free until you die, if you wish. In contrast, with traditional qualified accounts you are *required* to start taking minimum withdrawals from the account (and pay taxes on those withdrawals) once you reach the age of 70½ (see Chapter 7 for details on Required Minimum Distributions).

No requirement for distributions from Roth accounts gives a much greater flexibility and control to you over those funds and how and when you use them in the future.

○ **Tip** Because you are never required to make withdrawals from Roth accounts, they are an excellent tool for passing on an inheritance to your heirs. The money you put in a Roth IRA can grow for as long as you live and is then passed on to your heirs tax-free.

In addition, you are allowed to contribute funds to a Roth account no matter how old you are. With a Traditional IRA you are not allowed to make contributions after age 70½. Once you reach that age you are required to start taking withdrawals and so the government does not allow you to offset those withdrawals, making deductible contributions. With a Roth IRA you don't face that limitation. In this way you could continue to add to the amount available in the account as a tax-free inheritance for your heirs.

For a number of years the only Roth account available was a Roth IRA. Recently, Congress has allowed other types of qualified accounts to accept Roth contributions, such as Roth 401(k)s, 403(b)s, and 457(b)s. The same principles of tax-free growth and withdrawals apply to all Roth accounts, regardless of which type. However, the employer-sponsored plans have different rules than Roth IRAs relating to the amount of contributions you can make per year, as well as whether those contributions are limited by your income.

The Nuts and Bolts of How Roth Accounts Work

If you have a Roth contribution option available to you through your employer's retirement plan, there is no income-based limit on the amount that you can contribute to the plan each year. In contrast, your ability to invest in a non-employer–sponsored Roth IRA *is* limited by your Modified Adjusted Gross Income (MAGI). For example, in 2013 a single taxpayer whose MAGI is less than $112,000 can contribute the full amount allowable for the year. However, once that individual's MAGI goes above $112,000 her contributions are limited to a lesser amount. Her allowable contribution is eventually reduced to zero once her MAGI reaches $127,000. The formula that determines MAGI is below:

+ Adjusted Gross Income (AGI)

+ Social Security or Railroad Income not included in AGI

+ Deductions Taken for Traditional IRA Contributions

+ Deductions Taken for Student Loan and Tuition Expenses

+ Excluded Foreign Income and Foreign Housing Deductions

+ Excluded Interest from Education Bonds

+ Employer-paid Adoption Expenses

+ Deductions Taken for Domestic Production Activities

− Income from a Roth IRA Conversion

= Modified Adjusted Gross Income (MAGI)

As you can see from the formula, nearly every adjustment made to Gross Income in determining AGI is added back into the formula for MAGI. However, there are two very important exceptions worth noting. Any money that you contribute to a Health Savings Account (HSA) or to an employer-sponsored retirement plan—401(k), 403(b), 457(b), SEP IRA, etc.—reduces your AGI but is not added back into your MAGI. So, if your MAGI is within the phase-out ranges for a Roth IRA contribution, one of the best strategies for reducing your MAGI it is to contribute to an employer-sponsored retirement plan or to an HSA. Doing so could make a difference in the amount that you are allowed to contribute to a Roth IRA.

The phase-out is prorated evenly over the entire range. For example, the phase-out range in 2013 for a single individual is between $112,000 and $127,000, or a range of $15,000 ($127,000 − $112,000 = $15,000). If that individual's maximum allowable contribution were $5,500 for the year, the phase-out would limit that maximum contribution by $1 for every $2.73 that his or her MAGI is above $112,000 ($15,000 phase-out range ÷ $5,500 max contribution = $2.73 of excess AGI per $1 limitation). If a single taxpayer had an MAGI of $112,273 ($273 past the start of the phase-out), the maximum contribution would be reduced by $100 to $4,900. The phase-out ranges for Roth IRA contributions are shown in Table 10-1.

Table 10-1. Phase-Out Ranges for Roth IRA Contributions

MAGI Limits on Roth IRA Contributions for 2013		
Filing Status	Phase-Out Begins	Phase-Out Complete
Single and Head of Household	$ 112,000	$ 127,000
Married Filing Jointly	$ 178,000	$ 188,000
Married Filing Separately	$ 0	$ 10,000

If your MAGI is below the phase-out thresholds, you are allowed to contribute a maximum dollar amount to a Roth IRA per year. That maximum amount is adjusted each year by the IRS, based on inflation (as long as you have earned income equal to or greater than the amount of the contribution).

As mentioned previously, there is no income limit imposed on the employer-sponsored plans.

In addition, if you're 50 years old or older you are allowed to make an extra contribution of $1,000 over the normal maximum, which is known as a "catch-up contribution" to a Roth IRA. For the employer-sponsored Roth accounts the catch-up contribution amount is $5,500. The maximum allowable contributions to all Roth account types for 2013 are listed in Table 10-2.

Table 10-2. Maximum Allowable Contributions to all Roth Account Types

Roth IRA Maximum Allowable Contributions		
Tax Year	Younger than 50 Years Old	Age 50 or Older
2013	$ 5,500	$ 6,500

Employer-Sponsored Roth Account Maximum Allowable Contributions		
Tax Year	Younger than 50 Years Old	Age 50 or Older
2013	$ 17,500	$ 23,000

In order to contribute to a Roth account you must have "earned" income (income from employment) that is equal to, or greater than, the amount that you have contributed. For example, you cannot put $5,500 into your Roth IRA when you had only $3,000 of earned income for the year. This rule would preclude a person who is fully retired from transferring investments into an IRA each year.

O **Tip**   For parents and grandparents (or other relatives) who would like to help a child save for the future, there is an interesting planning technique based on these rules. The person contributing funds does not have to be the owner of the Roth IRA. If a child has earned income, another person can contribute money to that child's Roth account. For example, if a child earns $3,000 from a summer job, the child can keep the money for other uses and a relative can contribute up to that $3,000 maximum (based on the earned income) to the child's Roth IRA. It could be your family's personal "matching" program, helping the child save for a better future. (Also don't forget that "earned" income can come from the child doing legitimate work in a family business.)

Roth accounts have very specific rules about when you can withdraw money. You may not take withdrawals before you are 59½. You must also have the Roth for five years (even if you are older than 59½) before you take any withdrawals. This five-year period begins with the oldest Roth account that you own, meaning there is not a separate five-year period for each account (except in the case of Roth IRA conversions). If you break these rules you will be taxed on the proportion of the withdrawal that represents growth at ordinary income rates, plus an additional 10% penalty tax. (There are often state taxes and penalties associated with unqualified withdrawals, as well, increasing the total penalty paid.) There are a few exceptions to these rules, which allow for penalty-free withdrawals, which are detailed in Part 7 of this book.

➱ **Example**   Several years after Sean and Beth contributed $10,000 to their Roth IRAs the account value has doubled. When they see their account values at $20,000 they can't resist the impulse to withdraw the money and go on their dream vacation. They are in their 40s, so the growth in the account will be taxed and will also receive a penalty tax. If they are in the 25% tax bracket they would pay $3,500 in taxes and penalties on the $20,000 withdrawal [$10,000 growth withdrawn × (25% income tax + 10% penalty) = $3,500].

Converting a Traditional IRA into a Roth IRA

If you have money in a Traditional IRA that you wish were in a Roth, or if your income is above the phase-out thresholds for Roth IRA contributions but you would like to contribute if you could, there is a way available for you to put money in a Roth. You are allowed to change (convert) a Traditional IRA into a Roth IRA. You will need to pay income tax on the money that you move from a Traditional IRA to a Roth, but once the money is converted, it will have tax-free growth and withdrawals from that point forward (assuming you follow the rules).

➱ **Example**   Because Linda's income is far above the contribution threshold, she cannot contribute new money to a Roth IRA. However, she can still fund a Roth IRA by converting money she holds in a Traditional IRA into a Roth IRA. If she chooses to do this, the amount she converts to a Roth IRA will be added to her income for the year and be taxed at ordinary income tax rates—which in Linda's case adds up to 42.3%, considering both federal and state taxes. That may be too steep a price to pay for it to be a worthwhile decision for Linda, but for others in a lower bracket it could prove to be a great decision. Linda will need to determine if she has sufficient time for the investments to grow in order to make up for the taxes paid and the lost growth potential of the funds she used to pay the taxes, as well as estimate her future tax rates in comparison to her current rates.

○ **Tip** When deciding to convert a Traditional IRA into a Roth IRA, consider whether the additional income may push you into a higher marginal tax bracket. If the new tax bracket is 5% or 10% higher than your current bracket, it could really affect the results of your calculations in determining whether the conversion is advisable.

For individuals whose income precludes them from contributing to a Roth IRA and from taking a deduction for a Traditional IRA, there is an interesting strategy available for getting money into a Roth. Even when your income is too high to get a deduction for Traditional IRA contributions, you may still contribute to one without receiving the deduction (whereas with a Roth IRA this is not the case). When you make a non-deductible contribution to a Traditional IRA it creates a "basis" in that IRA, which means that when you withdraw money you will not be taxed on the portion that represents that non-deductible contribution. If you choose to convert the IRA (rather than make a withdrawal), you are not taxed on the basis portion of that conversion.

What if the only money that you had in a Traditional IRA was the amount that you contributed as non-deductible basis, and then you rolled that entire amount over to a Roth IRA? In that case, the conversion would be non-taxable. In essence, you would be making a Roth IRA contribution (which you are not allowed to do directly) by taking an extra step.

If you already do have money in a Traditional IRA and part of the money represents non-deductible contributions and the other part of it comes from growth or deductible contributions, then when you convert some or all of the money to a Roth the conversion will be prorated as part tax-free and part taxable.

⤳ **Example** Linda has made non-deductible contributions to her IRA for many years. The total of all her non-deductible contributions is $20,000. The actual value of all her IRA accounts combined is $100,000. So, the $20,000 in non-deductible contributions represents 20% of her IRA account value. If Linda decided to convert $40,000 of her IRA account into a Roth IRA, only $32,000 of that conversion would be taxable because 20% (the proportion of non-deductible contributions to total account value) would be considered non-deductible contributions.

꒾ **Note** Beginning with 2010, everyone is allowed to make a Roth IRA conversion. Before then, high-income earners and those who file separately were not allowed to make a Roth IRA conversion.

For a person with a large amount of money in Traditional IRAs, the non-deductible contributions to conversion strategy may not be very effective because the proportionate share of non-taxable contributions may be very small and not save much in taxes on the conversion. However, there is one other strategy that may work for this situation. If you have an employer-sponsored plan available to you—such as a 401(k)—you may be able to roll your IRA into the employer account. At that point you would not have any IRAs and could begin the non-deductible contribution to conversion strategy.

If you have a large Traditional IRA, it may not be wise to convert all of it to a Roth in one year because doing so could bump your total income into a higher tax bracket. Keep in mind that you need not convert *all* of the money in your IRA accounts. It is possible to do a partial conversion if that works best in your tax picture. You can choose to spread the total conversion out over many years. For some taxpayers, spreading the conversion out over many years can prove to be very rewarding.

⤳ **Example** Dan has quite a bit of money saved in an IRA but requires very little income to live on in his retirement. In fact, Dan pays no income tax each year because his income is lower than his exemptions and deductions. Each year Dan has me calculate how much money he can convert from his Traditional IRA to a Roth IRA before the additional income causes him to owe tax. I estimate as closely as I can the amount he should convert, and he then converts that amount, tax-free. By the time he reaches age 70½ and is required to make distributions from his IRA, he will have significantly reduced the amount he will have to take out, as well as reduced his taxes. He will also have never paid taxes on the money he converted from his Traditional IRA—he received a deduction when he put the money in a Traditional IRA, paid no taxes on the conversion, and he will pay no tax on that money or on the growth as he takes it out of the Roth IRA.

✒ **Caution** If you are younger than 59½ when converting an IRA to a Roth IRA, be sure to have the money available, outside of the IRA account, to pay the taxes on the conversion. If you use the money from the IRA to pay the taxes and convert only the net amount, you will be subject to an additional 10% penalty tax on that amount for taking an early withdrawal.

If you are 70½ or older and are subject to Required Minimum Distributions (RMDs) from your retirement accounts, you must still make an RMD in the year you convert a Traditional IRA to a Roth IRA. Be sure to withdraw the amount required, and do not contribute it to the Roth IRA with the rest of the conversion, unless you do it separately as a "new" contribution for the year.

If you make an IRA conversion in one year and later decide it was not a good idea, you can change your mind and switch it back. Although the initial conversion must be made by December 31, you can change your mind up to October 15 of the following year (assuming you file an extension) and revert the funds back into a Traditional IRA, in effect creating a situation as if nothing ever happened. The technical term for this is "recharacterization."

Why would you choose to do this? There are a few possible reasons. One would be if the money invested in the new Roth IRA declined significantly in value. You wouldn't want to pay taxes on a $50,000 conversion when the account is now worth only $25,000. Another possibility is that you may realize later (when preparing your tax return) that the tax consequences are more severe than you originally anticipated. I recently helped a client recharacterize a conversion that the client's investment advisor recommended because the tax consequences would have been devastating.

✒ **Caution**   If converting a Traditional IRA to a Roth IRA, do not withdraw money from that new Roth IRA within the first five years, or it will be subject to the 10% penalty. This five-year period for converted Roth IRAs is calculated separately for every conversion made and is not based on the oldest Roth IRA as it is for regular Roth IRAs. This could make things very tricky if you make partial conversions of your Roth IRAs over a number of years. I strongly recommend very accurate record keeping and separate accounts for each conversion, at least until the fifth year of the youngest converted account has passed.

Home Ownership

There is a significant opportunity in home ownership to achieve a tax-free return on your investment. Generally, any time that you purchase an asset for a given price, and then later sell it for a greater price, taxes are levied on that gain (the difference between the purchase and sale price). The tax code provides an important exception (or exclusion) to this rule when it comes to your personal residence. If you meet certain guidelines, the gain that you receive when selling your home can be tax-free. Many people have used this exclusion to periodically capture a tax-free gain from selling their home and, over time, use those gains to eventually pay for their new home entirely out of their tax-free gains, resulting in a huge cumulative tax savings.

↪ **Example** Chris and Courtney bought their first home for $150,000 shortly after they were married. Six years later they sold the home for $200,000 and purchased another home for $200,000, using the $50,000 gain as a down payment. Seven years later they sold the home for $300,000 and purchased a new home for the same price, rolling the cumulative $150,000 gain into the new home as a down payment. Five years later they sold the home for $400,000 and moved to a new area where they could buy a similar home for $250,000— an amount equal to the tax-free gains that they had accumulated through the three home sales. They paid cash for the home using only the gains, and never paid tax on any of that gain "income." If they had needed to pay tax on the gain with each sale it would have cost them $37,500 in taxes on those three sales, at a capital gains tax rate of 15%. That is a significant amount of money saved over time.

Three main guidelines must be met in order to achieve tax-free status on the sale of your residence. First, you must have lived in the home as your principal residence for two of the previous five years (from the date of the sale). The two years do not need to be continuous, as long as the home has been your principal residence for 730 days (365 days per year × 2 years = 730 days) of the previous five years.

Second, you must have owned the home for two of the previous five years. That may seem redundant, but it is possible to have lived in the home two years but not owned it for that long. This ownership test follows the same 730 guideline as mentioned earlier. Interestingly, the two years of ownership and two years of residence tests do not need to have happened at the same time—only within the last five years. So, you could have lived in it for two years, then purchased it and moved away for two years, and then sold it and you would have met both tests.

Third, you cannot claim this exclusion more than once in a two-year period. So, you cannot own two homes and meet the residence guideline by trading off living in each one six months at a time over four years and then sell both in the same year and claim exclusion for both homes.

🗂 **Note** This has been a very popular strategy with several people I have known, especially with those who are in the construction industry. They will build a home on the side, move into it for two years, then sell it and move into another home that they have built. It is sort of a slow, tax-free, home-flipping strategy.

The maximum gain exclusion per individual is **$250,000**, which translates to **$500,000** for a married couple. Any gain on the home greater than the maximum exclusion amount would be taxed. For married couples, the ownership test need be met by only one of them, but to claim the $500,000 exclusion, the personal-residence and one-exclusion-every-two-years tests must be met by both (otherwise it would be a $250,000 exclusion if only one spouse meets the tests).

○ **Tip**   A surviving spouse may claim the full $500,000 exclusion if three conditions are met. First, the home must be sold within two years of the date of death. Second, both spouses must have met the eligibility requirements of principal residence and no other exclusions within two years *before* the date of death. Finally, one of the spouses must have met the two-year ownership test before the date of death (the living spouse can claim the deceased spouse's length of ownership).

There are many additional rules and exceptions that apply—most of which are limited to very narrow circumstances. Most of these narrow exceptions are beyond the intended scope of this book and can become very complicated, but if you think you may have a special circumstance that would allow you to claim the exclusion, even though you do not meet the strict interpretation of the guidelines, it would be worth talking to a tax professional. There is a decent chance that your situation could meet the exception. With that said, there are three exceptions to the rules that apply to a sufficient number of people to warrant covering at this time.

First, the exclusion applies only to the use of the home as a personal residence. If during the previous five years you have used it as a rental property, or some other nonqualified use, the gain exclusion is prorated to the amount of time that it was your principal residence.

Second, if you have claimed depreciation on the house, the depreciation must be recaptured (and taxed) before applying the exclusion to any remaining gain.

↬ **Example**   Vince purchased a home for $200,000 and rented it out for two years. During that time he claimed $15,000 of depreciation on the home. After renting it for two years he moved into the home as his principal residence. He lived in the home for three years and then sold it for $300,000. At the time of the sale, the basis in his home was $185,000 ($200,000 purchase price − $15,000 depreciation = $185,000 basis). The total taxable gain on the home is $115,000 ($300,000 sale price − $185,000 basis = $115,000 gain). $15,000 of that gain represents the depreciation that he claimed and is taxed at ordinary rates. Of the remaining $100,000 of gain, $40,000 is taxable and $60,000 is eligible for the exclusion. This is because two of the five previous years (40%) were non-qualified use (rental property) and three of the five years (60%) qualify for the exclusion (personal residence).

The third exception applies to those who must leave their home due to a change of employment, a medical condition, or an involuntary or unforeseeable circumstance. For the change of employment exception to be met, the new job must be 50 miles farther away from the previous residence than the old job. For the health exception to apply, the move must be made in order to obtain, provide, or facilitate the medical care of oneself or a relative. For the unforeseen circumstance exception to apply, it must be for one of the following:

- Natural or man-made disaster damaging the home
- Condemning of the property by a government
- Death of the home owner
- Involuntary loss of employment, or change in employment status, making the owner unable to pay for the home
- Divorce or legal separation
- Multiple births from a single pregnancy
- Other similar circumstances may be considered.

This third exception (or group of exceptions) does not entitle an individual to the full exclusion amount. Rather, it allows him or her to claim a prorated amount of the exclusion, based on the amount of time that he or she met the guidelines.

↪ **Example**   Lance meets the ownership and residence requirements for one year (half of the two that are needed for the full exclusion), but is then transferred to a different part of the country by his employer. He qualifies for the change-of-employment exception, so when he sells his house 50% of the gain exclusion amount is available to him. This would mean that $125,000 in gains (one half of the full $250,000 exclusion) could be excluded from tax (or $250,000 if he were married).

Finally, the fourth exception is for those serving overseas. If an individual (or spouse) is on extended duty (greater than 90 days, or indefinite) outside the country, serving on official business for the military, foreign service, Peace Corps, or intelligence, the two-out-of-five—year rule can be suspended for up to ten years.

Agriculture and Livestock Development

If you have ever felt the inclination to grow your own food or raise your own livestock, maybe this "loophole" in the tax code will give you the final incentive that you need to become a part-time farmer. For a long time, gardening has been one of the most popular hobbies in the United States. More recently, a focus on organic and "local" foods has encouraged many people to take their gardening to the next level—creating mini-farms on their land and raising chickens for eggs. In addition to the health benefits, personal satisfaction, and taste-bud-pleasing attributes that this pastime can bring, there are also some rarely-thought-of tax savings that come from raising your own food.

↪ **Example**   The Johnson's monthly food budget is $750, which translates to $9,000 per year. Over time they develop fruit and nut trees, a substantial vegetable garden, and some egg-laying chickens. Before they know it, their mini-farm is producing enough food for their family to reduce their food purchases at the store by $4,000 per year. That reduction in the amount they have to spend on food is the equivalent of getting a $4,000 raise at work because they now have $4,000 more money available to use than they did before. The great thing is that the additional $4,000 in their pocket is tax-free (whereas the raise would not be). If they were in the 25% federal tax bracket and had a 7% state tax and 8% in payroll taxes (for a total tax of 40% of the $4,000 raise), $1,600 of that raise would go to taxes. By producing their own food they have saved $1,600 in taxes, or—put another way—they received a $4,000 tax-free return on their investment. Of course, there are costs in raising a garden, but you can buy a lot of seeds and trowels for $1,600 a year.

If you come to the point where you are producing more than you can eat, you can offer some of your tax-free "income" to your neighbors. Or you (or your children) can start a side-business offering locally grown organic fruits, vegetables, and eggs. Maybe you can sell just enough to cover your costs. Or perhaps you will dream big and realize that investing in an orchard or herd that grows over time can be a great tax-deferred investment (learn more about this idea in Chapter 15). Whatever the case may be, raising your own food can bring satisfying results to your table and to your pocketbook.

Taxable Investment Income

Know the Tax Rates, Strategies, and Traps of Each Investment Option before Going All In

There are many ways in which investments are taxed. It is important to understand how a particular investment will be taxed before jumping in because that taxation will have a real effect on the true earnings that you receive. This chapter focuses on the following areas of investment taxation:

- Capital gains income
- Dividend income
- Interest income
- Mutual funds—mutually confusing taxation
- Limited partnerships

Capital Gains Income

When you purchase an investment or business asset, and then later sell it, you generally must report the gain or loss from that sale on your tax return. If you sold the item for more than you paid for it, you have a gain. If you sell it for less than you paid, you have a loss. The price that you paid for an asset is called your "cost basis" (plus connected expenses, like commissions, minus things that lower the basis, like depreciation). It is your cost basis, compared to the sale price, that determines whether the sale resulted in a gain or a loss.

🖰 **Note**   It is important to understand that you are taxed on a gain or loss only after it has actually been "realized." That means that you have tax consequences only once a sale is complete. If you buy a share of stock for $100 that is now worth $300, you have a $200 gain in the value of that stock (sometimes referred to as a "paper" gain, because the value is only on paper—it has not been turned into cash in your hand). However, you will not be taxed on that gain (or loss, if that be the case) until you make it real—meaning the deal is done and the value (for you) will no longer fluctuate because you have sold it.

The tax code further distinguishes the sale of an asset as "short-term" or "long-term." If you have owned the asset for one year or less when you sell it, you have a short-term sale. If you have owned it for a year and one day (or more), you have a long-term sale. Long-term and short-term sales are treated very differently in the tax code. Short-term sales are treated as ordinary income, whereas long-term sales receive special treatment through lower tax rates.

The government has a vested interest in seeing the economy grow. An essential part of economic growth is the willingness of individuals to risk their money (or capital) by investing in business. Because of the critical role that business investments play in the health of the nation's economy, the tax code gives an added incentive to make those investments. If you do and you make money, you are taxed at a lower rate than you would be on other sources of income. This special treatment of investment income is known as "capital gains" income. However, only *long-term* gains get tax-favored treatment.

🖰 **Note**   Long-term capital gains have not always received special treatment in the tax code, and they may not in the future. There has been a lot of discussion in recent years about increasing the tax rates on gains for some, or all taxpayers. Some have even proposed taxing these gains at ordinary rates. Be aware of changes that are proposed and capture the low rates (by selling appreciated assets) before they go up, if that happens.

When considering selling any capital asset, from stocks to real estate, you should always be aware of how long you have held the asset. If the 12-month period is near, it may be worthwhile to hold the asset a little longer in order to significantly improve the tax consequences of the sale.

➼ **Example**   Jenny's broker called her one day to recommend selling a bond she owned. The value of the bond had risen significantly, and the broker thought it wise to capture the gain and reinvest the proceeds into another bond. Although this assessment may have been correct from an investment standpoint, the broker neglected to consider the amount of time she had held her bond. She sold the bond one week short of a year from her purchase date. Because of this, Jenny had to pay taxes equaling 33% of the gain, instead of the 15% she would have paid by selling it one week later. She likely would have made a similar gain from selling the bond a week later, but would have paid less than half of the tax.

▤ **Note**   Remember that taxes are only one factor to consider in your decision to sell an investment. Other factors may outweigh the tax consequences.

Long-term capital gains tax rates are at historical lows. The rate is 0% for those who are in the 10% and 15% marginal *income* tax brackets! It is amazing that for many people this income is not taxed at all. Regardless of your tax bracket, there is a significant difference in tax rates for long-term capital gains income compared to ordinary income. See Table 11-1 for a summary of the current long-term capital gains tax rates, based on Adjusted Gross Income (AGI).

Table 11-1. Long-term Capital Gains Rates Based on AGI

	Single or Married/ Filing Separately	Married Filing Jointly	Head of Household
0%	$0 to $36,250	$0 to $72,500	$0 to $48,600
15%	$36,251 to $400,000	$72,501 to $450,000	$48,601 to $425,000
20%	$400,001+	$450,001+	$425,001+

○ **Tip**   When you're investing in a mutual fund, rather than direct ownership of bonds and stocks, one important factor to consider is the ratio of long-term to short-term turnover of the assets within the fund. Mutual fund managers can differ significantly in their tax sensitivity as they manage the fund. Their choices in that regard will pass directly to your taxes and could significantly affect the net-of-tax return you earn on your investment.

As you plan for capital-gains income as a tax reduction strategy, be aware of the effect of additional capital-gains income on your overall income taxes. Even though capital gains are taxed at a lower rate, they are still a part of your AGI calculation, which in turn affects your ability to claim certain credits and deductions. It is possible to capture capital gains, assuming they will be taxed at a lower rate, but end up paying more income taxes than you expected because the effect of the gains on your AGI kept you from claiming certain deductions and credits.

⮞ **Example**   Mark and Melinda would have normally had an AGI of $167,000, except they sold some investments anticipating lower capital gains tax rates on the sale. The $20,000 in gains from their investments pushed their AGI up to $187,000. Consequently, their allowable itemized deductions were reduced by $200. Fewer allowable deductions translates into more taxes paid on ordinary income, and in Mark and Melinda's case, this meant that their marginal taxable income crossed into a higher tax bracket. In effect, the rate they paid by capturing capital gains income was actually higher than the long-term capital gains rate.

Although the example may not have translated to a much larger tax bill, it took into account only one affected deduction. If Mark and Melinda's increased AGI had reduced or eliminated other tax deductions or credits, the results could have been much more dramatic.

Loss Sales and Wash Sales

Because long-term capital gains receive favorable treatment in the tax code, capital losses have special limitations. If you lose money on the sale of a capital asset (you sold it for less than your basis), that loss is allowed only to reduce other capital gains income. If all of your capital gains for the year equaled $10,000 and all of your capital losses equaled $25,000, you would have an overall net loss of $15,000 ($10,000 capital gains – $25,000 capital losses = $15,000 net losses). You are allowed to take those losses against the gains, reducing the gains to zero, but the use of the remaining $15,000 in losses is limited. You are allowed to take a maximum of $3,000 in capital losses against other income (reducing your overall AGI), but no more than that. Any net losses remaining would carry over to be used in future years— either reducing the gains from that future year or reducing other income by a maximum of $3,000.

 ⇝ **Example**   Last year Angel had a net capital loss of $8,000. He was able to use $3,000 of that loss to offset other income, but the remaining $5,000 was carried over to the current year. This year Angel had $6,000 in net capital gains. He was able to use the $5,000 loss carryover to offset those gains, so the net amount of gain that he will be taxed on this year is $1,000 ($6,000 current net capital gains – $5,000 loss carryover = $1,000 net taxable capital gains).

If Angel had had $10,000 in net capital losses in the current year (instead of the $6,000 gain), he would be able to use $3,000 of losses this year against other income and would then carry over $12,000 in capital losses to future years ($10,000 in current losses + $5,000 in loss carryovers = $15,000 in total capital losses. $15,000 in total losses – $3,000 currently used = $12,000 in loss carryovers to future years).

Sometimes investors use a strategy called "harvesting losses." If an investor has 20 stock positions in his portfolio and has sold one that resulted in a gain, he may consider also selling another position for a loss in order to offset that gain and effectively pay no taxes.

 ⇝ **Example**   Ned sold 100 shares of IBM stock for a total gain of $600. Ned also owns 100 shares of Netflix stock, which currently are worth $600 less than he paid for them. If Ned is ready to sell the Netflix shares, he could do so and have a $600 loss on those shares that would offset the gains from the IBM stock. Doing this intentionally, to reduce taxes, is called harvesting losses.

Often, investors don't want to sell a stock for a loss. They hope to hold on to the stock until the price comes back and surpasses the price that they bought it at. Many times they still believe the stock is a good investment for the long term, but is just going through a slump in value. Many investors have eliminated gains by selling losing stocks and then immediately buying them back. In doing so they would realize a loss (in order to offset other gains), but would not lose their current position in that stock. This was a great idea—that is until the IRS said "No!" These shenanigans were not looked upon favorably, and so came into existence a rule known as the "wash sale." This rule states that anyone who sells a stock or option for a loss and buys that same asset within a 61-day period surrounding the date of sale is not allowed to use the loss for tax purposes. If the purchase of a substantially identical stock is made 30 days before or 30 days after the sale (or the same day—thus the 61 days) then the sale for a loss is a "wash," meaning it is counter-balanced by the purchase.

⮑ **Example** Marcus owned 100 shares of Exxon. He originally purchased them for $8,000 ($80 per share). When he heard about an explosion on one of their oil rigs he was certain the value of the shares would plummet, so he sold the shares as quickly as he could for $70 per share, for a loss of $1,000 (100 shares × $10 loss per share = $1,000 loss). Two weeks later it was clear that the explosion was not significant and Marcus repurchased 100 shares at $85 per share (for a total purchase of $8,500). Marcus will not be able to claim the initial $1,000 loss on his tax return this year because he repurchased the shares within the 61-day window governed by the wash-sale rules.

In a wash-sale situation, even though the tax laws do not allow the recognition of a loss, a real loss actually did occur. In the preceding example, Marcus really did lose $1,000 from his investment when he sold the shares. The tax code compensates for this real loss, only the recognition of it comes in a future time, rather than immediately. When a person has a disallowed loss, the amount of the loss is added to the basis of the newly purchased shares. In the future, when the shares are sold, there will be a lesser gain (or greater loss) recognized because of the additional basis.

⮑ **Example** In the preceding example, Marcus's second purchase of 100 shares of Exxon was for $85 per share, or $8,500. If there were no wash-sale rules his basis in the new shares would be $8,500 and if he later sold them for $100 per share, or $10,000, he would have a gain of $1,500 on those shares.

With the wash-sale rules, though, the previous loss is disallowed and is added to the basis of the new shares instead. In Marcus's case the unallowed loss was $1,000, so the new shares have a basis of $9,500 instead ($8,500 purchase price + $1,000 unallowed loss = $9,500 basis). Because of the adjusted basis, when Marcus sells the new shares for $10,000 he realizes a gain of only $500 instead of $1,500 ($10,000 sale price - $9,500 adjusted basis = $500 recognized gain). The $1,000 difference between the $500 recognized (taxable) gain and the $1,500 true gain on the sale makes up for the $1,000 loss that was previously disallowed.

The wash-sale rule does not occur in reverse. If you sell a stock for a *gain* and then buy it back within the 61-day window, you still must recognize that gain. Not fair? No, it's not, but it works well for the government, and they are the ones writing the rules.

There is a way to use this inequity to your advantage, though. If there is a reason that you expect your tax bracket to increase in the coming year (because you expect your income to increase, or you expect the tax laws to change and the rates to increase), then selling all of your appreciated stock positions for a gain and immediately repurchasing them could be very beneficial. For example, if you expect your overall income in the coming year will push you from the 0% tax on gains to the 15% tax, then selling your gains this year (and immediately repurchasing them, if you still want the stock) could save a significant amount of tax. If you have $5,000 in gains you would save $750 in taxes by realizing those gains this year instead of the next. (You may save even more than that, depending on where your total AGI is and whether the gains would eliminate some deductions or credits.)

Another situation in which recognizing gains could be beneficial is if you have a large amount of carried-over *losses*. Because the tax code does not allow you to claim more than $3,000 in net capital losses against ordinary income, many investors who have experienced large losses could have those losses carrying over to future years for a very long time. Those investors now have a great opportunity to capture those capital gains, tax free. You can take as many gains as you have in carryover losses without paying a penny in taxes (or even increasing your AGI). If you then repurchase those same stock positions you have effectively increased the basis in that stock so that your future gains (and taxes on those gains) are reduced.

One other reason that it may be advantageous to use up your carried-over losses is that the losses carry over only while you are alive. When you pass away the losses are lost forever. This is completely unfair because those losses were real but never recognized for taxes. However, whether it is fair or not, those are the rules. It would be a benefit to recognize gains to go against those losses while you can.

Long-Term vs. Short-Term Arbitrage

When calculating the tax on capital-gains income there is a set order that you must follow. First, every individual transaction (sale) is calculated on its own to determine whether it was a gain or a loss (as well as determining if it was long- or short-term). Next, all of the transactions are grouped into two categories, either long- or short-term. Then, all of the transactions in each category are added together to determine whether there was a net gain or loss for that category. Next you must net any short- or long-term loss carryovers from previous years with any net gains or losses for the current year in their respective categories.

The final step in the calculation is where it gets difficult, but it is also where there is an opening for strategic tax savings (*tax arbitrage*). Table 11-2 describes what happens next.

Table 11-2. The Final Step in the Capital-Gains Tax Calculation

		If you have:	Then:
I	1	Only long-term gains.	Those gains are taxed at favorable long-term rates.
	2	Only net short-term gains.	Those gains are taxed at ordinary income rates.
	3	Both net short-term and net long-term gains.	Each of those net gains is taxed separately at the appropriate rates.
II	4	Only long-term losses.	You may subtract up to $3,000 of those losses against other income; then any amount remaining will be carried over as long-term losses to future years.
	5	Only net short-term losses.	You may subtract up to $3,000 of those losses against other income; then any amount remaining will be carried over as short-term losses to future years.
	6	Both net short-term and net long-term losses.	You may subtract up to $3,000 of those losses against other income; then any amount remaining will be carried over as short- and long-term losses to future years.
III	7	Net long-term gains and net-short-term losses, with more gains than losses.	You may net the losses with the gains and the remaining gains will be taxed at favorable long-term rates.
	8	Net long-term gains and net-short-term losses, with more losses than gains.	First you will net the losses with the gains. With the losses that remain you may subtract up to $3,000 of those losses against other income; then any amount remaining will be carried over as short-term losses to future years.
	9	Net long-term losses and net-short-term gains, with more gains than losses.	You may net the losses with the gains and the remaining gains will be taxed at ordinary income rates.
	10	Net long-term losses and net-short-term gains, with more losses than gains.	First you will net the losses with the gains. With the losses that remain you may subtract up to $3,000 of those losses against other income; then any amount remaining will be carried over as long-term losses to future years.

The opportunity for tax arbitrage is found in rows 9 and 10 of the table, where you have net long-term losses and net short-term gains. Generally long-term losses offset long-term gains (which gains are taxed at higher rates) and short-term losses offset short-term gains (which are taxed at a higher rate). However, when you have net long-term losses and short-term gains, you are able to offset high-tax gains with low-tax losses, creating a special tax savings in the process.

If you have long-term capital-loss carryovers it could be very advantageous to sell positions for short-term gains, because you can use those carryovers against the higher tax short-term gains.

Special Rules for Collectibles

There is a category of assets that does not follow the regular long-term capital gains tax rules. If you have held a collectible for more than one year and sell it for a gain, that gain is taxed at a flat rate of 28%. The following items fall into the category of collectibles:

- Stamps
- Coins
- Precious metals*
- Precious gems
- Rare rugs
- Antiques
- Alcoholic beverages
- Fine art

Certain precious metal coins and bullion are considered regular investment assets and not collectibles.

In a strange twist of the norm, it would actually be beneficial for most taxpayers to sell a collectible for a short-term gain (held for one year or less) rather than long-term, since short-term gains are taxed at ordinary income tax rates. Those ordinary rates include the 15% and 25% brackets, which most taxpayers fall into, and would actually be lower than the 28% flat rate for long-term gains on collectibles.

An Opportunity to Double-Dip

Capital gains taxation includes one of my favorite opportunities for "double-dipping" in the tax code. That opportunity comes when you contribute appreciated assets, such as investments, to a recognized charitable organization. When you make a contribution of an appreciated asset, you can take a deduction in the same way you would if you had written a check to the organization at the asset's current market value. The bonus for contributing an appreciated asset, though, is that you will not have to pay capital gains taxes on that asset. You get a deduction for the full market value without ever recognizing (and paying taxes on) the gain. That's two benefits for the price of one—a very rare treat in the tax code.

↪ **Example**   Nicole purchased 10 shares of stock in August of year 1 for $100 per share (for a total cost of $1,000). In September of year 2 she sold the stock at a price of $300 per share, or $3,000. This transaction resulted in a long-term gain of $2,000. Her tax bracket for long-term capital gains was 15%, so she had to pay $300 in tax on the gain.

In year 2 Nicole also donated $3,000 to the Red Cross, her favorite charity. She did so by writing a check. This donation gave her a $3,000 deduction, resulting in a tax savings of $840 (she's in the 28% income tax bracket).

As an alternative, Nicole could have donated the $3,000 to the Red Cross in the form of her shares of Google stock, instead of selling the shares and writing a check to the Red Cross. If she had done so, she would not have had to pay the $300 capital gains tax and would still have received the $840 in tax savings from the deduction. This would have brought a combined $1,140 tax savings, or 38% of the value of the contribution.

This special tax treatment is available only for assets that have *long-term* gain. Donations of assets that have been held for a year or less (short-term gains), or of an asset that would bring ordinary income when sold (such as inventory) are not given this special tax treatment.

The total value (of deductions) that comes from donations of appreciated assets cannot exceed 30% of your AGI for the year. Any deductions of appreciated assets that are more than 30% of AGI can be carried forward for up to five years for future deductions. After five years the carry-forward disappears.

○ **Tip**   Do not use this strategy for assets that would sell at a loss. In that case it would be more beneficial to sell the position, capture the loss so that you can use it on your tax return, and then donate the cash to charity for the deduction. It is exactly opposite to the strategy for donating positions with capital gains.

The Effects of the Affordable Care Act (aka ObamaCare)

The key revenue-raiser in the Affordable Care Act (ACA) is the Medicare surtax (surtax is a tax levied on top of another tax). The surtax begins in 2013. There are actually *two* surtaxes in the law. The first is an additional 0.9% tax on all wages and self-employment income (earned income) over a certain threshold. The second is a 3.8% tax on unearned (investment) income.

↪ **Example**   Archie is a single, self-employed investment advisor. He spends a lot of his free time working on his personal investment portfolio. His total income for the year is $300,000, of which $250,000 came from his business and $50,000 from his investments. Because of the new law, Archie will pay a $450 surtax on his self-employment earnings and a $1,900 surtax on his "unearned" investment income (over and above the other taxes that he would normally pay on that income).

The 3.8% surtax of *unearned* income is somewhat alarming because it represents a significant shift in the tax rules. Before the ACA was enacted, Medicare taxes applied only to earned income. This change may signal a significant shift in the thinking of lawmakers: They are showing a willingness to apply employment taxes to income that does not come from employment in order to gather more revenue.

This new surtax will apply to nearly all unearned income, including interest, dividends, capital gains, rental income, royalties, and nonqualified annuities. It will not apply to income from retirement plan distributions—IRAs, 401(k)s, and so on—or to tax-exempt interest.

This tax will be levied only on taxpayers who have a Modified AGI (MAGI) greater than $200,000 for single individuals, or $250,000 for married individuals. It is important to note that the $200,000 and $250,000 thresholds are *not* indexed for inflation, so a greater percentage of people will be affected by the tax every year. The ACA surtax effectively increases the tax rates for long-term capital gains to as much as 18.8% for anyone in the 25%, 28%, 33%, or 35% tax brackets, and 43.4% for those who find themselves in the 39.6% bracket. The 3.8% surtax is applied to the smaller of:

- Total investment income, or
- The amount of MAGI that exceeds the threshold.

↪ **Example**   Doug and Maxine have an AGI of $280,000 and an investment income of $35,000. The 3.8% surtax will be applied to $30,000 of their ordinary income ($280,000 AGI − $250,000 threshold = $30,000, which is smaller than the $35,000 of investment income).

↪ **Example**   Scott, who is single, has an AGI of $230,000 and an investment income of $10,000. The surtax will apply to the $10,000 of investment income because it is a smaller number than the amount by which his total AGI exceeds the threshold for single taxpayers ($30,000).

📖 **Note**   This surtax gives an additional advantage to investing in municipal bonds, because the interest from these bonds is not counted as investment income. Since the tax is on the lesser of MAGI or investment income, if all (or most) of your investment income comes from municipal bond interest there will be little or no surtax.

📖 **Note**   There is a heavy marriage penalty in this surtax. Two unmarried individuals who live together could each earn $200,000 (for a combined income of $400,000) without paying the surtax, while a married couple can earn only $250,000 before paying it.

An Example of the Rigged Tax Code

Remember the discussion of unintended consequences in Chapter 5, showing that the way the tax code is written creates a compounding effect on the taxation of an individual as his or her income increases? The long-term capital gains tax is a prime example of this law in action.

Currently the tax rate on long-term capital gains is 0% for those in the 10% and 15% income tax brackets, and then it jumps to 15% for those in the 25% to 35% brackets, and then to 20% for those in the 39.6% bracket. This direct connection between the two tax brackets (capital gains brackets and income tax brackets) causes a "double whammy" effect on those individuals whose income increases to the point that they enter the 25% and 39.6% brackets. Each additional dollar of income is taxed at a rate of 25% (or 39.6%) *and also causes* a dollar of investment income to be taxed at 15% (or 20%) instead of 0% (or 15%). The true effective tax rate on that new dollar of income is 40% (25% income tax + 15% gains tax newly charged = 40%) or 44.6% (39.6% income tax + 5% additional gains tax charged = 44.6%).

Dividend Income

Generally dividends are regarded as ordinary, unearned income in the tax code. However, certain dividends are given a special "qualified" classification. This is significant because qualified dividends are taxed at the same rates as long-term capital gains. This special tax treatment is given to qualified dividends to encourage investment in the stock market, particularly investments in U.S. companies. The current rates for qualified dividends are listed in Table 11-3.

Table 11-3. Qualified Dividend Tax Rates Based on AGI

	Single or Married/ Filing Separately	Married Filing Jointly	Head of Household
0%	$0 to $36,250	$0 to $72,500	$0 to $48,600
15%	$36,251 to $400,000	$72,501 to $450,000	$48,601 to $425,000
20%	$400,001+	$450,001+	$425,001+

For your dividend to "qualify" for this special treatment, you must hold the stock for at least 60 days in the 121-day window surrounding the date the dividend was declared (meaning, during the 60 days before, the day of, and the 60 days after the dividend declaration). The dividend must also come from a qualified business, which is either a U.S. business or a foreign business the IRS has given qualified status to. The brokerage firm you use to purchase investments can tell you which dividends qualify.

As it was with capital-gains strategy, there are several important factors to consider with qualified dividends. First, when investing in a mutual fund be sure to note the ratio of qualified to nonqualified dividends the fund manager is choosing. A high amount of nonqualified dividends will significantly change the amount of taxes that you are paying on that income. Second, dividends of any kind will increase your AGI, so the apparently low tax rates may not be so low effectively if they change your ability to claim deductions or credits (because of AGI-based phase-outs). This could also be the case if the dividend's effect on your AGI causes other ordinary income to be taxed at a higher rate.

Finally, the surtax of the ACA applies to all dividends as well, potentially causing further erosion to the low tax rates offered on qualified dividends. For more details on any of these factors, read the details of the "Capital Gains Income" section earlier in this chapter.

Interest Income

In Chapter 10 I wrote about municipal bond interest, which is tax-free at the federal level, as well as at the state level if you live in the state of the bond's issuer. In addition to state and municipal bonds, any interest earned from bonds issued by the federal government or its agencies is not taxable at the state level. In high-tax states that distinction could make a fairly big difference in the net-tax earnings of your investment. Beyond government-issued debt, all other sources of interest income are taxed at the federal level at ordinary income tax rates (such as interest from savings accounts, CDs, corporate bonds, etc.).

There are two unique features in the tax code in relation to interest income worth noting. These items can make it so the tax you pay from your interest-bearing investment is based not only on the actual interest you receive, but on additional factors as well. These additional items are:

- Capital gains and bond swaps
- Original Issue Discounts (OIDs) and zero coupon bonds

Capital Gains and Bond Swaps

As mentioned in the "Capital Gains Income" section earlier in this chapter, regardless of the taxable (or non-taxable) nature of a bond, when the bond is sold it is still subject to the rules governing capital gains or losses. If you buy a municipal bond for $980 and later sell it for $1,000 you have a taxable gain of $20, even though the interest earned while you held it is not taxable. This is an important factor to remember when implementing a strategy for tax-free income.

Armed with this knowledge, however, you can use the capital gains rules to your advantage in something called a bond swap. A bond swap occurs when you sell one bond and buy another in its place. The tax advantage is found when you sell a bond for a lower price than you paid for it, realizing a capital loss. That capital loss can then be used to offset other capital gains (or ordinary income, to a limited extent). Then a new bond is purchased in its place in order to maintain the interest income that was being produced by the previous bond.

You are probably thinking that this tactic would fall under the "wash sale" rules discussed previously. After all, those rules state that if you sell an asset for a loss and then buy a substantially similar asset within a 61-day period surrounding the date of sale, you are not allowed to use the loss for tax purposes. The key to avoiding the wash-sale rule when it comes to bonds is the phrase "substantially similar."

The IRS considers a bond swap within the 61-day window to be a wash sale unless there are at least two features of the bond that are different. These features could include the issuer of the bond, the maturity date, the interest rate, or the rating. If at least two of these items are different then the wash sale rules will not apply.

⮑ **Example**   Stuart's investment portfolio includes a Chicago, IL school district municipal bond. The bond pays 6% interest, matures in July of 2035, and has an AA credit rating. He paid $10,000 for the bond when he bought it and it has a current market value of $9,500. Stuart sold the bond, realizing a $500 capital loss.

The next day Stuart purchased a Milwaukee, WI school district municipal bond. The bond pays 6% interest, matures in July of 2035, and has an A– credit rating (a lesser rating, but it is insured) for $9,500.

Even though both bonds are municipal bonds issued by school districts, both mature in 2035, and both pay 6% interest, this will not be considered a wash sale because two features of the bond are different: the issuer and the credit rating. In this way Stuart maintains a very similar investment in his portfolio while at the same time capturing the capital loss that he can use against other income.

Original Issue Discounts (OIDs) and Zero- Coupon Bonds

When an entity issues a bond, it takes a significant amount of time and effort to go through the regulatory and marketing process of selling that bond to the public. It is impossible for the entity to know what the going rate of interest on the market will be for the bond's issue date when the process is started months in advance. For this reason the entity will attempt to estimate what the rate will be and then let the buyers adjust between the market rate and the bond rate by purchasing the bond at a premium or at a discount.

⮑ **Example**   Widget Corporation needs to raise cash in order to produce its next great product. It decides to do so by offering bonds for sale on the market. Currently the market interest rate for corporations with their credit rating is around 9% per year. They move forward with their plans and print up bond certificates with a value of $10,000 each and an interest rate of 9%. Two months later, when they have received regulatory approval and marketed their bonds, the bonds actually go on sale. However, at the time they go on sale the going rate in the market has moved to 10%.

Who would pay $10,000 for a bond that earns 9%, when other bonds are available that pay 10%, all else being equal? The answer is that no one would. However, investors *would* be willing to pay $9,000 for that bond. Why? Because this discount makes the return of the two bonds equal. The Widget Corp. bond will pay 9% interest on the $10,000 face value, or $900 per year. However, if the investor only pays $9,000 for the bond and receives the $900 in interest, he is effectively receiving 10% in interest on his investment—the going rate on the market.

Widget Corporation is willing to sell the bond to him *at a discount* because it is the only way that they can sell the bond given the current conditions of the market. They will have to sell more bonds than they originally planned in order to raise the total sum of money that they needed for the new product's production.

(It is actually a little more complicated than represented in this example, but for the purpose of presenting the key concept as simply as possible I have left a couple things out. The end result is essentially the same.)

This discount on the original face value of the bond is called an Original Issue Discount (OID). This is important because the tax code actually taxes the holder of the bond on this difference as if it were interest. If an investor purchases a $10,000 face value bond for $9,000 and holds the bond until maturity, the issuer will pay the investor $10,000 as a return of principal on the investment. The IRS looks at the extra $1,000 between the original purchase price and the final return of principal as essentially interest, because the difference in price was used to change the effective interest rate on the bond.

Because the OID is viewed as interest the IRS requires the bond owner to divide up that total "interest" as if he were receiving it over the life of the bond, for tax purposes.

⟿ **Example** If the Widget bond in the previous example had a maturity of 10 years (meaning that 10 years after its issue the company would repay the initial face value to the investor and end the bond), then the OID of $1,000 would be divided up evenly over those 10 years and be recognized for tax purposes as $100 of interest each year ($1,000 OID ÷ 10 years = $100 per year).

The interesting part of this is that the "interest" that a bondholder is being taxed on for the OID each year is not actually flowing into the investor's account. He never sees an inflow of cash, but is taxed as if he did. It is a kind of "phantom" income that is created by the tax code. Each bond that is sold at a discount is registered with the IRS, so your investment broker will know if the bond you are purchasing is subject to this OID recognition before you purchase it.

Zero-coupon bonds are bonds that actually take the OID concept to the extreme. These bonds actually pay no interest during the years that the investor holds them. They are sold at a steep discount, and the return on investment that the investor receives is from a much larger "return of principal" at the maturity of the bond. (Another way to describe it is that the bond issuer doesn't pay anything until the maturity date, but at that date pays all of the principal and interest in one lump sum.) With this type of bond the investor will pay taxes on the "interest" evenly over the life of the bond, even though she does not receive that interest until the maturity date.

The opposite of buying a bond at a discount is buying it at a premium (paying more than the face value). This happens when the bond's interest rate is higher than the current market rate—investors will pay more to get the higher interest rate. When this happens, a bond owner has two options in how to deal with the premium for tax purposes.

The first option is to declare a capital loss on the bond when it matures for the difference between what you paid for the bond and the principal that you receive from the issuer (if you paid $11,000 for a $10,000 bond face value, you could declare a capital loss for the $1,000 difference). If you held the bond for more than one year it would be a long-term loss, offsetting the lower-tax-rate long-term gains. In this way you would be taxed at higher rates for the interest and lower rates for the loss—not the best case scenario.

The second option is to deduct a portion of that premium evenly over the life of the bond. If you do this you must also amortize the premium paid on any other bonds in your portfolio, in the current year and in future years as well. You must also reduce the cost basis in the bond by the amount deducted each year.

Tip   You do not need to begin deducting the premium in the year that you buy the bond. You can begin deducting it in a later year but then must continue doing so in each year after that.

Mutual Funds: Mutually Confusing Taxation

Very often I have clients who come to me confused by the way they are taxed on their mutual fund investments. The confusion comes most often when the value of the investment went *down* during the year and yet the investor is taxed for capital *gains*. Not many things are more frustrating for a person than to lose money on his investment and then pay taxes on top of that.

With mutual funds, three major factors cause the confusion. The first comes from the fact that the mutual fund is really a lot of individual investments wrapped into one. When you think of your investment in the *Ever Increase Fund*, you think of it as one investment. In reality, that investment is really lots of little investments in dozens of individual stocks and/or bonds. Each one of those individual positions has its own purchase date and price, and eventually will have its own sale date and price. The purchases and sales of positions within the fund go on all of the time as the fund manager changes its investment choices, even when you have not added or withdrawn any money from the fund. As each position is sold, it is sold for a gain or a loss based on the initial purchase price. At the end of the year your portion of that sold-position's gain or loss is passed on to you.

↪ **Example**   The *Ever Increase Fund* (EIF) holds $100,000,000 of investments. Tina has invested $1,000,000 in EIF (representing 1% of the fund's total investment) because she thinks it will bring her a great return. EIF's managers have purchased a portfolio of stock positions of 50 companies, one of which is NewCastle Products, which makes beach toys. EIF's total investment in NewCastle is $5,000,000 (which means Tina's 1% share of that position is $50,000 of NewCastle stock).

When a new study comes out that people are having fewer children, NewCastle's stock plummets because it is expected that the company will not be able to sell as many beach toys in the future. EIF's position in the stock goes down to a market value of $3,000,000, at which point EIF sells its entire position in NewCastle for a $2,000,000 capital loss ($5,000,000 purchase price − $3,000,000 sale price = $2,000,000 loss). At the end of the year, Tina's 1% portion of the capital loss ($20,000) will be passed on to her to report on her taxes (even though Tina did not sell her position in the fund—the loss is based on the individual position, not her overall investment in the fund).

When the gains and losses of individual positions that were *sold* during the year are passed on to the investor it can cause an interesting illusion. At the end of the year the investor sees the fund's current market value on the year-end statement. In that person's mind, whether she made money is based on whether the fund is worth more at the end of the year than it was at the beginning. In the mind of the IRS, whether an investor made money is based only on the individual investments that were sold during the year, not on the value of the investments held at year end. This can make it so that what the year-end statement shows and what is reported on the tax return can seem very contradictory.

↪ **Example**   Despite the big capital loss that EIF experienced with the NewCastle stock, the fund as a whole actually did very well. In fact, all of the other 49 stocks in the fund increased in value. Cumulatively the fund doubled in value by year end. When Tina received her year-end statement it showed that her account value had doubled to $2,000,000. While she was thrilled with the results, she also cringed a little when she thought of the taxes she would have to pay on those gains. However, when she received the tax forms it showed that she had a $20,000 loss for the year. This is because EIF only sold one position during the year (NewCastle), so that is the only capital loss that is realized for tax purposes.

The second factor that makes mutual fund taxation tricky is that your position in the fund is a proportion of what the fund does as a whole, and not what you do with your shares of the fund. In addition, the fund must react to the orders of individual investors, which will, in turn, affect you. For example, imagine that the stock market begins to drop rapidly, so much that there is widespread investor panic. If individual investors begin withdrawing money from the fund, the fund managers must sell assets in order to raise the cash to send to the panicked investors. Even if you keep a cool head and decide to weather the storm, keeping your money invested, all of the gains or losses that the fund incurs because of the panicked investors will be passed on to you for your share of the fund. You did not sell anything, but because others did you will be taxed as if you did.

⮑ **Example**   A few years later the EIF fund has doubled in value again—reaching a total fund value of $400,000,000 and bringing Tina's account value to $4,000,000. Then a major economic recession hits the world and the stock market begins to plummet. By year-end investors are in a panic and withdrawing money from the market indiscriminately, including withdrawing funds from EIF. The EIF fund is forced to sell many of its positions in order to deliver the money to investors who want out. At the end of the year the total value of EIF is half of what it was, and Tina's account value is $2,000,000.

Tina is devastated to see her account value decimated, but then becomes irate when she receives tax forms showing capital gains of $300,000. How could she lose $2,000,000 from her account value and have $300,000 in capital gains?! Even though the market value of EIF plummeted, the positions that the fund sold were actually sold for a higher price than their original cost. As such, a gain on those positions is realized and passed on to Tina for tax purposes.

It is important to note that if none of the investors in the EIF fund had sold out, and if EIF managers had held their positions, there would be no tax implications of the market downturn. There are tax consequences only when positions are sold, and then those consequences pass on to every investor in the fund whether a particular investor sold shares or not.

The third factor affecting the taxation of mutual funds is the timing of when the funds pass gains (and other income) on to the investors. Funds are required to pass this income on to investors only at the end of the year. This accounting method could have a significant effect on an investor who buys into a fund at year end. The individual could end up paying taxes on gains that he never received.

⮑ **Example**   By December 15 the market crash has reached its bottom and Ned, a savvy investor, recognizes that it is about to go up. Ned feels that the EIF fund is a great investment and believes that it is an ideal time to buy into the fund before it starts to increase in value. He makes a $200,000 investment in the fund, representing 0.10% of the fund's total value. When Ned receives his tax forms in the following year he will have a $30,000 capital gain to report (and taxes to pay on those gains). This is because the EIF fund issues the capital gain distribution on December 30t. Even though Ned didn't own the shares when the gains occurred, he owned them when the gain was passed on and so he is taxed on a gain that he never saw.

It probably goes without saying, but make sure to know about potential income distributions in a fund before investing, especially when investing near the end of the year. It is a much wiser tax decision to wait until after those distributions are made before investing.

These three factors make mutual fund taxation fairly unique. Understanding how the income distributions of a fund work can help you make better decisions and help you avoid the frustrations that come from confusion. In addition, there are many funds that specifically tailor their decisions, as much as possible, to minimize the income that is passed through to their investors. All else being equal, it would be best to invest in one of these tax-minded funds.

Limited Partnerships and REITs

An alternative form of investment is found in owning shares of a Limited Partnership (LP) or of a Real-Estate Investment Trust (REIT). In essence, investing in an LP or REIT is the equivalent of buying part-ownership in a business, similar to buying stock in a corporation. There are, however, some key differences between the taxation of LPs and REITs versus the taxation of corporate stock.

One significant difference is that with an LP or REIT there is no "double-taxation." With a corporation, the business pays tax on its profits and then the shareholder is taxed when the business distributes its profits in the form of dividends—resulting in a double-taxation of the same money. On the other hand, LPs and REITs are not taxed at the business level. Instead, all of the tax attributes (income, deductions, etc.) are passed on to the owners of the partnership and are taxed only once, at the level of the individual.

Because the tax attributes of an LP or REIT are passed through to the individual owners of the business, it makes the taxation of the "income" unique. Some of that income could come in the form of capital gains, some could be ordinary income, and some could be non-taxable return of capital. What usually occurs is that the overall tax rate of the income is reduced, at least in the short term.

⮑ **Example**   Jason invested $10,000 in an LP, which pays him an 8% distribution each year, or $800. Of that $800, $300 is taxed as ordinary income, $100 is taxed as capital gains, and $400 is not taxed because it is a return-of-capital.

The reason for this division of taxation is that the money came from different sources. The $300 represents Jason's share of the business's actual net income. Because it is from business income, it is taxed at ordinary rates. The $100 is Jason's share of a capital gain that the business received from selling a large piece of equipment for more than its basis, or for a profit. Jason will pay tax at capital gains rates for that part of the income, because that is where the money came from. Finally, the $400 represents money that the business distributed to Jason (and other owners) that was over and above the profits that it earned that year. Since this portion was not from profit, it is seen as a return of a portion of the original amount of money that he contributed to the business ($10,000). With that return of capital, Jason's basis in the investment will be reduced $400, becoming a basis of $9,600 in the LP investment.

The reduction in basis that comes from a return of capital will eventually lead to greater capital gains (or fewer losses) when the investor sells the shares in the business, or when the business closes. This form of investment usually results in fewer taxes per year on the distributions received (than what you might pay on other income sources), but eventually could result in a larger tax bill in the year the shares are sold.

Deductions from Investment Income

Deduct Your Investment Expenses from Your Income, Even from Ordinary Income

As the saying goes, "It takes money to make money." With investments it is no different. The good news is that there are several opportunities available to reduce your income by deducting your investment expenses, and there are even a couple tax credits available as well. In this chapter I focus on five categories of opportunities for tax deductions and credits that come from investments:

- Investment interest
- Withdrawal penalties
- Foreign tax credit
- Miscellaneous deductions
- Professional trader status

Investment Interest

At times investors borrow money in order to make an investment. This is done most commonly in "margin" accounts when a broker lends money to an investor in order for them to buy positions in the market. Some investors like this because they can make money on an investment using someone else's money. The return on the investment can be much greater by employing this strategy.

⇝ **Example** Beth is a skilled stock trader. She has a track record of spotting great deals in the market and taking advantage of them. Beth knows that she can make even more money from her investments if she has a greater amount of capital to invest.

One day she recognizes a growth opportunity in XYZ stock. She has $10,000 available to invest in it and she also borrows an additional $10,000 from her broker for a total of $20,000 to invest in the stock.

It turns out that her hunch was correct and XYZ stock shoots up 25% in its value over the next three weeks, bringing her original position in the stock from $20,000 to $25,000. At that point she sells the stock and pays back the loan of $10,000 to the broker.

By borrowing the $10,000 Beth was able to achieve a capital gain of $5,000, whereas the gain would have been only $2,500 had she used only her own money. In effect, Beth achieved a 50% gain on *her* money when the stock went up only 25%. Though the broker charges interest on that loan, it is far outweighed by Beth's gain from the stock that she purchased by borrowing.

Another form of investment interest is incurred when an individual borrows money to buy a business (not to be confused with money that is borrowed to run a company). This interest can be used as an interest deduction as well. It is not the source of the loan that determines the status of the interest, but how the money is used (if it is used to make an investment).

Investment interest expense is deductible *up to* the total amount of net investment income reported on the return. For the purpose of this deduction, net-investment income includes all investment income that is taxed at ordinary rates (such as ordinary interest, ordinary dividends, and short-term capital gains). Any unused investment interest is carried forward to be used against investment income in future years.

↪ **Example**   Chuck purchased a business four years ago using loans for a large portion of the purchase. Over those four years, Chuck has paid $35,000 in interest. Because it qualifies as investment interest, Chuck could earn short-term capital gains, interest, and dividends up to $35,000 and pay no taxes on that income because it would be offset by the investment interest deduction.

The investment interest expense deduction could actually be used to offset qualified dividends and long-term capital gains as well. To do so you must make an election on your tax return to treat the dividends as ordinary (not qualified) and the gains as short-term (not long). Why would you do this? If you are in the upper income brackets that trigger the 15% or 20% tax on long-term gains and qualified dividends you could use this deduction to reduce or eliminate that tax. A 0% tax is still better than 15% or 20%. However, if you anticipate having ordinary investment income in the future, it may be more beneficial to you to let the unused interest expense roll over to future years.

It is important to note that the interest expense deduction is taken on Schedule A. This means that if you do not have enough total deductions on Schedule A, you will not be able to use the interest deduction.

Withdrawal Penalties

Interest from Certificates of Deposit (CDs) issued by banks is taxed as it is earned, not when it is paid. If you have a CD with a maturity date in a future year you will be taxed on the amount of interest attributable to the current year. This is much like the treatment of Original Issue Discount (OID) interest discussed in Chapter 11.

If you withdraw money from a CD before its maturity date, most banks will charge you a penalty for the early withdrawal—sometimes as much as the interest earned. If this happens, you are allowed to deduct that fee as an above-the-line adjustment to income. This deduction essentially makes up for the tax that you paid in previous years for interest that you never really received, because of the fees.

Foreign Tax Credit

The United States taxes income that you earn from any source, including foreign sources. However, to reduce double-taxation of income, the tax code provides a credit for the income taxes that you are required to pay a foreign country. For a diversified investor it is not uncommon to have foreign taxes withheld from interest or dividends earned from foreign sources. Most often these taxes are reported on the 1099 that is provided by the investment company.

To calculate the credit, a comparison is made between the tax that the investor would pay on the income under U.S. tax law and the tax that is charged by the foreign country. A credit can be claimed on the taxes paid, up to (but not exceeding) the tax that would have been charged under U.S. law.

↪ **Example**   Vanessa owns 1,000 shares of a company based in France, which pays her $2,000 in dividends each year. France requires that the company withhold 20% of all dividends paid as a tax on that income, totaling $400 in withholdings for Vanessa ($2,000 dividends × 20% tax = $400 withheld). Under U.S. law, Vanessa would owe 15% in taxes on that same dividend income, or $300. However, because she has paid $400 in taxes on that income to France, Vanessa can claim a $300 credit on her U.S. income tax return—the lesser amount of what she paid to a foreign country or what she would have paid to the United States on that same income.

The Foreign Tax Credit is non-refundable, so it cannot be larger than the total income tax for the return. If it is greater, the excess portion can be carried back and used one year previous to the year of the return, or carried forward for up to ten years.

Miscellaneous Deductions

As a general rule, expenses that are incurred for the purpose of producing income are deductible against that income. At times, those deductions are reduced, or limited. There are several investment expenses that can potentially be claimed as deductions against your income. Here is a list of some of the more common ones:

- Fees to a financial advisor for investment advice or management of investments

- Software and online services used to manage your investment accounts

- Financial publications

- Custodial fees of qualified accounts (such as IRAs) *if* paid outside of the account

- Accountant or attorney fees paid to determine taxable income.

- Safe deposit box rental fees, if used to store investment-related documents or actual investments (such as bullion)

- Travel to your broker or financial advisor's office

All of these expenses are claimed as Miscellaneous Itemized Deductions and are subject to a limitation on their deductibility based on your Adjusted Gross Income (AGI). You may only claim those expenses that are greater than 2% of your AGI. For example, if you have $3,000 in miscellaneous deductions and your AGI is $100,000 you will be able to claim $1,000 of those expenses as a deduction (2% of $100,000 AGI = $2,000 limitation. $3,000 of miscellaneous expenses − $2,000 limitation = $1,000 deductible miscellaneous expenses). This limitation is applied only once to all miscellaneous deductions. It may be that other miscellaneous deductions (such as unreimbursed employee expenses or tax preparation fees) have already crossed the 2% limit and then other miscellaneous deductions like investment expenses would be fully deductible.

In addition to the 2% of AGI limitation, all of your itemized deductions (of any kind) must add up to more than the standard deduction to be of any value. In essence, there are two factors limiting your deduction for investment expenses—the 2% AGI limitation *and* the total value of all of your itemized deductions combined. Even with these limitations, many taxpayers are able to take advantage of these deductions to reduce their taxable income.

Caution   Certain investment expenses are not deductible, such as commissions paid on investments, travel to shareholder's meetings, and any expenses paid that are related to tax-exempt income.

Professional Trader Status

Are you a "day trader?" Do you actively and regularly trade stocks in your own account? If you do, you may qualify as a *professional trader* for tax purposes and, as such, receive significant tax benefits.

One major benefit that professional traders receive is the ability to deduct all of their trading-related expenses directly from their investment income. These deductible expenses are not limited to the ones listed in the Miscellaneous Deductions section, but also include all normal business expenses, such as computer and equipment purchases, Internet service, mileage, meals and entertainment, cell phones, trader chat-room fees, subscriptions, home-office expenses, educational courses, and so on. These expenses are not listed on Schedule A, where they would be limited by the 2% of AGI floor, but rather are listed on Schedule C (for businesses) where they are deducted directly from income. Margin interest is also directly deductible and not subject to the limitations of the investment interest deduction rules.

> **Caution**   A very common deduction claimed by traders is the cost of educational courses they take to become better traders. Though this deduction is allowed as a continuing education expense, it is not allowed for those learning how to get into the business. For educational expenses to be taken as a business deduction it must be for courses taken to improve one's skill in an already-established profession, not to qualify an individual for a *new* business or profession.

Another benefit is that the deduction of net capital losses is not limited to $3,000 per year. If a professional trader loses $20,000 in a bad year, the entire amount can be deducted against all other income because it is considered to be business income. This difference alone can have a dramatic effect on the individual's total tax bill.

> **Caution**   To be able to take the full deduction, a trader must notify the IRS of her status as a professional trader and elect Mark-to-Market accounting treatment. This is a fairly complex process and it would be wise to consult a tax professional for help.
>
> If you have loss carryovers from previous years you may be better off waiting to elect the professional trader status until you have used up those losses by offsetting future gains. Otherwise a gain on the professional-trader business side of your return will be taxed and cannot be offset by the loss carryovers from previous years.

Even though the income and expenses of a professional trader are reported as business income on Schedule C, the trader is not subject to self-employment tax on that income because it comes from capital gains and other investment-related income. It is significant that the professional trader is afforded all of the tax treatments, deductions, and benefits of a business owner and yet does not have to pay the self-employment tax. In fact, I am really surprised that this is the case.

One other significant difference for professional traders is that they are not subject to the "wash-sale" rules. This too is significant, and can open up some real tax-planning opportunities for a trader each year by offsetting income with losses. In addition, the professional trader doesn't need to report individual trades on his tax return, but can simply report the net results for the year of gains and losses.

Qualifying as a professional trader also allows the individual to set up an employer-sponsored retirement plan, such as a Simplified Employee Pension (SEP) IRA, Savings Incentive Match Plan for Employees (SIMPLE), or a defined benefit plan (among others). All of the benefits of owning a business become available for a trader who elects professional status.

Are you a professional trader? Here's what it takes:

With all of these great benefits available to professional traders you can bet that there have been a lot of people who have tried to claim this status just so that they can be better off come tax time. The IRS is keenly aware of this temptation and has aggressively fought such abuses. To claim the status of professional trader you have to meet some stringent guidelines, based on the results of important court cases on this subject.

First, you must trade on a regular basis—very regular. In fact, if you are not actively trading a minimum of 50% of the available trading days in the year, you probably don't qualify. In fact, you need to not only be trading most days, but also transacting multiple times on those days. An average of three trades a day is probably the minimum amount it takes to pass muster. In reality, the number of trades that you make per year should be in the thousands, not in the low hundreds, in order to safely pass this test before the IRS and the courts.

Second, you must be trading for short-term swings in the market, not for long-term growth. Leaving your investments to grow for a year or more makes you more of an investor, not a trader. You must also have an established margin account that you use for pattern trading.

Third, you must be making these trades for your own account, not for clients. If you are managing the accounts of clients you are in a different kind of business, which doesn't enjoy the benefits of the professional trader status.

Finally, as mentioned in the caution note previously, there is a formal process of paperwork and elections that must be made to the IRS in order to claim the professional trader status.

Education Investment Strategies

Where the "Smart Money" Invests for Education

There are a number of tax-benefited ways to fund a college education, each with its own set of rules. In addition, many non-investment tax strategies help with the cost of higher education. These other strategies are discussed in Chapter 20 and Chapter 30. This chapter focuses on the methods for reducing the taxes on investments set aside for education expenses, including the following:

- 529 plans and Qualified Tuition Programs
- Coverdell Educational Savings Accounts
- Education Savings Bonds
- IRAs and Roth IRAs
- Gifting appreciated items

529 Plans and Qualified Tuition Programs

529 plans and Qualified Tuition Programs (QTPs) are programs run by a state or by an educational institution, such as a private college or university, designed

to help families save for future higher-education tuition costs. QTPs are basically pre-paid tuition plans, in which an institution accepts tuition payments at current prices in payment for future tuition costs for the beneficiary. 529 plans are savings instruments, similar to IRAs, which can be used for tax-deferred growth, which becomes tax-free growth if it is used for qualified educational expenses.

At the federal level, no tax deductions are given for contributions made to 529s and QTPs. However, some states do offer a tax deduction for contributions made to the state-sponsored plan, assuming you pay income taxes to that state. Growth on the investments in the plan is tax-deferred, and withdrawals of the funds (both principal and growth) are tax-free when used for qualified expenses. Expenses that qualify for tax-free treatment are:

- Tuition
- Books
- Fees
- Supplies
- Equipment (if required for enrollment or attendance)
- Room and board (if enrolled at least half-time)

There is no dollar-based limitation placed on the amount of money that can be invested in a 529 or QTP. The only limit is that the amount invested cannot be greater than the amount that is necessary for the beneficiary's qualified tuition expenses. There are also no limits placed on who can contribute to a plan—no matter what an individual's Adjusted Gross Income (AGI), he or she may contribute to a 529 or QTP.

You may have only one beneficiary per 529 account, so, each child will need to have his or her own. However, if the beneficiary of the account does not use the funds because he or she chooses not to go to school, earns a scholarship, or whatever the reason, the beneficiary can be changed to another family member without triggering the tax.

You must decide who the owner will be, as well as the successor owner in the event that the owner dies. The choice of successor is important because he or she will have the ability to change the beneficiary; choose one who will have the child's interests first.

Contributing funds to a QTP or 529 is considered a gift for gift-tax purposes. The annual gift-tax exclusion is available for these contributions. That means that in 2013 an individual may contribute up to $14,000 to a QTP or 529 per individual beneficiary. A married couple may elect to treat their contributions separately, each giving $14,000 to an individual, for a total possible gift of $28,000 per beneficiary per year.

Tip If an individual or couple would like to contribute more than the annual-exclusion amount in one year, they may do so by electing to spread that gift over five years for tax purposes. A gift-tax return must be filed to make this election, and care must be taken to not make gifts in the following five years to the same beneficiary in an amount that would exceed the extended exclusion. In this way a couple could contribute as much as $140,000 ($14,000 exclusion × 2 individuals × 5 years = $140,000) in one year to a single beneficiary's 529 or QTP. Also note that the gift-tax limitation is per contributor, not per recipient. In theory, many people could contribute substantial amounts to an individual's 529 or QTP and there would be no limit on the total contributions, other than the total qualified educational expenses that the beneficiary will need.

Discuss with your financial advisor the important investment limitations placed on 529 plans, such as what investments can be chosen and how often they can be changed. In addition, most state-sponsored plans are run by a mutual fund company and, as such, have only the funds of that company available to choose from.

Should you decide to pull money from a 529 account for nonqualified reasons, the growth of the investment will be taxed at the beneficiary's applicable income tax rates *plus* an additional 10% penalty tax (plus any taxes and penalties imposed by the state). Because of this penalty you should use caution to not invest more money into the plan than will be used for education.

Coverdell Educational Savings Accounts

Coverdell Educational Savings Accounts (ESAs), formerly known as Education IRAs, are a more limited vehicle for tax-benefited college savings, other than the 529 plans and QTPs. However, two features of these accounts make them intriguing in certain circumstances.

First, the funds in these accounts are not limited to higher education, but can also be used for qualified elementary and secondary education expenses (such as for private school) and many other school-related costs. This opens up additional possibilities for parents and grandparents who are seeking tax-preferred ways to enhance their children's or grandchildren's education. The list of qualified educational expenses includes:

- Tuition for all levels of education from elementary school through graduate level
- Books
- Fees
- Supplies

- Equipment (if required for enrollment or attendance)

- Room and board (if enrolled at least half-time)

- Tutoring (for K-12)

- Transportation (for K–12)

- Uniforms (for K–12)

- Extended Day programs

Second, funds can be contributed to 529/QTP plans *and* Coverdells in the same year, which opens up additional planning opportunities.

A maximum of $2,000 per beneficiary may be contributed to a Coverdell account (or combination of accounts) per year. It does not matter how many people contribute, or how many accounts there are; the grand total of contributions per beneficiary cannot exceed $2,000. In today's world this is not very much money, even for a private elementary school—much less for higher education. However, the amount allowable is not indexed for inflation, so has remained the same since it was last changed in 2002 (prior to that it was $500).

The contributions are not deductible. However, the growth in the account is tax-deferred, and if used for qualified purposes when withdrawn it is tax-free. A person's ability to *make* contributions is limited by his or her AGI. The allowable contribution is phased out for married couples in the $190,000 to $220,000 range of Modified AGI (MAGI). The phase-out is between $95,000 and $110,000 for single filers These contributions are considered gifts, so the amount given must be included in the annual gift-tax exclusion with any other gifts given to the same individual.

If funds are withdrawn from an ESA for nonqualified reasons the growth portion of the investment will be taxed at the beneficiary's applicable income tax rates *plus* an additional 10% penalty tax (plus any taxes and penalties imposed by the state). However, the 10% penalty does not apply if the distribution is less than the amount of a scholarship received by the beneficiary. It also does not apply in the event of the death or disability of the beneficiary. In these cases, though, regular income tax on the growth will be due—only the penalty is waived.

The ESA must be established before the beneficiary's 18th birthday. In addition, all funds must be withdrawn from the account by the time that the beneficiary reaches the age of 30. However, the beneficiary can be changed to a family member in the same (or previous) generation if that new beneficiary meets the age requirements.

Education Savings Bonds

The federal government issues Education Savings Bonds as "zero-coupon" bonds, meaning they are sold at a discounted rate, pay no interest during the holding period, and then pay a higher principal amount than the original selling price when they mature. For example, you might purchase a savings bond for $800 that will pay you $1,000 when it matures in 5 years (and no interest). The higher amount paid at maturity is the implicit interest on the bond, which in this case would be 5% simple interest ($800 × 5% = $40, $40 × 5 years = $200 increased price at maturity).

As you learned in Chapter 11, the implicit interest in this type of bond is usually taxed each year on a pro-rata basis. However, with Series EE and Series I federal savings bonds you can elect to not recognize the interest until you sell the bond or until it matures. Further, if you use the proceeds of the bond for qualified higher-educational expenses you don't ever need to recognize the interest—it is tax-free.

To qualify, the purchaser of the bond must have been at least 24 years old before the bond was originally *issued* (not when it was purchased). The proceeds of the bond must be used for the educational expenses of the bond owner or the owner's spouse or dependents. Qualified expenses include only tuition and fees that are required for enrollment or attendance at an eligible educational institution.

The exclusion of interest income is subjected to a MAGI-based phase-out as well. For 2013, a married couple's ability to exclude the interest income is phased out when MAGI is between $112,050 and $142,050. For all other taxpayers the phase-out is between $74,700 and $89,700 MAGI. MAGI is calculated using the following formula:

+ AGI

+ Non-taxable Social Security

+ IRA deductions

+ Qualified adoption expenses

+ Student loan interest deduction

+ Tuition deduction

+ Foreign income exclusion
_____
= MAGI

IRAs and Roth IRAs

Saving for an education using an IRA or Roth IRA is not an ideal method. However, if the situation arises such that the only funds available for necessary educational expenses are in one of these accounts, it is good to know that the normal 10% penalty on early withdrawals will not apply. If you withdraw funds from these accounts regular income taxes *will* be due, but no additional penalty.

For this exception to apply the money must be used for the higher education expenses of the IRA owner, or the owner's spouse, child, or grandchild. Qualified expenses include tuition, fees, books, supplies, and equipment necessary for post-secondary education. Note that room and board are not included in the list.

A Word of Caution (and Coordination)

It is important to understand that there is no double-dipping allowed with the qualified expenses used for any of the four savings strategies listed above. If you count certain expenses toward the qualified withdrawal of funds from one type of account you may not use them toward the exclusion of funds from another account. In other words, you cannot spend $1,000 on tuition and use that as the sole reason that you withdrew $1,000 from a 529, $1,000 from an IRA, and $1,000 from an ESA. Only one of those withdrawals will receive the tax benefits and the others will not.

Because each type of savings strategy has a different list of qualified expenses, coordinating those expenses with withdrawals from the proper accounts will allow you to maximize the amount of withdrawals that can be taken without negative tax consequences. In addition, all of these expenses used against the withdrawals must also be coordinated with any tax credits that are claimed, as discussed later in Chapter 30.

Gifting Appreciated Items

One additional method for reducing taxes on educational savings is to give the student a gift of an appreciated item (such as shares of stock). When an individual receives a gift, the tax basis that she has in that gift is the same as that of the giver. When the student sells the item the gain will be calculated from that basis. However, the tax rate paid on that gain will be at the recipient's tax rate. In this way the net-of-tax amount realized from the gift could be much greater.

➥ **Example**   Many years ago, Grandpa Joe purchased 100 shares of XYZ stock for $1,000, or $10 per share. Today the market price of XYZ shares is $60, making the total value of the 100 shares $6,000.

Grandpa Joe would like to help his granddaughter, Cindy, pay her college tuition, and needs to liquidate some of his investments to do so. If he were to sell the XYZ shares he would pay 15% capital-gains tax on the $5,000 gain, or $750, based on his current tax bracket. However, because Cindy has no significant income he could save on taxes by giving the shares to Cindy and then having her sell them. Cindy would still need to recognize the $5,000 capital gain, but her income places her in the 0% tax bracket for those gains, so the $750 in tax that Joe would have paid can be avoided, making more net-of-tax income available to her as a gift.

Retirement Investment Strategies— The Basics

Tax-Deductible and Tax-Deferred Retirement Plans

Contributing to a tax-deductible retirement account is a well-known way to reduce taxes. There are a multitude of deductible retirement account types, such as Traditional IRAs and 401(k), 457, and 403(b) accounts. Each of these account types has its own little twists in the rules that govern it, but the basic concepts behind each type of retirement account are the same. Each account type offers a deferral of taxes on any growth and a tax benefit for contributions. The government created these "tax qualified" savings vehicles to encourage people to save for their own retirement by giving them tax incentives for doing so. In this chapter you will learn how each of these retirement accounts works, what thorns you may encounter when using them, and when their use could actually turn to your detriment instead of your gain. You will also learn about how the new health care laws affect your retirement accounts, as well as a little known credit for retirement contributions that can bring amazing benefits to those who qualify for it.

Tax-Deductible Contributions

Most of the government-sponsored retirement plans offer an income tax deduction for contributing money to the plan. This means that the money that you contribute during the year is subtracted from your total income when calculating your Adjusted Gross Income (AGI), effectively reducing your taxable income and potentially allowing you to take more deductions and credits if your AGI is at or near some of the phase-out thresholds.

☛ **Example**   Mary manages a dentist office. Her taxable income is $40,000, placing her in the 25% marginal tax bracket. If Mary contributes $5,000 to her IRA account this year, she will reduce her taxable income to $35,000, saving her $1,250 in federal taxes (25% × $5,000 = $1,250). Depending on the state she lives in, her contribution could reduce her state tax liability as well.

The flipside of taking a deduction in the current year for contributions is that you will be taxed on that money in the future when you withdraw it. The prevailing notion is that you will benefit from doing this because your income needs in retirement should be less than your current income, so you will be taxed at a lesser rate in the future on those contributions.

☛ **Example**   Sandi is 48 years old and is saving all that she can to prepare for her retirement in the future. She is currently in the 28% marginal income tax bracket. Each year she contributes the maximum amount that she is allowed to in the 401(k) plan offered through her work, which in 2013 is $17,500. By doing so Sandi reduces her current year's taxes by $4,900 ($17,500 × 28% marginal tax rate = $4,900 fewer taxes paid).

When Sandi retires in 20 years she intends to have her home mortgage paid off, her children established and financially independent, and many of her other current expenses taken care of. As such, she will need less income per year to cover her cost of living and estimates that she will be in the 15% marginal tax bracket during retirement. When Sandi withdraws money from her retirement accounts in the future she will pay only $2,625 in tax on a $17,500 withdrawal ($17,500 × 15% marginal tax rate = $2,625 in taxes). By taking a tax deduction for contributions during her working years, Sandi saved $2,275 in taxes on that income ($4,900 tax deduction − $2,625 eventual tax = $2,275 tax savings).

While you do receive an income tax deduction for contributions to a qualified plan, you do not receive a deduction for payroll taxes. You will still pay the employee portion of payroll taxes on your full income, regardless of whether you make a contribution (as well as the employer portion of those taxes if you are self-employed).

Tax-Deferred Growth

As discussed in Chapter 11, the tax code requires you to pay taxes on investment income realized during the year—even if you reinvested that income. Whether the income is from interest, dividends, or capital gains, the government wants its share of your earnings, and wants it now. Having to pay taxes on the growth each year can really cut into your overall investment earnings over time. If you didn't have to pay taxes on the growth, you could instead put that money toward other investments and benefit from the additional compounding effect of the growth on those earnings.

The exception to this rule is when the investment income is held within a tax-qualified retirement account. In this case the government does not tax any growth within the account until you actually withdraw money from it. This allows the entire value of the account to grow untouched, freeing up other money to make additional investments (the money that would have gone to taxes).

Buyer Beware

Deductible retirement plans have their place, and in many instances they will reduce the total lifetime tax bill of an individual. However, there are many factors and assumptions at play in this analysis, and a change in one or more of those assumptions could actually cause you to be giving more money to the government in the end. Some of the potential outcome-changing issues are:

- Tax rates may not be the same in the future.

- You may need more income in retirement than you think.

- Required Minimum Distributions (RMDs) force taxation on these accounts.

- Withdrawals from retirement plans are taxed at ordinary rates, even the portion of the withdrawals that come from gains (and would have otherwise received favorable capital-gains tax treatment).

If the last three decades are any indication, it would be pretty safe to assume that there will be many tax law changes in the coming years and decades. These days it seems that the only constant feature in tax laws is change. Those changes can be beneficial, but they can also be harmful. If you are contributing money to a deductible retirement fund now and the tax rates increase significantly in the future you could wind up paying a lot more taxes in the end, and be doing so at a time in your life when you have little control over your net-of-tax income because you are no longer working. In the case of Sandi, in the previous example, if tax rates go up in during her retirement (instead of remaining steady as in the example) the projected tax savings from the contributions could be turned on their head and wind up being a significant increase instead.

In my experience with clients I have also found that many are surprised by how much income they need in retirement. They expect their costs to be reduced, but they don't anticipate many things that keep their income requirements as high, or sometimes even higher, that when they were working. For some, all of the extra time on their hands leads them to spend more on projects, leisure activities, or hobbies. Others travel a lot more than they thought they would. A few begin to have significant increases in medical expenses. And others find that their children and grandchildren cost them as much as when they lived at home. Whatever the reason, if your income needs in retirement rival the income you required in your working years, your tax rates will not go down significantly, even if the tax laws remain the same—thwarting the tax-benefited calculations of retirement savings contributions.

Another factor affecting the true tax benefit of deductible retirement account contributions is that you must take Required Minimum Distributions (RMDs) from the account once you reach age 70½. If you have the ability to live on other income sources (pensions, part-time work, other savings, etc.), you could end up paying more taxes than otherwise necessary because of these RMDs. See Chapter 7 for a thorough discussion of RMDs and their tax consequences.

In addition to these factors, it can prove to be significant that retirement account distributions are taxed at ordinary income rates, even though a good portion of the value of the account may have come from capital gains. It may be more beneficial in the long run to pay capital-gains tax rates than to receive the tax deduction. The following scenario follows a likely pattern for many people, and illustrates the potential dangers of falling in line with the tax-deductible contribution bandwagon.

↝ **Example**   Troy begins working for ACME Corp. at age 30 and immediately signs up to have $1,000 per year of his wages contributed to the company's 401(k) plan. Troy never really thinks about the 401(k) very much again until he leaves the job 30 years later. At that time Troy withdraws the entire balance of the 401(k), pays taxes, and uses the net-of-tax amount to cover his cost of living while he seeks new employment.

During the first 15 years at the job Troy's income increased steadily, but not significantly. In fact, during those years he never left the 15% tax bracket. However, during the second half of his tenure at the company his career began to take off as he climbed the corporate ladder, and his income climbed with it. In years 16–20 he was in the 25% tax bracket, then he moved to the 28% bracket in years 21–25, and finally he jumped to the 35% bracket in his final five years with the company. His 401(k) grew at an average annual rate of 7.2% over those 30 years.

When Troy withdrew the funds from his 401(k) the account value was $105,000 and after paying taxes at a rate of 35% he was left with $68,200 to live on.

If Troy had decided in the beginning to not use the 401(k), but instead take the net-of-tax income and invest it in a taxable account, he would have had more money in the end to use In the first year he could have taken the $1,000 of income instead of putting it in the 401(k), paid the 15% tax ($150), and invested the remaining $850. Then he could have continued that pattern for 30 years, investing the net-of-tax amount. In the end when he withdrew the funds he would have paid capital-gains taxes on the growth, instead of ordinary income tax on the entire balance as he did with the 401(k).

In this scenario he would have had an account balance of $85,600 and a net-of-tax withdrawal of $76,200 to live on. That is $8,000 more, net-of-tax, or a 12% increase. While $8,000 may not seem like much (because of the small dollar value being invested), a 12% difference is significant. If he had been investing $15,000 per year, instead of $1,000, the 12% difference would translate to $120,000 more in his pocket, after tax.

Incidentally, if he had increased his contributions (even doubled them) as his income increased (reflecting what some people do), he would still have come out with more money outside of the 401(k) than in it.

While I have greatly simplified several factors in this example, the point remains valid and clear: there are times and scenarios (perhaps many) where it would be more beneficial to invest outside of a tax-deductible qualified account than it would be to use one and receive the deduction. In this example the keys to the given result were an increasing tax rate over his working years, a continued high tax rate when he made withdrawals, and a low capital gains rate.

I have a friend who, as a CPA, often recommends that clients not invest in qualified accounts and put the money in tax-free bonds instead. The investment then earns tax-free income (just like the tax deferral of qualified accounts) and has no tax upon withdrawal of the funds (as long as the bonds are held to maturity). In addition, there are no other rules attached to the investment, such as being penalized for withdrawing funds early or forced to make RMDs later in life (and be taxed on them, of course), even if you don't need them.

Do not misunderstand the point of this section. I am not saying that you should never consider making contributions to a qualified account. There are just as many scenarios where it could be more beneficial to do so. The point that I am making, though, is that it is not as straightforward as many people make it appear. Making contributions to a qualified account should be a carefully thought out decision, not one made as a tax-time, knee-jerk reaction to finding a way, anyway, to reduce the current year's taxes. Just like making a spontaneous purchase on a credit card, you may end up paying a lot more for that decision in the end.

Types of Deductible Plans Available

There are many types of retirement plans that "qualify" for tax-deductible treatment by the IRS. All individuals are able to contribute to Individual Retirement Accounts (IRAs). In addition to IRAs there are numerous other retirement accounts that are sponsored by employers. Depending on the type of entity that employs you (government, for-profit business, non-profit, etc.), you may have access to one or more of these plans. Here is a list of some of the more common ones available:

- 401(k)
- 403(b) (Tax Sheltered Annuity)
- 457(b) (Thrift Savings Account)
- Simplified Employee Pension (SEP) IRA
- Savings Incentive Match Plan for Employees (SIMPLE) IRA
- Traditional IRA (not employer-sponsored)

At their core all of these plans function in basically the same manner. They are designed to allow an employee or business owner to contribute a portion of earnings toward saving for retirement and receive a tax deduction in the current year for that contribution. Each of these plans provides tax deferral on the growth in the account until the funds are withdrawn. And each of these accounts provides a means for the employer to make additional contributions into the employees' accounts.

There is some variation in the rules between the different types of accounts when it comes to the amount an employee and employer are allowed to contribute to each year. The following sub-sections give some important individual details of the rules governing each type of account.

401(k), 403(b), and 457(b) Plans

401(k), 403(b), and 457(b) plans are almost identical in the rules that govern them, especially in regard to contributions allowed each year. The main difference is the type of employer (government, business, etc.). For the remainder of this subsection I refer only to 401(k) plans (to make it easier to read), but know that everything that I cover in this sub-section applies equally to 403(b) and 457(b) plans.

Each type of plan is set up by an employer and can receive contributions from both the employer and the employee. An employee may contribute up to 100% of his or her income, up to a maximum amount each year. The contributions are fully deductible for income tax purposes, but not deductible for payroll taxes.

The employer has the option of making three types of contributions. The first is a "matching" contribution, in which the business's contribution is based on the employee's contribution. For example, the match may be 50% of the employee's contribution, up to $6,000. In this case, if the employee contributed $4,000 during the year the business would contribute an additional $2,000 to the employee's account (50% match × $4,000 employee contribution = $2,000 employer match).

The second option for an employer is to automatically contribute a certain percentage of the employee's income, often 2%–3%, regardless of whether the employee contributes. This method allows the employer to accurately project what the company's contributions will be for the year, as well as ensure an equitable contribution for all employees.

The third optional contribution for employers who sponsor a 401(k) is making a "profit-sharing" contribution. This is just a contribution of a fixed dollar amount, not based on the employee's contribution or salary. Contrary to its name, the business does not actually need to make a profit during the year in order to make a "profit-sharing" contribution.

Similarly to the rules for employees, the employer is subject to a maximum amount that it can contribute to an employee's account during the year. The IRS sets a total contribution maximum for each year, which is the highest combined amount that may be contributed to an employee's account between the employee and employer. So, the amount an employer may contribute is determined in part by what the employee contributed. For example, if the combined maximum is $50,000 and the employee contributes $15,000, then the employer may not contribute more than $35,000 to the account ($50,000 maximum allowed − $15,000 employee contribution = $35,000 allowed for the employer to contribute). In addition to this limit, the employer may not contribute more than 25% of the employee's wages (or 20% of a self-employed individual's gross income before the contribution).

Individuals who are 50 years old (or older) by the end of the year are allowed to contribute an additional amount each year, over and above the "maximum." This additional amount is known as a *catch-up contribution* and is meant to help those who are nearing retirement to put more money aside for that purpose. The catch-up amount allowed is adjusted each year for inflation and is also added to the total maximum amount that governs the employer contribution.

There are also rules governing a 401(k) plan that attempt to make the playing field equal between employers and employees by not allowing for discrimination between highly compensated employees and lower-paid individuals. These rules ensure that the plan is not limited to owners and executives in the business, as well as ensuring that profit-sharing and matching provisions are equitable. Any business owner contemplating the establishment of a 401(k) plan will need to be familiar with these rules and the financial implications that they bring. Many "safe harbor" provisions are available to ensure that the rules are followed, such as the automatic employer contributions mentioned previously.

401(k) plans give a business owner the opportunity to defer a significant amount of income each year. For example, a business owner who is 50 years old and makes $250,000 could contribute as much as $56,500 in 2013 to the plan, between employee and employer contributions (compared to a maximum contribution of $6,500 in a Traditional IRA). The business owner must take care to follow the non-discrimination rules if the business has employees, and the contributions to employee accounts must be weighed in the calculation of the overall tax benefits of the plan to the employer. Very often, though, the employer will be able to save enough money from the tax deferral of the plan that the savings far surpass the money spent on contributing to employee accounts. If the business owner has no employees (or a few low-wage employees, or employees who don't save), the benefits can be even more significant.

There is also an option available to allow for Roth 401(k) contributions. It is up to the employer to decide if this option will be available in the business's plan. Under this option the employee contributions that are designated as Roth contributions are not tax deductible, but rather taxable in the current year. However, the contributions and growth of these contributions are not taxed when they are properly withdrawn in retirement.

Only employee contributions can receive the Roth designation. Any employer matching or profit sharing must be made to the tax deductible, traditional 401(k) account. The plan must also maintain a separate account for the Roth contributions in order to keep a clear accounting of which assets are taxable and which are not.

For corporations (or businesses taxed like a corporation), the employer's portion of the contribution must be made by the end of the year. However, for individual business owners (or businesses that are taxed like individuals), the contribution can be made as late as the filing deadline (including extensions) for the return. However, the plan must be in place before the end of the year. Table 14-1 shows the various limits of employer and employee contributions allowed during the year.

Table 14-1. Employer and Employee Contribution Limits for 401(k), 403(b), and 457(b) Plans

401(k) 403(b) 457(b)	Maximum Employee Contribution	Catch-up Contribution	Total Maximum Employee Contribution	Maximum Account Contribution, Including Employer Contribution	Maximum Account Contribution, Including Catch-up Contribution
2013	$17,500	$5,500	$23,000	$51,000	$56,500

The regulatory requirements and non-discrimination testing that are required for 401(k) plans can be fairly expensive to comply with. For this reason many small employers have shied away from 401(k) plans and used other, less cumbersome plans instead. In recent years, however, a solution has been created in the tax code that makes 401(k) plans for business owners who have no employees much simpler to administer. These plans are sometimes referred to as a "Solo K" or "Single K" plan. If you have an employee, though, you will need to figure the cost of administration as a factor in weighing the benefits of a 401(k) versus some other plans, such as the SEP and SIMPLE IRA plans.

SEP IRA Plans

For business owners with no employees (as well as those with family-member employees), the most popular choice of retirement plans has been the SEP IRA. This is because of the minimal administration costs involved with the plan, coupled with high contribution limits.

SEP IRAs are contributed to solely by the employer. Contributions are based on a percentage of income and must be the same percentage for every eligible employee. Having to contribute the same percentage for employees as owners is a large factor in why these plans quickly lose their popularity among businesses with employees. If an employer would like to contribute 25% of his income to the plan, for example, he must also do that for each employee, which quickly eliminates the benefit that the employer gets from his own contribution.

The maximum total annual contribution for SEP IRAs is the same as it is for 401(k) plans, although it comes entirely from the employer side. The contribution can be up to 25% of an employee's income, which is capped by an upper limit each year ($51,000 in 2013 or $56,500 for employees over 50 years old).

The calculation becomes more difficult for the owners of a sole-proprietorship. These individuals must calculate the net income of their business, and then subtract one half of the self-employment tax to arrive at "net self-employment income." The business owner may then contribute any amount between 0% and 20% of net self-employment income.

An employer can set up a SEP IRA as late as the extended filing deadline for his or her return, as well as make contributions up to that date. This is more flexible than a 401(k), which must be set up before the end of the year.

While a SEP IRA is easier (and less expensive) to administer, a 401(k) will often allow a small business owner to contribute more money to the plan each year. This is because the 25%-of-income limit is placed on the entire contribution in a SEP IRA, while is only placed on the profit-sharing portion of the 401(k) contribution. If your income is not high enough to max out the total contribution limit, you may be able to combine the employee and employer contributions for a higher total amount.

↪ **Example**   Zack is the sole proprietor of a small business and pays himself a W-2 salary. He has no employees and his total net business income is $150,000. The maximum contribution he would be allowed to make to a SEP IRA is $27,705 [($150,000 net income − $11,475 half of self-employment income = $138,525) × 20% max contribution = $27,705].

On the other hand, the maximum contribution that he could make to a 401(k) is much larger because he can contribute as both an employer and an employee. His total maximum contribution with a 401(k) would be $44,000 ($17,500 employee contribution + $26,500 = $44,000 total contribution).

The amount an employer contributes to a SEP IRA can vary year to year and, in practice, is often determined during the process of preparing the employer's tax return. In this way also the SEP IRA is a very flexible plan for employers.

SIMPLE IRA

For the most part, the SIMPLE IRA lives up to its name. It is similar to a 401(k) plan in the sense that both the employer and the employee can contribute to it. However, the rules that govern the contributions, and the number of options available, are reduced. In addition, there is little to no administrative oversight needed for SIMPLE plans.

Employees may choose to contribute any amount, from $0 up to the maximum allowed for the year. The employer, on the other hand, is required to choose one of two contribution amounts and the election is applied across the board for all eligible employees. The business may either match employee contributions up to 3% of their wages or make contributions equal to 2% of employee wages, regardless of whether the employ makes a contribution.

⮑ **Example**   Sally's Salon offers a SIMPLE IRA plan for its employees and matches their contributions up to 3% of the employee's wages. One of the employees, Rachel, earns $40,000 per year and contributes $6,000 of her earnings to her SIMPLE IRA. Sally's Salon must contribute an additional $1,200 to Rachel's account to meet the 3% match requirement (3% × $40,000 wages = $1,200).

Mack's Car Wash also offers a SIMPLE IRA to its employees. Mack, however, has chosen the automatic 2% of salary contribution. James works for Mack and does not contribute anything to his account. Even so, Mack must deposit the equivalent of 2% of James' $30,000 salary to his account, or $600.

The maximum contributions allowed for a SIMPLE IRA are much lower than with the previous plans. In 2013, for example, an employee can contribute a maximum of only $12,000 (plus an additional $2,500 catch-up contribution for those who are 50 and older). The employer can contribute only the additional 2%–3% of the employee's salary. Though the plan is very easy to administer, it is very limiting to those who would like to contribute the higher amounts that are available in other plans.

🗐 **Note**   Most of the retirement plans can be "rolled" into other plans. For example, on leaving an employer you can roll your 401(k) plan into a Traditional IRA to have more control over it and consolidate accounts. You could also roll it into another 401(k) plan with your new employer. This is not the case with a SIMPLE IRA, however. Funds from a SIMPLE IRA cannot be combined with the funds of a different type of account, nor can other accounts be rolled into it.

Traditional IRA (Not Employer-Sponsored)

If you have no employer-sponsored plan at your disposal, you can opt for the Individual Retirement Account (IRA). A few people qualify to contribute to both an employer-sponsored plan and an IRA, but only if their income is below the phase-out thresholds (see Tables 14-2a and 14-2b).

Table 14-2a. IRA Income Limits (Contribution Phase-Out Range) for 2013

Filing Status	Phase-Out Begins at:	Phase-Out Complete at:
Single, Head of Household, MFS—employer plan available	$59,000	$69,000
Single, Head of Household, MFS—<u>no</u> employer plan	$112,000	$127,000
Married—a spouse eligible for employer plan	$95,000	$115,000
Married—a spouse <u>not</u> eligible for employer plan	$178,000	$188,000
Married Filing Separately	$0	$10,000

Table 14-2b. Maximum Allowable IRA Contributions

Tax Year	Younger than 50 Years Old	Age 50 or Older
2013	$5,500	$6,500

Each year limitations are set on the amount individuals can contribute to an IRA. For 2013 the IRA contribution limit is **$5,500 ($6,500 if you're 50 years or older)**. Unlike employer-sponsored plans, you can make the contribution any time up to the tax deadline for filing your return (usually April 15). You cannot extend this contribution deadline by filing an extension for your tax return.

✎ **Caution** To avoid penalties, contribute no more than the maximum amount to an IRA. The penalty is 6% of the amount of excess contribution for *each year* the excess contribution goes uncorrected. The good news is that if you accidently contribute more than you are allowed, you have until April 15th to remove the excess, penalty-free.

Your contributions to an IRA may not be greater than the total amount of your *earned* income for the year. For example, if you have only $2,500 in earned income for the year, you may not contribute more than a total of $2,500 to qualified retirement accounts.

There is one exception to this rule. If your spouse does not work, but you have sufficient earned income to contribute to IRA accounts, you can contribute to your spouse's account. For example, if the wife earned $30,000 during the year and her husband had no earned income, the wife could contribute the maximum amount both to her own account and to her husband's account.

If you have sufficient earned income to qualify for an IRA contribution, that contribution need not come *from* your income. For example, you could simply transfer money from a savings account to an IRA. Also, some parents and grandparents will contribute to a child's IRA or Roth IRA as a gift, which allows the child to use his income toward other goals. Be aware, though, that the giver gets no tax deduction for such a contribution.

For the purposes of IRA contributions, alimony income qualifies a person to contribute to an IRA even though it is not considered earned income. So a former spouse who does not work, but receives alimony, can contribute to an IRA.

If you or your spouse has access to an employer-sponsored retirement plan, your ability to contribute to an IRA may be limited or even eliminated. For example, in 2012 a single taxpayer's IRA deductions are limited when his Modified AGI (MAGI) reaches $59,000. His ability to contribute to an IRA is completely eliminated at an MAGI of $69,000. Here is the formula for calculating MAGI.

+ Adjusted Gross Income (AGI)

+ Social Security Income or Rail Road Benefits not included in AGI

+ Deductions taken for contributing to a Traditional IRA

+ Deductions taken for student loan interest or tuition expenses

+ Foreign income you have excluded and deductions for foreign housing

+ Interest from series I and EE bonds previously excluded

+ Employer-paid adoption expenses

+ Deductions taken for domestic production activities

= Modified Adjusted Gross Income (MAGI)

For married taxpayers the phase-out limitations become a little more complicated. There are two possible scenarios. First, if both spouses have an employer-sponsored plan available, the phase-out begins when MAGI reaches $95,000 and is eliminated at $115,000, in 2013.

⏎ **Example**   Troy and Lily are married, and both are eligible to participate in an employer-sponsored plan. They have a combined MAGI of $85,000. Because their MAGI is below the phase-out threshold of $95,000, they can both contribute the maximum amount allowed for an IRA.

Max and Kathleen are married, and both are eligible to participate in an employer-sponsored plan. They have a combined AGI of $185,000. Because their MAGI is above the maximum phase-out range of $115,000, neither of them can contribute to an IRA.

The second scenario occurs when only one spouse has an employer plan available. In this case the MAGI phase-out range changes again. The spouse who has a plan available is subject to the limits described previously. However, the spouse who has no plan available has a much higher eligibility threshold, which is from $178,000 to $188,000, in 2013.

⏎ **Example**   Mitch and Trisha are married. Trisha has an employer plan available to her, but Mitch doesn't. They have a combined AGI of $150,000. Trisha could not contribute to an IRA because the couple's MAGI is above $115,000 and Trisha has a plan available to her. However, Bob can contribute fully because he has no plan available to him and the couple's cumulative MAGI is less than $178,000.

Anthony and Jenny are married. Jenny has an employer plan available to her, but Anthony doesn't. They have a combined AGI of $200,000. Anthony cannot contribute to an IRA, even though he has no plan available to him, because the couple's MAGI is above the $188,000 threshold.

✒ **Caution**   Notice that the limitation rules apply if you are *eligible* to contribute to an employer-sponsored plan. It does not matter if you *actually* contributed.

Even if you are above the MAGI limits that allow you to claim a deduction for an IRA contribution, you can make non-deductible contributions. Although you get no immediate tax benefit for making such a contribution, you do get the benefit of tax-deferred growth in the account, meaning any gains on the investments are untaxed until they are withdrawn. You also pay no taxes on the portion of your IRA withdrawals that represent non-deductible contributions. (If you have a non-deductible IRA, see Chapter 10 for additional tax strategies.)

Before making a non-deductible IRA contribution, first consider contributing to a Roth IRA. This is a better choice if you are eligible to make such a contribution, since you get the benefit of not only tax deferral but also future withdrawals that will be 100% tax-free (assuming you follow all applicable rules).

✒ **Caution**   Keep impeccable records of your non-deductible contributions, IRA withdrawals, and tax returns forever (not the usual seven years), because you may need to substantiate your non-taxable portion of the IRA.

Penalties for Early Withdrawals

I once prepared a return for a client who had taken several thousand dollars from her retirement account, subjecting her to a 10% penalty on all of the money she had removed—in addition to the income tax she owed on the withdrawal. There was, however, a silver lining to the story, which I discovered as I worked on her return. She had spent a significant amount of money that year on medical bills (which are one of the exceptions allowed for penalty-free withdrawals) and, because of that, she was able to avoid most of the penalty.

The government does not want you to take money out of your qualified retirement accounts before you reach retirement age (i.e., 59½). If the government did not prevent you from removing funds from your retirement account, you would be able to manipulate your tax return by claiming deductions for contributions in a high-tax year and then withdrawing those contributions in a lower-tax year. For this reason, a 10% penalty tax is imposed for withdrawing money early from a qualified account.

✒ **Caution**   In the case of the SIMPLE IRA, the 10% early-withdrawal penalty is actually increased to 25% if the money is moved out of the plan in the first two years.

📖 **Note**   457(b) plans are the only type of qualified retirement account that does not have a 10% penalty for early withdrawals.

The tax code does provide opportunities to make penalty-free withdrawals in certain circumstances. These exceptions available for employer-sponsored retirement plans are:

- Withdrawals that are rolled into another retirement plan within 60 days (this may only be done once per year)

- Distributions upon the death or permanent disability of the account owner

- Distributions upon separation of employment if the account owner is 55 years old (or older)

- Distributions to a spouse by a court order in a divorce

- Distributions up to the amount of deductible medical expenses during the year (whether or not deductions are itemized on the return)

- Distributions due to an IRS levy (at least they don't *penalize* you when they take your retirement money)

- Distributions made as substantially equal periodic payments over the expected lifetime of the owner

---

💰 **Caution**   The exception that allows for "substantially equal" withdrawals of the owner's expected lifetime can be very tricky to orchestrate and carries significant financial risk. If you plan to withdraw funds under this rule be sure to hire a very competent professional to help you.

For non-employer–sponsored, Traditional IRA accounts, all of the exceptions above apply, except the one regarding separation from service after age 55. In addition to those on the list, there are a few other times when you can remove money from a Traditional IRA without incurring the penalty. They include:

- Insurance premiums for unemployed individuals

- First-time home buyer's expenses. (The exception is for withdrawals up to a maximum of $10,000, and only once in an individual's lifetime. It is also worth noting that a "first-time" home buyer is one who has not owned a home in the previous two years—not necessarily limited to the truly first-time buyer.)

- Education expenses (discussed more in Chapter 13)

○ **Tip**   If you need to withdraw money from an employer plan, such as a 401(k), but do not qualify for the exceptions, you may still have another option. If you are no longer working for the employer who sponsors the plan you can first roll the money into an IRA and then withdraw the money under one of the IRA penalty exceptions.

If you *are* still employed with the company, check with the Human Resources department to see if the retirement plan allows for loans to be taken from the funds. Many plans do allow for loans, which gives you the opportunity to withdraw funds without incurring taxes or penalties.

○ **Tip**   To qualify as a first-time home buyer, you can purchase the home for yourself, your spouse, your children, your grandchildren, or a living ancestor of you or your spouse. The "first-time" status is based on the *purchase*r, not the resident or owner.

○ **Tip**   The first-time home buyer exception is for a principal residence. So you could own a rental property and not own a principal residence, and you would still qualify for the exception when you buy a new home.

When withdrawing money from a retirement account, be sure to withhold enough taxes from the withdrawal to cover your additional tax liability at the end of the year, in order to avoid penalties and interest that are imposed on late payments of taxes. Also, if you take an early distribution, be sure to pay for all your medical bills and other "exceptions" before the year's end to ensure that you utilize as much of the exemption as possible.

A More Subtle Penalty

While it is not a penalty per se, the Affordable Care Act (aka ObamaCare) could essentially penalize withdrawals from qualified retirement accounts by increasing taxes on other income. Withdrawals from IRAs will increase gross income, possibly triggering the 3.8% tax that is levied on income over the Modified AGI (MAGI) threshold of $200,000 for single individuals and $250,000 for married individuals. This tax is discussed in greater detail in Chapter 11, but it is worth noting its effects if you plan to withdraw money from tax-qualified retirement accounts.

Retirement Savings Contribution Credit

The tax code offers an added incentive for low-income earners to save money for retirement, in addition to incentives I've discussed previously. If your AGI is within the acceptable thresholds, you will not only receive the normal deductions for retirement contributions, but you'll also be eligible for a special tax credit that is meant to sweeten the deal. This credit in and of itself is a "double-dip" opportunity.

If you have a 2013 AGI of less than $28,750 if you're single, or $57,500 if you're married, the credit offers an incentive to save at least $2,000 in a qualified retirement plan ($4,000 for married couples). The contribution can be to an IRA, a Roth IRA, or an employer-sponsored plan—including a 401(k), 403(b), SEP plan, SIMPLE, or 457(b).

Tip Take note that one of the ways to become eligible for the credit is to contribute to a Roth IRA. You get a significant tax credit when you contribute to the account, and then you get tax-free growth and withdrawals in the future. This is an amazing opportunity to never be taxed on the money, and even be given more money (in the form of a tax credit) for making the contribution.

The Retirement Savings Contribution Credit is non-refundable, meaning it can reduce your tax liability to $0, but no less. You can take the credit against income taxes as well as the Alternative Minimum Tax (AMT), although if you qualify for the credit you wouldn't be subject to the AMT as it currently stands.

The credit is calculated as 50% of the amount you contribute, up to a maximum credit of $2,000. So contributing more than $2,000 will not benefit you as far as the credit is concerned. The credit is phased out in steps, rather than evenly, which makes it important to use very careful planning. The maximum credit (50%) is available if your AGI is below $17,250 if you're single, and below $34,500 if you're married. If your AGI is above those numbers but below $18,750 or $37,500 (single or married, respectively), the credit is reduced to 20% of the contribution (instead of 50%). The credit steps down again, to 10% of contributions, when your AGI is above those thresholds. And the credit is no longer available once your AGI reaches $28,750 or $57,500 (single or married, respectively).

If your AGI falls within the parameters of this credit, you should recognize how significantly the credit increases the benefit of saving in a qualified retirement account. At times the credit will bring an even greater tax savings than the deduction.

➮ **Example** Dan and Emma are newlyweds who have just started a pet-grooming business together. Their AGI for the year is $30,000, and they each contributed $1,000 to an IRA, for a total of $2,000 between them. They receive an above-the-line deduction for that contribution, which saves them $300 in taxes. They also receive the retirement savings contribution credit, which saves them $1,000 in taxes! The deduction and credit combined bring a total tax savings of $1,300. In essence, they really contributed only $700 to their retirement accounts, and the government contributed $1,300. That is an instant 285% growth on the $700 net investment. That can't be beat.

Remember the two components that determine the amount of the credit you receive. First, the credit is a percentage of the contribution. So the amount you contribute to a retirement account will affect the amount of the credit you receive. Second, your AGI will affect the percentage rate that is used for the credit—it can be 50%, 20%, or 10% of the contribution. Do not be dismayed, though, if your AGI makes it so that you receive only a 20% credit instead of a 50% credit. In this scenario you can still receive the maximum $1,000 credit by contributing $5,000 to your retirement accounts, instead of $2,000. The proportionate tax savings may not be as great, but a $1,000 tax credit on top of the deduction is still a significant savings.

🖝 **Caution** If your AGI is on the borderline of the thresholds that determine whether the credit is for 50%, 20%, or 10% of your contribution, take special care in your planning. Just $1 of AGI over the threshold could reduce the credit from $1,000 to $400. In this scenario it would not be worth earning the first $600 of income over the AGI threshold, because you would be worse off financially for having earned it. If you are at the borderline of the AGI range, look for ways to limit your income or increase your above-the-line deductions so you can maximize the credit. For example, if your AGI were $100 over the 50% threshold mark, an additional $100 contribution to the retirement account could result in a $600 savings in taxes.

Because the tax code allows both a deduction and a credit for the same contribution, this is a double-dip opportunity. Based on the example of Dan and Emma (with their pet-grooming business) in the previous section, a tax savings of 65% was achieved for a person in the 15% tax bracket. This very significant savings makes this credit worth serious consideration for anyone in or near the qualifying AGI ranges. There are three additional things to be aware of when planning for this credit. First, you must be 18 years old or older by the end of the tax year to claim this credit. Second, before contributing to a retirement plan in order to receive this credit, be sure that you will have a tax liability. Because the AGI thresholds are so low for this credit, many who qualify for it owe no tax. Without tax liability, the credit affords no benefit, because it is non-refundable.

Third, the credit will not be so sweet if you withdraw money from a qualified retirement account two years before your contribution or one year after your contribution (up to the due date of the tax return, including extensions). If you make such a withdrawal, the amount of the contribution that qualifies for this credit must be reduced by the amount of the withdrawal or withdrawals.

Retirement Investment Strategies— Alternatives

Non-Traditional Tax Strategies for Saving for Retirement

In addition to the traditional tax-sheltered retirement accounts discussed in Chapter 14, there are many alternative options available for individuals to invest for the future in ways that bring tax benefits. Excellent means of doing this are through Roth IRAs, Roth IRA conversions, and Non-Deductible IRAs as discussed in Chapter 10. Another way is through life insurance products, such as annuities and cash-value life insurance policies.

Some strategies are best for people who have already contributed the maximum amount available to them in the traditional retirement accounts. Other strategies are focused on finding alternative investments to the traditional stock-market-based options. A few strategies combine the two. While there are many tax-preferred opportunities for alternative retirement savings strategies, there are four in particular that I cover in this chapter:

- Self-directed IRA accounts

- The secret of Health Savings Accounts

- Deferred compensation and defined benefit plans (pensions)

- Livestock, agriculture, and land

Self-Directed IRA Accounts

All retirement accounts are maintained in the name of a custodian. A custodian exists, in part, to assure the IRS that you have not tapped into your accounts during the year (thus triggering taxes and, possibly, penalties). In addition, these custodians often assume a level of fiduciary responsibility. As a fiduciary, they limit the investments that you can choose from so that they are not held liable for allowing you to invest in something "crazy." For example, traditional custodians would not allow you to use money in a retirement account to invest directly in a piece of real estate or to buy shares of a non-public corporation.

A few custodians, however, offer what is called a self-directed IRA. In this case the custodian withdraws its fiduciary responsibility and allows you to choose the investments that *you* think are appropriate. With this option, you can take the money that is in your IRA—or in a 401(k) from a previous employer that you roll into an IRA—and use those funds to purchase investment property, precious metals, or even a new business. The ability to use these funds in such a way opens your investments up to significant risks, but also offers two great benefits that would not otherwise be available.

The first benefit is probably obvious from what has been said so far. You are able to invest the money in your retirement savings account in almost any way that you feel is best. You can choose the investment that you think will bring the greatest success in preparing for your future needs, and you have a source of money to make such investments that would not have otherwise been available to you.

⤳ **Example**   Chelsea has not been happy with the results of the investments she has made in her retirement accounts. For a long time she has wanted to invest in real estate— believing that she could have better results from owning rental property than from owning shares of a mutual fund. However, all of the money that she has available to invest is tied up in her IRA account and her IRA custodian does not allow direct investments in real estate. If Chelsea were to move her money to a custodian that offers self-directed IRAs she would be able to use the money in her IRA to purchase property and begin building her rental portfolio.

The second benefit may not be quite as obvious, but could prove even more beneficial. Since the real estate (or business) is held within an IRA, all income and gains on the investment are tax-deferred. You don't need to pay taxes each year on the rental or business income—it is deferred to a future time. You keep the income within the IRA account and reinvest it elsewhere, or have it in reserve for future expenses.

Even more exciting is that when you decide to sell the property or business and buy another, or even if you just keep the gains and invest in something else, it isn't necessary to deal with the headaches of a 1031 exchange (to avoid taxes on real estate) or pay capital gains. Because of this, the timing of buying and selling assets can be when it is optimal to do so, without having to figure in the effect of taxes or be tied down to the strict timing connected to 1031 exchanges.

⤳ **Example**   After 15 years, Chelsea has been able to use the cash flow from the rental property in her IRA to purchase two additional properties. She has not needed to pay any taxes on the income and, instead, used the money to reinvest in other opportunities as they have arisen.

At this point in time she believes that there are some looming problems with the neighborhood of the first property a-nd wants to sell the house before the market values in the area decline. The great news for Chelsea is that when she sells the house she will not have to pay any taxes on the gain and can use the entire proceeds from the sale to reinvest in another home when she finds the right deal.

Of course, you must use great prudence and caution when investing your retirement savings. It would probably be best to not "put all of you eggs in one basket" by using all of your money to buy one property or one business. You must also be aware of the many risks that are inherent in real estate, including a measure of illiquidity.

It is very important to recognize that the IRA owns the asset. It is critical that you keep your non-IRA money (as well as your time and labor) separate from every aspect of the ownership in the real estate or business. For example, if you need to make repairs or replace the roof of a rental property, the money to fund these projects *must* come from the IRA. Otherwise, if you pay for anything out of pocket, it is considered a contribution to your IRA (subject to all of the maximum annual contribution limitations and income thresholds of an IRA). Putting more money in the IRA than the contribution limits allow subjects you to an annual penalty tax. Therefore it would be wise to have a significant portion of your IRA money in reserve (not invested in the property) so that you are free to make adjustments as needed.

You must also need to be aware of some special rules regarding self-directed IRA that limit your involvement in the investment. For example, in the case of rental real estate you must use an independent property manager to receive the income from the property and pay the expenses. You are not allowed to touch the money in your IRA; otherwise it is considered a distribution, and in this situation any money involved in the investment would count. The property manager would collect income and send it to the IRA custodian and would bill the custodian for the property's expenses. The custodian will also charge a fee for this service. You *are* allowed to have control over the property manager; you just can't touch the money. The rules for owning a business within an IRA become even more complicated. Your involvement in the business must follow strict guidelines. When investing in a business or rental property, it is critical that you work with an experienced and competent tax professional who can guide you through all of the potential land mines.

With all of that said, the tax benefits of a self-directed IRA can be enormous. If you have sufficient funds in a Roth IRA, the benefits from self-directing can be even greater because a Roth IRA can lead to tax-free income in your retirement. Investments in a small business or portfolio of rental properties within a Roth IRA could eventually lead to a retirement with a steady stream of tax-free income that is withdrawn at whatever pace you deem appropriate.

The Secret of Health Savings Accounts

The main purpose of *Health Savings Accounts* (HSAs) is to encourage individuals to choose higher-deductible health plans and save for future medical expenses. It is believed that the more a person is paying for medical expenses from his or her own account (instead of with the funds of an insurance company) the more careful the person will be. This in turn would lead to lower medical costs overall. In addition, if people have saved significant amounts of money for their own health care needs they will likely be less dependent on the government to cover those expenses in the future. For these reasons the government has created tax incentives to save for medical expenses, including the HSA.

The general concept of how an HSA works is that you receive a tax deduction for making contributions, the growth is tax-deferred, and if the funds are used for qualified medical expenses they are tax-free when withdrawn. It is like the best features of a Traditional IRA and Roth IRA combined—deductible contributions *and* tax-free withdrawals. HSA accounts are the best tax-saving opportunity around. While all of the ins and outs of HSAs are discussed in detail in Chapter 26, there is one specific aspect of an HSA that I want to discuss in this chapter as it pertains to alternative retirement strategies.

Generally, HSAs are intended to help pay for medical expenses and you will be penalized for using the funds for other purposes. However, once an individual reaches retirement age (59½), he or she can make non-medically related withdrawals from the HSA and they will be treated the same as a withdrawal from a Traditional IRA (meaning the money is taxed, but there is no penalty for using the funds for non-medical purposes). If you don't need the HSA money for medical expenses, but do need an additional funding source for your retirement, you have an additional resource available to draw upon.

This rule is made even more beneficial by the fact that contributions to an IRA or 401(k) do not limit your ability to contribute to an HSA. If you have made the maximum contribution to an IRA, an HSA could be a great way to significantly increase the contribution you can make to an IRA-like account each year. In addition, HSA contributions have no high-income cap. High-income earners, who might not be allowed to make contributions to an IRA can contribute to HSAs no matter what their Adjusted Gross Income (AGI) happens to be.

↪ **Example**   Maggie earns $250,000 per year. She contributes the maximum amount to her 401(k) each year, but cannot contribute to an IRA because her income is too high. She is also subjected to many phase-outs for deductions and credits because of her high income and does not have many ways available to her to reduce her tax burden. However, Maggie is able to contribute to an HSA account and receive the full deduction because there are no income limits on HSA contributions and they are not affected by other contributions to retirement plans. The HSA provides a great opportunity for Maggie to put more money away for retirement and reduce her taxes.

Stan is married and works for a small business that does not offer a retirement plan. Stan is 55 and wants to put as much money into retirement savings as he can, but his only option is to invest in an IRA that has a pretty low maximum contribution per year. Stan could more than double the contributions he makes to his IRA by also funding an HSA account.

The maximum contributions to an HSA that are allowed each year are set by the IRS and increase annually, based on inflation. Table 15-1 shows where the annual contribution limits are currently set.

Table 15-1. Maximum Allowable HSA Contributions in 2013

Tax Year	Younger than 50 Years Old	Age 50 or Older
Individual	$3,250	$4,250
Family	$6,450	$7,450

HSAs present a tremendous opportunity for individuals to capture significant tax savings, both when the contribution is made and when the funds are withdrawn. They are governed by special rules, so be sure to read more about them in Chapter 26 before investing. I have found, though, that even under these rules the HSA is one of the greatest gifts that Congress has given the American taxpayer in decades—and that the HSA is also one of the tax world's best-kept "secrets."

Deferred Compensation and Defined Benefit Plans (Pensions)

Business owners have an opportunity to shelter a significant amount of income by deferring compensation through *defined benefit plans,* or what some people refer to as pensions. Most employer retirement plans are based on *defined contributions*—meaning an employee can contribute up to "X" amount and the employer will, in turn, match those contributions by a fixed amount as well. In such plans there is no guarantee of what the value of an employee's account will be upon retirement; the contributions are made and the end result is completely dependent upon the performance of the investments made in the account.

In contrast, a *defined benefit plan* is based on the projected outcome and not as much on the amount of contributions made. Each year the plan is subjected to actuarial scrutiny to determine what contribution needs to be made in order to meet a predetermined retirement income. Based on that projected income and the number of years until the planned retirement, the actuary will determine what the contribution for each employee needs to be.

With defined contribution plans—such as a 401(k)—there is a fairly low ceiling set for allowable contributions ($17,500 by the employee and $51,000 total between the employee and employer). If an individual wants to put more money into a retirement plan, his or her options are fairly limited beyond that amount., With a defined benefit plan, however, the total allowable contribution can be as high as $205,000 in 2013! That is a significant difference, and, for the older business owner who wants to put away as much as possible, the defined benefit plan offers a great opportunity to do so.

The reason that the contribution limits are so high for these plans is that you are required to meet a fixed future benefit. If there are not sufficient funds in the plan to meet that benefit there must be flexibility in contributing significant amounts of money in order to make up for the shortfall. However, an individual cannot just arbitrarily decide to contribute the maximum amount each year—the contribution must be determined by an actuary, based on several assumptions.

Tip The ideal situation in which to use a defined contribution plan is when the owner of the business is nearing retirement and his or her employees are few in number and young in age. This scenario allows for the highest possible contributions for the owner, with very limited contributions required for the other employees.

A significant downside to a defined benefit plan is that whatever the required contributions are in a given year, they must be made, regardless of whether the business was profitable in that year. This can pose a significant hardship for businesses that have cyclical ups and downs in their revenue, or that have a sudden downturn in their revenue stream. Defined benefit plans are much better suited to businesses whose revenue streams are relatively steady and predictable from year to year.

Tip Though contributions to the plan are required each year, there is a certain amount of flexibility allowed in how those contributions are determined. An actuary has to make assumptions about the projected growth rate of investments, the individual's retirement age, and the income stream needed in retirement. Each of these assumptions can be adjusted up or down within a reasonable range, depending on the need for the contribution requirement to be increased or decreased.

Livestock, Agriculture, and Land

In Chapter 10, I wrote about creating a tax-free income stream through investing in livestock or agriculture, by creating a source of food for your family that you do not have to purchase with taxable income. These are also potential opportunities for tax-preferred retirement investments that allow you to contribute as much money as you desire each year into building a herd or orchard and defer the income to a future year. When you do begin to draw upon these investments, you are able to do so at the rate that you choose, instead of being forced to withdraw specified minimum amounts.

As an example, let's examine the idea of developing a herd of cattle. I am not a rancher, but from what I am told a herd can triple in size every 3–4 years. Each cow can be bred and nurture a calf every year, and a new calf can be bred when she is 18–24 months. Depending on the breed, cows can mother a new calf each year for 15–20 years. Assuming half of the newborn calves are male and sold off, and the females are kept to build the breeding herd, the size of the herd would grow at around 37% per year. At this rate of growth, the original herd of 20 cows would turn into around 360 in 10 years, 1,700 in 15 years, and more than 8,000 in 20 years (by which time the original 20 cows are no longer breeding). Of course, you would need to have a lot of land for that many cows. Also, the cows are worth more when they are younger (but not calves). But it gives you an idea of the growth potential available. See Figure 15-1 for a visual representation of how quickly a herd can grow.

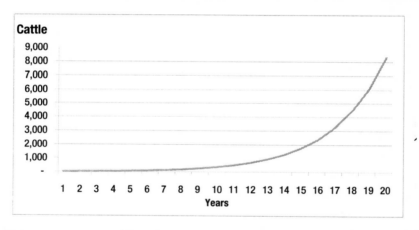

Figure 15-1. Tax-deferred growth of a cattle herd from 20 original cows over 20 years

The great tax news that comes from such a scenario is that the growth in the cattle herd is tax-deferred—you don't pay any taxes on the new cows as they are born. You only recognize income when you sell the cows. If you are 10 years from retirement and in a high income tax bracket, you could put money into raising cattle for 10 years and not recognize any significant amount of income from the growth of the herd until you are (presumably) in a lower tax bracket in retirement. At that point you can sell off the herd over a period of time (in order to keep your income down), or even maintain its size and sell only the increase in size as a nice supplement to your retirement income.

In addition to the tax-deferred growth of the herd, you are also able to deduct many of the expenses, such as feed, fertilizer, and other supplies, as they occur. These deductions can help offset any income that you receive from selling male calves or other incidental items. Immediate deductions, coupled with tax-deferred growth and the ability to choose the timing of income recognition, combine to form a fairly significant tax savings opportunity. The opportunities presented in this example of a cattle herd can be repeated with other animals as well, such as sheep or alpacas. The possibilities don't stop with animals, either.

There are similar opportunities for tax deferral in planting trees. I know a few individuals who have built great wealth (mostly tax-deferred) through lumber. They purchase a large tract of land with mature trees, and then harvest enough trees from the land that the profit from the trees covers the original cost of the land. At that point they own the land free and clear, plant new trees to grow for future years, and sit back while the value of the land grows (literally) over the years, all tax-deferred. It takes a long time for new trees to develop into mature trees that are large enough to bring a significant price when they are harvested—but if you have the time it is a great way for your wealth to grow and have complete control over how and when it gets taxed.

Fruit and nut trees offer a similar opportunity, but on a shorter time scale. Most fruit and nut trees take 5–8 years to begin producing a full harvest. If you are about that far from retirement, or from lowering your income into a better tax bracket, planting an orchard could be a great way to invest money now and reap tax-preferred benefits later (while deferring all the taxes on the growth in the value of those trees).

Finally, another asset that is great for tax-deferred growth is land. Real estate has proven to be one of the most reliable investments for long-term growth. Real-estate taxes that you pay on investment property are tax-deductible each year, and the growth in the value of the land is deferred until you sell it. In fact, there are ways to sell real estate and roll the proceeds into another property without paying any tax. And when you eventually sell the land it is taxed at capital-gains tax rates as long as you have owned it for more than one year. Real estate happens to be one of the favorite investments of wealthy members of Congress, as well—which should probably tell us something about its current tax benefits and the security of maintaining those benefits in the future.

Business Income and Deductions

Owning your own business can be tremendously satisfying. It can also be amazingly confusing and frustrating. One area that is particularly confusing to business owners is how to use the tax code effectively to their advantage. When you start dealing with business issues, taxes can become very complicated very quickly.

On a positive note, one of the greatest opportunities to reduce your taxes is found in converting your personal (non-deductible) expenses into deductible business expenses. The ability to recognize these opportunities can bring huge savings. With careful planning and record keeping, you will be able to use these deductions to your advantage and actually keep more of the money you work so hard for.

Part IV is full of money-saving opportunities—so many, in fact, that if you don't own a business you may find yourself considering it after reading these chapters. There is no other circumstance with more opportunities for saving money on taxes than by owning a business.

Business Taxation

Some Things You Should Know

Who says you can't mix business and pleasure? Owning a business provides one of the greatest opportunities to reduce your taxable income by transforming non-deductible personal expenses into deductible business expenses. There are a multitude of opportunities to do so with personal expenses such as meals, transportation, travel, health care, education, your home, and so on. The key to doing this is in understanding what constitutes a legitimate business expense and the appropriate way of accounting for it.

What if you don't own a business? Are all of the opportunities in this section out of your reach? Never fear. Owning a business can be very simple and easy. All you really have to do be in business is to say that you are. In fact, many times a person's hobby or pastime can be converted into a legitimate business without much effort at all. Once you establish that you are pursuing an activity with a profit motive, all of the strategies in the seven chapters of Part 5 are opened up to you.

There are a few things about running a business, from a tax perspective, that you should know before diving into the individual strategies that are outlined in the following chapters. This chapter is devoted to helping you understand two key concepts:

- Income and expense recognition
- Losses and hobby rules

Income and Expense Recognition

There are two main methods of accounting that are used for the taxation of businesses. The first method is called the "Cash Accounting" method. Basically this method recognizes income when it is received and expenses when they are paid. A simple way of understanding this method is by thinking of your checkbook. If you write one check on December 31st, Year 1 and a separate check on January 1, Year 2, the first check would be an expense on Year 1's tax return and the second check would appear as an expense in Year 2.

The second method of accounting is known as the "Accrual Accounting" method. With this method, income and expenses are recognized when they are incurred, not necessarily when they are paid or received. For example, if you purchase a new item for the business on December 15th, Year 1, but do not actually pay for the item until the vender sends you a bill on January 10th, Year 2, you would recognize the expense in Year 1 for accrual accounting purposes even though you did not pay for it until Year 2. The same scenario applies to income – you must recognize the income when you have earned it, not when you are paid for it.

Most sole proprietors can choose which method of accounting they will use. However, once you choose a method you may not change that method without permission from the IRS. This prevents businesses from bouncing back and forth between methods each year in an effort to game the system.

In addition, you cannot simply play games with invoices and income at the end of the year in order to manipulate the recognition of income. For example, if a cash-based business received a bunch of checks at the end of the year, it cannot simply wait until the following year to deposit them in the bank and count them as income for the following year. If you have control over the receipt of income it is considered the same as having been received.

To claim an expense as deductible for business purposes it must meet three criteria. It must be:

- Ordinary and necessary
- Paid or incurred during the taxable year
- Connected to the conducting of the trade or business

"Ordinary and necessary" has been interpreted by the tax courts to mean "reasonable and customary." To be customary, an expense needs to be customary to the industry that you are in, as well as for the location where you operate your business. It doesn't mean that the expense needs to be customary in your own business (meaning something you do all of the time), only that it is not unusual for a business similar to yours. In fact, it is okay even if you have only had the expense one time in the history of your business.

The expense must also be connected to the conduct of your trade or business. For example, even if you are a florist who buys hundreds of flowers every day to sell in your store, you cannot deduct the purchase of a dozen roses for your wife as a business expense because those particular flowers are not connected to conducting your trade or business.

Losses and Hobby Rules

Income sources are separated into different categories, such as investment income, passive income, earned income, and so on. In many cases a loss in one income category cannot be used to offset income in another category. This is not the case with business income. If your business loses money, that loss will reduce your total income and help reduce your taxes. In fact, if the loss is greater than your total income from other categories it can be carried back to offset income from the two previous years, or carried forward to offset income in a future year.

With that said, there is one catch. The IRS does not allow you to continuously claim a loss from a business year after year after year. If it were not so it would be easy to claim you favorite pastime as a business and write off all of your expenses as losses, since you have little or no income. What a fantastic way to reduce your taxes by deducting personal expenses! Too bad it doesn't work.

↪ **Example** Dean operates a mountain expedition business where he takes tourists on week-long backpacking trips. Mike isn't very good at marketing, so he rarely finds anyone to go on the trips. Each year, however, Mike takes four week-long trips (by himself) in places around the world in order to become familiar with the locations in case he ever has a customer who would like to go there and claims all of his expenses for the trip as deductions for his business. These expenses add up to thousands of dollars in losses each year since he has no income to offset them. After four years of claiming these losses for his "business" the IRS caught up to him and determined that he was not really running a business—he was really just pursuing a hobby—and they disallowed all of the previous losses from his "business."

Of course, your business does not have to make a profit every year to be considered a legitimate business. The IRS and the courts only need to see that you have a true profit motive in your business in order to allow you to claim a loss. As a rule of thumb, the IRS will automatically presume that you have a profit motive if you earn a profit in three years out of any five-year period. In fact, if you lose money in the first years after starting a business you can insist that the IRS can defer a challenge to your business losses until you have completed a five-year period.

The three-out-of-five year rule is not absolute; it is more of a safe haven. It is okay to lose money in more years than that as long as you can prove a true profit motive for the activity that you are undertaking. More accurately, you must prove that you have an honest profit objective—even if there is not a reasonable expectation of actually earning a profit. In determining whether you have as your motive the intent to make a profit, the following things will be considered:

- The manner in which you carry on the activity

- The time and effort you spend in the activity

- Your success in carrying on similar activities, as well as other profit-motivated activities

- Your history of income and loss related to the activity

- Your expertise in the activity, as well as the expertise of you advisors

- The expectation that the assets in your business may appreciate in value

- How high your profits are when you are profitable

- Your personal financial status

- The elements of personal pleasure and recreation involved in the activity

It does not matter if you are employed full-time in another business. Only the demonstrable profit motive will determine the deductibility of losses. If the IRS successfully shows that your "business" does not have a profit motive, however, you will be subject to the back taxes, penalties, and interest that come from the reduced taxes that you didn't pay because of those losses.

There are many hobbies that can be successfully turned into a profit-motivated business. If you can find ways to derive income from those hobbies (or at least reasonably expect income) you can claim the expenses. If it turns out that you are continuously showing a loss and you don't want to have a run-in with the IRS, just be sure not to claim all of your deductions in three of the five years so that you show a little income. In this way you will be able to write off a lot of your personal expenses that would otherwise bring you no tax benefit.

Business Use of the Home

The Way to Deduct "Personal" Expenses on Your Home through Your Business

Wouldn't it be nice to write off some of your personal expenses, such as utilities, home repairs, or even lawn care? It would be even better if you could write off these expenses against both income *and* self-employment taxes. Under normal circumstances the tax code explicitly categorizes these types of personal expenses as *non*-deductible. However, if you work at home, or even store things at home for your business, you may be able to claim a tax deduction for some of your otherwise "non-deductible" expenses.

You may have heard of this deduction as the Home Office deduction. A more accurate name, however, is the Business Use of the Home (BUH) deduction. As the accurate name indicates, you can claim this deduction in many more ways than simply having an office in your home. You may also qualify for this deduction if you store inventory, have a greenhouse or workshop on your property, have a lab or studio, run a daycare service, or even work from home for an employer. Don't limit your possibilities for this deduction by thinking you have to have an office in your home. Any use of your home or property for business purposes may qualify you for the deduction.

↪ **Example**   Mike is an elementary school teacher. He also has a side business making wooden toys that he sells at craft fairs. Mike converted an old shed on his property into a workshop that he uses exclusively for his business several nights a week. Because of this exclusive business use, Mike can deduct from his business income a portion of his mortgage interest, utilities, and cost of improvements on the shed. This deduction lowers his income and self-employment taxes by $1,500 each year.

There are so many ways in which the BUH deduction opens up opportunities for tax savings. For one, it allows you to write off expenses that are normally non-deductible. For another, it allows self-employed individuals to reduce their income *and* self-employment taxes, resulting in an extra 15% tax savings on top of their marginal income tax rate. Most personal deductions, if allowed at all, can be taken only against income tax.

Yet another benefit of the BUH deduction is that it provides opportunities to avoid the limitations that are often placed on the deductions of personal expenses. Itemized deductions on Schedule A are often limited by Adjusted Gross Income (AGI) as well as by the total value of the deductions combined, compared to the standard deduction. The BUH deduction can reduce the effects of those limitations. For example, if your AGI is too high, the amount of real-estate taxes you can deduct from Schedule A is reduced by the Alternative Minimum Tax (discussed in Chapter 31). If you can claim a portion of those real-estate taxes as business expenses instead, a portion of the deduction can still be claimed (and also used to reduce self-employment tax).

The mortgage interest deduction also illustrates how the BUH deduction can reduce the limitations placed on personal expenses. Normally you are allowed to deduct mortgage interest only on loans up to $1,100,000. However, with the BUH deduction you can claim the excess interest if you can show that the excess interest is necessary as a result of the business.

Another great benefit: if your home office is your principal place of business you can claim a mileage deduction for any distance you travel for business purposes. Under normal circumstances, the distance of the commute between your home and your office is considered a personal expense and cannot be deducted; only trips conducted after the arrival at the office can be claimed. However, when your home *is* your office, *any* business travel can be claimed. It is not uncommon for this additional mileage deduction to be worth even more than the BUH deduction.

First Things First

The BUH deduction is one of the most commonly used deductions by small-business owners. In my experience it is also one of the least understood and most abused deductions around. Because it is so commonly used and abused, it is also one of the most consistently audited deductions on a tax return. Before claiming this deduction you must be sure you fully understand the pros and cons associated with it, as well as its very specific rules.

Determining the BUH deduction is a fairly complicated, multistep process. To claim the deduction you must satisfy many requirements. In addition to meeting those requirements you must also make a complex series of calculations (using as many as three tax forms) in order to determine the value of the deduction you are entitled to. So, take a deep breath, sit back, and try to take in the rest of this section as best you can. This is one area of taxes that has a lot of thorns clinging to it, but with care it can be navigated successfully and bring sweet returns.

Determining Whether Your "Business Use" Qualifies for the BUH Deduction

The first thing to understand about this deduction is that it is contained in a part of the tax code known as the *disallowance* section—because in most circumstances the expenses related to your residence are specifically *not* allowed as deductions. Then, within that section of the code are narrowly defined exceptions to the rule. With this in mind, you must answer several questions to figure out whether your use of the home is considered "business use," as defined by the tax code. The following sub-sections address these key questions.

1. Is the activity a "business" in the eyes of the IRS?

The mere fact that a certain activity brings a profit does not mean it is a business. You must determine that the IRS considers your income-making-activity to be a legitimate business and not a hobby or other activity. If it is not considered a "business," you cannot claim the deduction.

↩ **Example**   Mike's wife, Susan, is a retired chemist. She devotes a significant portion of her time each week to managing her stock portfolio. She does this in an office in her home for several hours each day. She cannot claim this as a business use of her home, however, because, for tax purposes, personal investment management is not considered a business. Even though Susan makes a profit from her trades, this use of the home is not eligible for the BUH deduction.

---

2. Is the space you use for business part of a "home"?

You must determine whether the space you use is part of a home, or "dwelling unit," as the code refers to it. You'll need to consider several factors. First, the term "dwelling unit" includes any property that provides basic living accommodations, such as a toilet, a place to sleep, and a place to cook. From this description you can see that even some RVs and boats fall into the category of dwelling units, or homes. In addition to these minimal requirements, the place must actually be used as a residence (not just qualify as one).

○ **Tip** I have some clients who use this broad definition of a home to their advantage. They claim some of the expenses related to their RV as legitimate business expenses and write them off under this deduction.

A tricky part of this "dwelling unit" rule is determining how to treat structures that are *not* connected to the dwelling unit—such as Mike's shed in the earlier example. If a structure (like a shed) is "appurtenant" to a dwelling unit, it is considered a part of it. "Appurtenant" means that the structure is related to, or belongs to, the main property. In fact, all such structures *must* be deducted under the BUH rules, even though they are not actually a part of the home.

If the space you're using for business purposes is a dwelling unit, or is appurtenant to one, the special rules for BUH must be applied before you take any deductions for that space. This is important because the deductions that are allowed will be in proportion to the total square footage of the home and other structures combined, which will make the deduction more limited than if you could write off 100% of the expenses related to the separate structure.

↬ **Example** Mike's workshop shed is not considered a dwelling unit, in and of itself, because it has no bathroom, kitchen, or place to sleep, and because he does not use it as a residence. However, the shed is on the same lot as his home. It has no separate address and is not separate from the home in its expenses, such as property taxes, utilities, and insurance. For these reasons the shed is considered appurtenant to (belonging to or related to) the home and as such, is subject to the rules of the BUH deduction.

If, on the other hand, the shed were on a separate piece of land that Mike owned, which had its own real-estate taxes and utility bills, Mike could deduct the shed expenses directly from his business income, without being subject to the BUH deduction guidelines.

---

3. Do you use the space *exclusively* and *regularly* for the business?

"Exclusively" means that the space is used for no other reason than its business use at any time during the year. For example, if a computer and desk are used for the business during the day and for video games at night, the use of the space for business purposes is not deductible. If you use the space for personal reasons *at all* during the year, it is not eligible for use for this deduction.

↪ **Example**   If Mike uses his workshop all year for his business, but in the fall he also uses it to make gifts for his grandchildren, he cannot claim any of the expenses for the space under the BUH deduction. No personal use of the space is allowed during a year in which the deduction is claimed.

"Regular" use requires that the area be used more than occasionally or incidentally. Mike satisfies this requirement because he uses the workshop several times each week. If he used it only a few times each year he may not qualify for the deduction.

Did you answer yes to the first three questions?

The first three questions regarding business use of your home are:

- Is the activity a "business" in the eyes of the IRS?
- Is the space you are using part of a "home"?
- Do you use the space exclusively and regularly for business?

If you were able to answer yes to each of these three questions, you are close to being able to claim the BUH deduction. All that remains is meeting *one* of the following three requirements:

1. Is it your principal place of business?

You satisfy the "principal place of business" requirement *if*:

- You use the space to conduct administrative or management activities for the business, *and*
- There is no other fixed location where you conduct substantial administrative or management activities for the business.

Under certain circumstances it may *appear*, by a strict interpretation of the preceding definition, that you do not meet these two requirements. However, you may still qualify based on additional guidance that the IRS has given. Based on this guidance you may still meet the preceding requirements if one of the following cases applies to you:

- You oversee administrative and management activities, but other people take care of them at a location other than your home. (Administration and management activities include overseeing outsourced bookkeeping, payroll, or billing.)

- You perform administrative and management activities at other locations (such as in a hotel or a car) that are not fixed locations of the business, in addition to doing them at home.

- On a minimal and occasional basis, you perform these activities at another fixed location of the business.

- You perform a significant amount of non-administrative and non-managerial activities at another fixed business location.

↪ **Example**   Mike's neighbor, Drew, is a traveling vacuum-cleaner salesman. To spend as much time as possible selling his products, Drew outsources his bookkeeping. After filling out invoices at customers' homes he sends all of the paperwork, along with expense receipts, to his bookkeeper downtown. However, he still has a few administrative tasks that he must do on his own, such as ordering new supplies. Drew handles all such administrative tasks when he gets home, using a spare bedroom that he has set aside exclusively for the use of his business. In this scenario, Drew can claim the spare bedroom as his principal place of business, because it is where he conducts his administrative activities (including overseeing those that he has outsourced).

○ **Tip**   I have found that the "administrative and management" criteria are excellent ways for many small-business owners to qualify for the BUH deduction. If you carefully study the preceding guidelines, you may find that structuring your business in a way that meets these guidelines is your ticket to being able to claim this deduction and thereby write off expenses that would otherwise be non-deductible.

2. Do you use the area to meet or deal with customers?

Even if your "home office" is not your principal place of business, as defined earlier, you may still be able to claim the deduction if you regularly use the office to meet with customers, clients, or patients. To meet this requirement you must meet with customers in the home office during the regular course of business and these meetings must constitute a substantial and integral part of your business. In addition, the meetings must be in person—phone calls and e-mails don't count. Courts have consistently held firm on the stance that, for the purposes of the BUH deduction, a meeting is a meeting only if it is in person.

↬ **Example** Mike's other neighbor, Russ, is an optometrist. He has an office near the hospital, where he conducts appointments with most of his patients. However, about 20% of his patients are friends and family, with whom he conducts his appointments in his home office on Fridays. Even though the home office is not his principal place of business, nor is it the location of his administrative duties, he can claim the business use because he meets with patients there regularly, and because these appointments constitute a substantial part of his business about 20%.

---

3. Is the area you use in a structure separate from the home but still part of the home under the "appurtenant" rules?

If the space you want to claim for business use is separate from but appurtenant to your home, the building needs to be used only "in connection" with the business to qualify for the deduction—it doesn't have to be the principal place of business or a place where you meet with customers. Remember, though, that the area must still be used exclusively and regularly for the business.

↬ **Example** Mike's woodworking business began to really take off, and he decided to quit his teaching job and open up a storefront downtown, where he could sell things every day—not just at craft fairs. This storefront would likely be considered his principal place of business. However, he would still be able to claim a deduction for the shed where he creates all of his woodwork because it is used "in connection" with his business, and it is appurtenant to the main structure of his home (not under the same roof).

Can you claim the deduction?

If you answered yes to all of these questions:

- Is the activity a "business" in the eyes of the IRS?
- Is the space you are using part of a "home?"
- Is the space used exclusively and regularly for business?

And you answered yes to at least *one* of these three questions:

- Is this the principal place of business?
- Do you use the area to meet or deal with customers?
- Is the area you use in a structure separate from the home but still part of the home under the "appurtenant" rules?

Then you probably qualify to claim a business use of your home and deduct the related expenses. Of course, there are always exceptions to tax rules. Before making a final determination on your eligibility based on the six questions above, you should consider three more questions to see if you fit the criteria of some important exceptions to the rules.

1. Are you claiming the business use as a business owner or as an employee?

If you are claiming business use of your home as an employee, not a business owner, you must satisfy one more rule. The use of your home must be for the convenience of the employer. Using your home for business purposes must benefit the employer for some reason, and that reason cannot be solely that it is more convenient for the employee.

↪ **Example**   While Mike was still teaching, he used a spare bedroom in his home, regularly and exclusively, to grade homework and tests. The school provided a place for Mike to do this work, but he preferred to do it at home. Because it was Mike's choice to use his home in this way, for his own convenience and not for the convenience of the employer, he could not claim this as a business use of the home.

If, however, Mike had been employed as a teacher for an Internet-based home school program, and the school required all of its teachers to work from home because it did not maintain a campus, then Mike would have been able to claim the BUH deduction.

○ **Tip** If your employer requires you to work from home for the convenience of your employer, I would highly recommend getting a letter from them stating that this is the case. Although the possession of such a letter is not a guarantee, it should add great support to your case if you are audited by the IRS in regard to this deduction.

2. Is the business use you are claiming related to storage space?

The rules regarding storage space can actually be a little easier to satisfy than those related to other business uses of the home because the area is *not* required to be used *exclusively* for business. However, to qualify for the deduction for storage space, you must satisfy *all* of the following requirements:

- The storage space must be used for inventory or product samples of items that you sell through your business.

- The storage space must be separately identifiable from other areas and must be suitable for storage.

- The home must be the only fixed location of the business, and the storage space must be used regularly.

Some of the key determinants for "business use" do not apply to storage space. For example, the home does not need to be the principal place of business (but it must be the only fixed location), nor do you need to meet with customers there. Also, the space does not need to be used for business *exclusively*—it only needs to be used for that purpose regularly. Remember, though, that the items you are storing must be inventory of goods you sell in order to use these more lax rules.

↬ **Example** As an accountant, if I used space in my home to store client files I could not claim the space used for storage because I am not in the business of selling client information—it's not inventory (thank goodness). However, if I tried to maintain a supply of 5,000 copies of my book , *Tax Insight*, on hand (in order to meet high demand), I *could* claim the space for a deduction because the book is an item I sell.

3. Is your business a daycare service?

The question is not, "Does your home business *feel* like a daycare service?" However, if you actually run a daycare service in your home, special rules apply to you in regard to claiming the business-use deduction. You must meet each of the following requirements:

- You must be licensed or otherwise approved by your state for the type of care you provide.

- Your primary service must be the custodial care of children, adults older than age 65, or those who are physically or mentally unable to care for themselves.

- The care you provide must be limited to certain hours of the day—it cannot be 24-hour care.

If your business is a qualified daycare there is no exclusivity rule, as there is with other businesses. So, if you use your kitchen and living room for the daycare, but also use it for personal reasons as well, you are still able to claim the deduction. (There is a specific formula that must be used in this circumstance, which I discuss in the next section.)

Which Expenses You Can Deduct

Once you determine that you are eligible to claim expenses related to the business use of your home, the next step is to determine which expenses are deductible, and to what extent. Expenses fall into three potential categories, which in turn determine the deduction you can take. These three categories of expenses are:

- Directly related expenses
- Indirectly related expenses
- Unrelated expenses

Under the following three subheadings I discuss each of these categories of expenses in detail.

Directly Related Expenses

Directly-related expenses are those which benefit the business-use portion of the home exclusively. Two examples of directly related expenses are improvements or repairs to the area used for the business, or additional insurance on the business property in that room.

⤳ **Example**   The improvements Mike made to the shed in his backyard, when he converted it to a workshop, are directly related to the business because they did not benefit any other part of the house. For this reason they are fully deductible business expenses.

○ **Tip**   Whenever possible, separate out receipts and bills into business and non-business portions. If you are having your home interior painted, for example, ask the contractor to specifically separate on the bill, or on separate bills, the cost for painting the home office. In this way you will have a clear way to distinguish the business-use expense and you will be able to count that portion as a fully deductible business expense (rather than a pro-rated amount).

Indirectly Related Expenses

Indirectly related expenses are those that benefit both the business and non-business portions of the home. Some examples of these kinds of expenses are utilities, roof repairs, mortgage interest, insurance, or real-estate taxes. These expenses can't easily be divided between the personal and business portions of the home on a direct basis—only in a pro-rated fashion.

Generally, these types of expenses will be deducted proportionately to the amount of space used for business in the home. If the home office is 250 square feet, for example, and the home is 2,500 square feet, 10% of indirect expenses can be deducted as business use (250 sq. ft. of office space ÷ 2,500 total sq. ft. in the home = 10% of the total sq. ft. used for the office). However, certain expenses may be treated differently than this because it does not make sense to divide the expense proportionately.

One indirect expense that may receive special, non-proportionate treatment is utilities. If the nature of the business lends itself to using a disproportionately high or low percentage of the utilities, the amount deducted should be adjusted to reflect the actual usage.

⮎ **Example**   The tools Mike has in his workshop use a lot of electricity. In fact, based on the difference in his electricity bill between months when he is spending a lot of time making crafts, and those when he is not, he estimates that 35% of his annual electricity usage is related to the workshop. Although the shop makes up only about 8% of his home's total square footage (the combined square footage of the shed and home together), he will actually deduct 35% of the electricity bill for tax purposes.

On the other hand, he really doesn't use any water for his business. Practically all of the water used at his home is for personal reasons. Because of this he won't deduct any portion of the water bills as business use.

○ **Tip**   If you are going to claim a disproportionate amount of utilities as deductible business use—especially if you're claiming a higher amount—be sure that you can substantiate that claim with good records and evidence. In the preceding example, Mike should keep records of all of the electric bills and mark months in which he used the shop less so that the difference in usage can be substantiated.

Another indirect expense with special treatment is homeowners' insurance, if it is paid annually. The IRS allows only the portion of insurance premium that applies to the current year to be deducted in that year. So, if you make an annual payment for your insurance on October 1, this year you can deduct a quarter of that premium (3 out of 12 months' worth of insurance), multiplied by the proportion of square-footage that the business uses. You would deduct the remainder of the pro-rated annual premium in the following year, since it pertains to insurance coverage in that year. Of course, this year you could also claim the 9 months' worth of premium that you paid the previous year and were unable to claim.

Finally, the IRS allows no deduction for the first phone line into the home— period. The cost of basic local service, plus taxes, for the first phone line is considered 100% personal, *even if* you could prove that it was used 100% for business. However, the cost of additional services on that phone line, such as long-distance service or voice mail, can be used as business deductions to the extent that they can be shown to be for business use (or any portion thereof).

Unrelated Expenses

Unrelated expenses are those that benefit the home, but not the business portion of the home. If, for example, you run an Internet-based search-engine optimization business and you replace your kitchen stove, you can't claim any portion of that expense as a business deduction because it has nothing to do with the business.

One unrelated (disallowed) expense that I want to highlight is landscape installation or maintenance. The IRS does not allow you to pro-rate a portion of these expenses as business-related *unless* you see clients, customers, or patients in your home, or if the business use is renting out a portion of your home.

How Much of a Particular Expense Can I Deduct?

If an expense is directly related, you can deduct all of it. A caveat to that statement is that if the expense was for an item that falls under the rules of depreciation, such as furniture, equipment, or permanent upgrades to the home, you must follow the depreciation rules. Depreciation deductions will be taken on a different portion of the tax return.

If the expense is indirectly related, you can deduct the amount that is proportionate to the amount of space your business uses in the home (see the explanation and example in the preceding "Indirectly Related Expenses" sub-section).

If your business is a daycare service, you must follow one additional rule for indirect expenses. As is the case with all businesses, you must first multiply the percentage of space used by the expense (for example, 10% of all utilities). Then, as an additional step, you must multiply that value by the percentage of hours used the space is used for the business.

↪ **Example** Mike's mother, Nancy, runs a daycare service in her home 10 hours per day, 5 days per week, 50 weeks per year. This makes a total of 2,500 hours per year that she is "open for business." There are 8,760 hours in a non–leap year, so the daycare service is run 28.54% of the available hours in a year. If Nancy makes 50% of her house available to the children in the daycare service, and her annual electricity bill is $1,800, she can deduct $257 of her electricity bill as business use (50% of home used × 28.54% of the time × $1,800 = $257).

○ **Tip** If you run a daycare service, you should be aware of several other special deductions that are available to you. Be sure to consult a tax advisor or the IRS publications.

Depreciation

Once you establish a qualified business use of the home, you can begin to depreciate the business-use portion of the home as an additional deduction. Depending on the value of your home, this could be one of the larger deductions available to you under the business-use rules. To claim depreciation you must first establish a "basis" in the home, or in other words, the home value on which you can base the depreciation.

For the purpose of the BUH deduction, the basis of the home is the *lesser* of either:

- The original cost of the home, plus the cost of improvements, minus any depreciation previously taken

  or

- The fair market value of the home when you started using it for business

Given the conditions of the housing market, your current home value may be less than what you paid for it. If this is the case, you must use that smaller value in your depreciation formula.

○ **Tip** Get a third-party valuation of your home at the time that you begin to take this deduction. An appraisal would obviously be the best documentation—one that is hard to dispute. But I think that even a realtor's evaluation or a website such as Zillow.com would be better than nothing. I don't know how these latter sources would hold up in an audit, but you could at least show that you had reasonable evidence for the depreciation value you chose.

Once you have established the total cost of the home, or its current value (if less), you must subtract from that number the value of the land the house is built on (because land cannot be depreciated). The best way to establish the value of your land (other than an appraisal) is by referring to your real-estate tax bill. It will usually show the value the county assessor has given the land, separate from the value of the building or buildings. After you have subtracted the land value from the total property value, you arrive at the home's depreciable basis.

The next step is to multiply the home's basis by the percentage of the home used for business purposes. This will give you the net depreciable basis of the home for business purposes.

⤻ **Example** Mike's home is 2,300 square feet, and the workshop is 200 square feet, making a total of 2,500 square feet for business-use calculations. This means that 8% of his home (200 ÷ 2,500 = 8%) is qualified for business-use deductions.

Mike purchased his home for $200,000 and has made $40,000 in improvements, for a total cost of $240,000. His home was appraised at $600,000 when he recently refinanced. The cost of $240,000 is lower than the appraisal, so this cost will be used as the basis. The depreciable basis for Mike's home is $19,200 (8% × $240,000 = $19,200). All depreciation for the business use of his home will be based on this number.

If you began using your home for business after 1993, your home office will be depreciated over 39 years. (If you began using your home for business purposes during or before 1993, you need to consider other rules that I will not cover here. See a tax advisor or the IRS publications for assistance.) That means you would take 2.564% (1/39th) of the depreciable basis each year as a deduction.

The exception to the standard annual depreciation rate would be in the first year depreciation is claimed (or in any year the business does not use the space for that full year). In the first year, you can claim a deduction only for the portion of the year in which you used the property for business. Table 17-1 lists the percentage you should use for depreciation in the first year of business use.

Table 17-1. First-Year Depreciation Percentage Rates

Month	%	Month	%	Month	%
January	2.461	May	1.605	September	0.749
February	2.247	June	1.391	October	0.535
March	2.033	July	1.177	November	0.321
April	1.819	August	0.963	December	0.107

⤻ **Example** The first year Mike used his workshop for business, he began using it in September. In that year he could claim $144 in depreciation expenses ($19,200 depreciable basis × 0.749% from the table = $144). In all other years he could claim $492 ($19,200 × 2.564% = $492) until the basis is fully depreciated.

Claiming the BUH Deduction

If you're a business owner, use Form 8829 to calculate and report expenses related to the business use of the home. On this form is where most of the number crunching occurs; it shows the IRS how you arrived at the deduction you are claiming. Once you determine the total deduction, the number then flows to the Schedule where you report the other business income and expenses. That would be Schedule C if you're self-employed, and it would be Schedule E for the partner, S-corporation owner, or rental-property owner.

If you're an employee claiming this deduction, report the expenses on Form 2106. Your expenses will then flow to Schedule A and are subject to the 2%-of-AGI threshold for miscellaneous deductions, as unreimbursed employee expenses. An employee is not required to use Form 8829 to compute the deductible expenses. Instead, the IRS provides a worksheet to help you calculate the deductible amounts, which you should keep with your other tax records.

○ **Tip** Employees who claim a BUH deduction should not include any mortgage interest or real-estate tax as part of that deduction. Rather, those expenses should be reported as completely personal expenses on Schedule A. The IRS instructs taxpayers to do this because it will bring a potentially greater benefit to you: those personal expenses are not subject to the 2% floor that employee expenses are subject to, and so they are better used outside of the BUH deduction.

The Simplified Home Office Deduction

Beginning with the 2013 tax year, the IRS is offering taxpayers a much simpler way to calculate their Home Office Deduction. The simplified version does not change any of the rules that determine whether you qualify to claim the deduction. However, what it does simplify is the calculation of the deduction and the record-keeping requirements.

There are several benefits to this option. First, you will not need to keep records of all of your business-use expenses. You will simply claim $5 in expenses per square foot of business-use space. The maximum space allowed to be claimed is 300 square feet, for a maximum $1,500 deduction. If your previous deductions have been much greater than $5 per square foot (or your square footage is much larger than the 300 foot cap) you may want to continue using the traditional method for claiming the deduction. On the other hand, if your true expenses are less than $5 per foot, you will get a greater tax benefit by using the simplified method than you would by doing it the traditional way.

Second, you may switch between using the simplified method and the traditional method every year. This allows for deduction arbitrage, where you time expenses to be heavy in the year that you claim the traditional method and light in the year that you use the simplified method. If in the light years your expenses are less than $5 per foot, you can still claim $5 and get a larger deduction than you really "deserve."

Third, if you use the simplified method, you do not have to allocate any of your mortgage interest or real estate tax to the business use deduction, allowing the entire amount to be deducted from your personal itemized deductions on Schedule A.

A few other things to note: You cannot claim depreciation on the home when using the simplified method (which is often better, anyway), and you cannot use the method for two separate houses in one year (although you can still use the traditional method for the second house).

This new, simplified method is a huge breakthrough in the tax code for taxpayers. It will make many people's record-keeping tasks much easier and it will also result in a larger deduction for some.

Your BUH Deduction May Be Limited

Although you are allowed to deduct expenses related to the business use of your home against business income, you are not allowed to claim a *loss* because of those deductions. In fact, you must deduct each expense in a specific order to determine which expenses will be allowed and which will not. The order is as follows:

1. From your gross business income, you must subtract all business expenses that are not related to your home. For example, expenses for things such as office supplies, wages, meals, and depreciation of business assets (not including the home) would be subtracted from income first.

2. Deduct expenses related to your home that you would be able to deduct regardless of business or personal use. These expenses include mortgage interest and real-estate taxes.

3. If a positive net income remains, you can then subtract other expenses related to the home that would not be allowed as deductions if they were solely personal expenses. Some examples of these expenses are utilities, insurance, repairs, and maintenance. None of these deductions can lead to a negative net income. Once the net income reaches $0, these deductions must stop.

4. As long as sufficient net income remains, you can deduct depreciation on the business-use portion of the home. As with the previous deductions, the deduction for depreciation cannot exceed the net income that remains after all previous deductions.

At no time will the deductions claimed in the third and fourth group be allowed to produce a loss. However, any unused deductions can be carried forward to a future year when you have sufficient income from which to deduct them.

⮑ **Example**   In Year 4 Mike had a hard time selling his woodwork because of a down economy. Although he made a profit, it wasn't as much as he was accustomed to. In fact, his income wasn't even enough to be able to claim all of his BUH deduction:

Year 4 Gross Income	$25,000
Ordinary Business Expenses	– $21,000
Net Income Remaining	$4,000
Business % of Mortg. Int. & Taxes	– $2,300
Net Income Remaining	$1,700
Other Business-Use Expenses	– $1,500
Net Income Remaining	$200
Depreciation on the Home	– $492
Net Income	– $292

Depreciation on the home is not allowed to create a negative net income. For this reason Mike had to carry over $292 of BUH deductions to a future year when he had sufficient net income to deduct it and still leave a positive balance.

As you can see from this example, even if you meet all of the qualifications for the BUH deduction you may still be unable to claim it all in the current year. This reduces the benefit of claiming the deduction at all—unless in most years your income is more than sufficient to allow you to claim the full deduction.

○ **Tip**   If your net income after non–home expenses is low enough that you cannot even claim all of the business-use portions of your mortgage interest and property taxes, consider the possibility of not claiming a business use of your home at all. You may have a greater benefit in being able to claim all of your mortgage interest and real-estate taxes on Schedule A (itemized deductions), rather than carry forward the business deductions to a future year. You will discover which option is best only by the result of both scenarios in the current year.

Multiple places of business complicates the calculation

The preceding scenario (deductions limited by the amount of income) becomes even more complicated when you have multiple places of business. This is because the deduction is actually limited by the amount of income derived from the business use of the home. So if you run most of your business elsewhere and perform administrative duties only at home, for example, it may be difficult to claim sufficient income derived in the home to cover the expenses claimed.

↪ **Example**   Mike's neighbor Russ, the optometrist, sees 25% of his patients in his home. Because this is the only business activity he performs in his home, he can use only the income from those in-home visits against the expenses he claims for the business use of the home.

○ **Tip**   When allocating income to the home, take into account the amount of time you spend at each business location, the amount of money you spend on capital assets at each location, and any income that is easily attributed to each location (meaning, you wouldn't have to estimate where the income was earned because it clearly came from a specific location).

Warning I: The BUH Deduction May Haunt You Later

You'll want to give thoughtful consideration to the future tax consequences of claiming a deduction for the business use of your home. By declaring that a part of your home is, in essence, business property, you can lose some of the tax benefits of home ownership when you sell the home.

In most cases, when you sell your principal residence you can realize up to $250,000 in gains ($500,000 for couples who file jointly) on the home without paying taxes on those gains. Specific rules govern this exclusion of gains and are covered in Chapter 10. For the purposes of this chapter I will assume that you would otherwise qualify for the exclusion.

⌐ **Example**   Mike and Susan purchased their home in 1990 for $200,000 and made an additional $40,000 in improvements. They sold their home in 2011 for $603,000—a gain of $363,000. If they had realized a gain from the sale of any other asset, they would be required to pay taxes on that gain. In this case the taxes for Mike and Susan would add up to $54,450 ($363,000 gain × 15% capital gains tax bracket = $54,450).

However, because this asset was their home, the tax code offers an exclusion from tax on the first $500,000 of capital gains if all of the rules are met. Under normal circumstances this would mean that Mike and Susan would not be required to pay the $54,450 in taxes.

When part of the home has been treated as business property (instead of personal property) the rules that govern the tax exclusion change. The primary difference is that any depreciation you have taken on the home must be "recaptured."

The idea behind depreciation is that over time an asset becomes less valuable. The tax code allows you to expense, or deduct this theoretical loss in value over the estimated useful life of the home. However, if you sell the home for a higher price than its basis (the price you bought it for, plus improvements, minus depreciation) the home has not really gone down as much in value. For this reason you are required to "recapture" the depreciation you have claimed and then pay taxes on that amount, because you paid fewer taxes in the past by claiming it.

When this depreciation is recaptured, it is taxed at rates determined by special tables. The maximum rate for this recapture is 25%, as opposed to the maximum 15% capital gains rate. The reason for the higher rate is that you have previously deducted depreciation from ordinary income (and in some cases from self-employment income as well). In recapturing this depreciation you will pay taxes on a portion of the gains from the sale of your home which would have normally been tax-free (because of the homeowner exclusion).

➥ **Example**   Mike used his shed for about 6½ years before he and Susan sold the house. During that time he claimed $3,000 in depreciation as a part of the BUH deduction. Although the gain he realized from the sale of his personal residence would normally be excluded from taxes, he will have to pay up to $750 in tax on the recaptured depreciation ($3,000 recaptured × 25% maximum rate = $750).

If the space you claim for business use is within the main walls of your residence, this is the only adjustment you will need to make to the treatment of gains when you sell the home. However, if you claimed business use of a structure appurtenant to your home, as Mike did with his workshop, you'll need to make an additional adjustment on the taxation of the gains. When the portion of the home you depreciated is separate from the "dwelling unit," you must divide the gain on the home and pay taxes on the business portion of that gain, in addition to the recaptured depreciation. The taxable gain is based on the total gain, minus depreciation that has been recaptured.

➥ **Example**   Mike claimed on his tax return that 8% of his home was used for business purposes. Because his workshop is a separate structure from his home, he will have to claim 8% of the gain on the sale of his home as taxable, although it would otherwise be excluded under the personal residence rules. This will cost him an additional $4,320 in taxes [($363,000 gain on the sale of the home – $3,000 depreciation recapture) × 8% of the home used for business × 15% capital gains tax rate = $4,320]. This brings the total tax paid on the sale of the home to $5,070 ($750 depreciation recapture tax + $4,320 capital-gains tax = $5,070 total tax).

As you can see, there are some potentially significant tax consequences when you sell a home that you have claimed for business use. These consequences could be compounded further by the fact that when you sell the home, the full tax impact happens in one year, whereas the tax benefits of the deduction have been split over multiple years. The impact of the sale could even change your marginal tax bracket or cause you to become ineligible for certain tax deductions in that year because your income becomes too high.

In addition, you cannot fully anticipate future tax rates. You could end up saving a little each year from the deductions in a lower tax bracket that the brackets you pay the tax in when you sell the home, if the rates change (or your income changes) before you sell. Take all of these factors into consideration before deciding to claim a BUH deduction.

○ **Tip**   The gain on a home sale, the excluded portion of the gain, and the recapture of the depreciation need to be reported in special ways. I recommend working with a tax professional or studying the IRS publications before finalizing a tax return that includes this type of transaction.

Warning II: The BUH Deduction Will Increase Your Chances of an Audit

As I mentioned at the beginning of this chapter, the BUH deduction is *one of the most commonly audited deductions on a tax return.* The IRS has not officially admitted that this is the case, or that the deduction increases your chances of an audit. However, in a couple of instances high officials in the IRS have stated in public forums that this is the case. I have personally been told by an IRS auditor that the computer system ranks the BUH deduction higher on the list of reasons to audit. In addition, IRS statistics show that self-employed individuals are twice as likely to be audited as other individuals. Claiming the BUH deduction only adds to that risk.

This fact alone is a reason to consider carefully whether to claim the deduction, even if you are entitled to it. The cost of defending yourself in an audit, both in time and in money, plus the potential for the IRS to find other deficiencies while examining your return, can add up to a lot more than the deduction is worth. If the tax benefit you get from the deduction is not significant it may not be worth claiming it at all.

If you choose to claim the deduction you can do things to prepare yourself for a possible audit in order to have a more successful outcome. Why go through all of the work to calculate and claim this deduction, only to have the IRS disallow some or all of it and add penalties and interest to boot? If you are going to do it, make it stick. Some of the ways you can protect yourself are:

- Have a floor plan of your home that shows the dimensions of each room, drawn to scale. Most of the time the IRS agent will never see your home. A floor plan will help the agent see that you have correctly allocated the space between business and personal use.

- The old mantra for the three most important considerations in real estate—location, location, and location—can be re-coined for taxes and IRS audits as documentation, documentation, and documentation. I can't stress enough how important good records are in an IRS audit. They can literally make all the difference. For every expense you claim, be sure to have the documentation (bills, bank statements, and so on) to back it up.

- Take pictures of the space you use for business, from different angles. Print these pictures each year, making sure the date is printed on the picture. The audit of your return will usually happen two to three years after the actual year of the tax return. In that time you may have moved, changed the layout of the room, or gone out of business and repurposed the area for personal use. A picture of the way your room looked during the tax year will help a lot when your return is examined.

- Those who claim to use more than 20% to 25% of their home for their business are far more likely to be questioned. If you are going to claim more than that, be extra certain that you can back up your claim.

- If you are renting, send a 1099 to the landlord for the business portion of the rent to help substantiate the expense.

- If you conduct business anywhere besides the home, keep a log book that shows the amount of time you spend in the home office during the year.

- Be careful not to double-deduct expenses. I have seen people take a deduction for the business portion of their mortgage interest and real-estate taxes and then deduct the full amount of those expenses on their Schedule A as well. This is a simple error, but the IRS computers will quickly pick up on the fact that you have claimed more mortgage interest than the bank reported and will create an automatic flag on your tax return.

- Avoid having multiple years of "losses" on your business and then having other years of $0 income because of the home business deductions and carryovers. In my opinion it would be better to show income for your business and pay some taxes than to have losses and $0 income. If you have several years of losses, the IRS may say that you have a "hobby," not a business—and that can mean a lot of taxes, penalties, and interest.

○ **Tip**   In most cases you can deny the IRS entry into your home if they request a visual examination of your business-use space. Doing so, however, will likely result in the disallowance of all business-use deductions. If the IRS actually wants to see your home, I would strongly recommend getting help from an experienced tax professional who has power of attorney to represent you before the IRS.

Travel Expenses

How to Get the IRS to Buy You a Car, and Other Great Tidbits

Business travel expenses can add up to a significant amount of money. They can prove to be a great deduction when used correctly. In fact, there are even opportunities to deduct a larger amount than you actually spend. These deductions are very popular among businesses, and are often abused. The IRS is aware of this abuse and has put very strict rules and guidelines in place that govern which expenses are deductible, to what extent, and what records need to be kept. They are also very inclined to audit travel expenses that have an appearance of abuse. Even so, certain businesses will gain a lot from understanding how these deductions work and taking advantage of them on their returns.

This chapter focuses on two types of travel expenses: First, mileage and vehicle expenses for business driving and, second, expenses such as airfare, hotels, and other incidental items that are incurred for travel away from home. While meals and entertainment expenses can also be associated with travel, they are given a chapter of their own, Chapter 20.

Mileage and Vehicle Expenses

Early in my career as a tax preparer, I was discussing with a client the standard mileage rate deduction for business use of a vehicle. He was considering the purchase of a fuel-efficient vehicle for his business driving and wanted to know the after-tax costs of the vehicle. As we spoke I ran some quick calculations and excitedly told him it looked like the government would be paying him to buy the vehicle! It turned out that with his high tax bracket, the low price he was going to pay for the car, and the great gas mileage that it got, he would actually come out with more cash in his pocket from claiming the standard mileage deduction than he would spend on the purchase of the vehicle and fuel.

This amazing scenario is not very common, but it *is* common for business owners (as well as some employees) to obtain significant after-tax savings from the mileage deduction. In fact, the right combination of a high tax bracket and a cheaper vehicle with great gas mileage can make it so that the after-tax cost of operating the vehicle is minimal.

↪ **Example**   On January 2, 2013, Jasper bought a five-year old Volkswagen Jetta in great condition and with average miles for $9000. He expects the vehicle to last for 4 years, after which he will dispose of it. Jasper drives around 1,000 miles per month, mostly on the highway. Based on customer ratings and his driving habits, he estimates that he will average about 25 miles per gallon (mpg). At $4 per gallon that would translate to $160 in gas per month (1,000 miles ÷ 25 mpg × $4 per gallon = $160). The monthly car payment and gas costs combine for a total operational expense of $348 per month.

Jasper is in the 35% marginal federal tax bracket, 5% state bracket. and, as a business owner, he also pays 15.3% in self-employment taxes—for a total combined tax bracket of 55.3%. The standard mileage rate for 2013 is $0.565 per mile. Driving 1,000 business miles per month brings him a $565 mileage deduction ($0.565 × 1,000 miles = $565). This deduction results in a tax savings of $312 (55.3% × $565 deduction = $312 tax savings).

With a tax savings of $307, Jasper's true out-of-pocket, after-tax cost for purchasing the vehicle and driving it 1,000 miles each month is $36 ($348 monthly costs − $312 tax savings = $36 net cost). If Jasper had found a better deal on the car, purchased a car with even better mileage, or driven more business miles than planned, his net cost would be even closer to $0.

For many small business owners, vehicle mileage is one of their biggest deductions—especially for those whose business requires a lot of travel. If you are willing to keep good records, this deduction could prove to be a real money saver.

The tax code provides two options for deducting business-use vehicle expenses. You can either use a standard mileage rate for the deduction or you can deduct your actual expenses. At times the actual-expense method can result in a larger deduction—but not always. If you didn't pay very much for the vehicle, have a fuel-efficient vehicle, or drive a lot of miles each year, the standard mileage rate may prove to be more valuable. The actual-expense method requires significantly more recordkeeping than the standard mileage method as well. For some people the recordkeeping requirement alone makes the standard mileage method more appealing than deducting actual expenses, even if it doesn't save you as much money—especially since the difference in tax savings between the two methods is sometimes insignificant.

◆ Caution If you want to use the standard mileage method for a vehicle you must elect to do so the *first* year you use the vehicle for business. If you use the actual-expense method in the first year, you are stuck using that method for as long as you have the car.

○ Tip If you use the standard mileage method in the first year, you are allowed to switch back and forth each year between actual costs and the standard rate. If you are not sure which method to choose, it may be advisable to choose the standard mileage method in the first year so you can decide each year which method is best, based on a comparison of the actual deductions available through each of the methods each year.

◆ Caution If you lease your vehicle, you may not switch back and forth between methods. Whichever method you choose in the first year is the one you have to use for the life of that vehicle.

If you plan to calculate each year which method brings the greatest deduction, keep a few things in mind. First, you must adjust the value of the vehicle for depreciation by the depreciation portion of the standard mileage rate that has been previously applied to the vehicle. Also, in the years when you claim actual expenses, you must calculate depreciation by using the straight-line method (which gives you an equal amount of depreciation each year) instead of the accelerated depreciation method (which gives you a much greater amount in the early years of the vehicle's use). Finally, you cannot claim any bonus depreciation or a Section 179 deduction (which is another special kind of rapid depreciation) on the vehicle. Each of these factors must be weighed in determining the best method to choose for deducting your vehicle expenses.

When claiming the standard mileage deduction, you simply deduct a predetermined amount (set and adjusted by the IRS) for every business mile driven. The rate in 2013 is $0.565 per mile. This fixed deduction per mile is based on an average cost for fuel, repairs, maintenance, and depreciation of a vehicle. It does not matter what your actual expenses were, or what type of vehicle you drive; the standard deduction does not change. The portion of the standard rate that accounts for depreciation must be subtracted from the basis of the vehicle each year, which affects the amount of gain (or loss) on the vehicle when it is sold.

As you can see, most of the actual costs of owning and operating a vehicle are covered by the standard deduction. However, there are four vehicle-related expenses that you can deduct in addition to taking the standard mileage deduction. These are:

- Tolls

- Parking fees (but not those at your place of business)

- Interest on a loan to purchase the vehicle

- Any value-based tax paid when purchasing the vehicle

Of these additional deductible expenses, the most significant may be the interest on a loan, which can add up to a large amount of money, and which many people neglect to deduct. (It is important to note, though, that you can deduct only a portion of the interest based on the percentage of business versus personal use of the vehicle.)

It may seem obvious, but if you decide to claim actual expenses, rather than the standard deduction, you can deduct only the expenses that you actually incur (including depreciation). If you have a lot of repairs, low gas mileage, or can take a high depreciation deduction, the actual-expense method may bring greater dividends.

✒ **Caution** When I have illustrated the potential cost savings of the standard mileage deduction to clients, as in the example about Jasper, above, a couple quick-minded clients have asked me about the possibility of using scooters. Some scooters get 100+ miles to the gallon and are very inexpensive to buy. Driving a scooter for business purposes and deducting the standard mileage rate could actually result in a nice profit—a business itself!

The first time the idea came up in a conversation I thought it was brilliant. However, when I looked into it I found that other, more brilliant minds had already thought of it and shut it down. Unfortunately, the IRS and Congress were aware of this scenario and have made it so that the standard mileage rate is not available for motorcycles, scooters, or bicycles (bicycles being the most brilliant idea). It applies only to passenger vehicles.

The standard mileage rate is also not available if you use five or more vehicles for your business in one year (such as with a fleet). In this case you must use the actual-expense method for deducting your vehicle expenses.

It is important to note that travel from your home to your office is not considered business miles—it is considered personal commuting miles. The same goes for traveling from home to another business location within the area of your home if it is effectively your commute. Once you have made your commute, then other miles that you must travel for business purposes during the day are deductible.

I have an acquaintance who drives a mile or two to a coffee shop near his home and does some work on his phone or computer while there. Then he continues on to the office from there. Since he has begun to work at the shop he says that the distance to the shop is his commute and the remaining miles are then considered business miles. It's a cute idea, but something tells me it won't fly in an audit or in tax court.

○ **Tip**　If you have a home office that qualifies as your principal place of business, you can deduct any trips you make from your home to another location for business purposes. With careful planning of your trips from home, you can write off a significant number of miles each year. See Chapter 17 for details on what qualifies a home as a principal place of business.

Employees can also claim the vehicle expense deductions. If they claim the deduction directly, it is done as a miscellaneous expense on Schedule A, subject to the 2%-of-AGI threshold. However, an alternative to claiming the deduction is to be reimbursed by the employer for the actual expenses, or a fixed rate per mile up to the standard mileage rate.

○ **Tip**　If your employer reimburses for mileage at a rate that is lower than the standard rate set by the IRS it is possible to receive the reimbursement and then claim a deduction for the difference.

If you are receive a temporary assignment that is distant from your home or office you can count that commute as business miles. It is considered temporary only if it is expected to last one year or less. As soon as it is reasonable to expect the assignment to last longer than one year the travel becomes a commute and not business miles.

If you have two jobs you can actually deduct the miles driven from the first job to the second one if you go straight from one to another. However, if you go to the first on one day and to the second on a separate day, both are considered to be commuting miles.

Record Keeping and Audit Risk

The key to maximizing either mileage deduction is keeping accurate records of *every* business trip. Each time you travel from one location to another, for business reasons, you should record the following information:

- Date
- Starting odometer reading
- Ending odometer reading
- Business reason for the trip

You must record this information for each individual trip. If you travel to five different locations during the day, each for a business purpose, don't just write down the total mileage for the day. You need to break out the record keeping for each segment of the route and the purpose for each piece. Although this may seem cumbersome, it is what the IRS requires and what they will be looking for in an audit. This requirement is still easier than the actual-expense method, which requires all of that same detail plus individual records (receipts) for *every* expense incurred.

In addition to those daily records you should also obtain a third-party record of your vehicle's mileage at the beginning of each year (such as the receipt from an oil change). This will substantiate your beginning and ending odometer reading for the year for the IRS.

Several products are available to help you track your mileage. Some people simply use a notebook in their car. You could also buy an inexpensive mileage log from any office-supply store. Mobile phone apps are available for this purpose as well. Whichever way you choose to track your mileage, just be sure to record all of the key information and to keep the records safe and accessible for three years after the year you file your tax return.

The deduction for vehicle mileage is one of the most heavily audited deductions by the IRS. Three factors lead to this heavy scrutiny:

- Notoriously bad record keeping by business owners
- The high dollar value of the deduction
- A history of abuse

The mere fact that you have claimed the deduction will increase the likelihood that your tax return will get a second look by the IRS. In addition, if your return is selected for an audit for *any* reason, you will almost certainly have to defend the mileage deduction as well. Good records will help you keep the deductions you have claimed. I have found that an IRS agent's lenience with this deduction correlates closely to the level of detail and accuracy in the taxpayer's records. The more detailed and complete your records are, the less scrutiny the IRS tends to give the deduction you claimed and the more likely that it will stand.

Travel Away from Home

When the reason for traveling is entirely for business purposes, all reasonable travel expenses will be deductible. However, if there is a combination of business and personal purposes for the travel (determined by what is done on the trip), then the deductibility of the expenses on the trip may be limited—sometimes severely. The rules for deducting travel expenses differ depending on what portion of the trip was for business, and whether the travel is within the United States or if it is in a foreign location. In addition, there are special rules for conventions and luxury water travel (i.e., cruises).

Travel within the United States

Travel within the United States that is entirely for business is fully deductible, including the costs of getting to and from the destination, as well as related expenses while you are there. If the trip is not entirely for business, it will fall into one of two other categories: primarily-for-business or primarily-for-personal reasons.

Primarily business. If your trip was primarily for business and, while there, you extended your stay for a vacation, make a personal side trip, or had other personal activities, you can deduct only your business-related travel expenses. In this case, the entire costs of traveling to and from the business location are deductible. The only items that cannot be deducted are those that you would not have incurred had you solely engaged in business while on the trip.

⮑ **Example**   Lance, who works in Los Angeles, takes a business trip to Omaha, NE to meet with an important client. He spends five days in business meetings and then drives two hours east to Des Moines, IA, to visit with his sister for a couple days before returning home to L.A. The cost of the entire trip was $2,800, $300 of which was for the rental car and some food during the visit to his sister. Because the trip was primarily for business purposes, Lance can deduct all of the expenses of the trip except the $300 associated with visiting his sister.

Primarily personal. If the trip is primarily for personal reasons the entire cost of the trip is non-deductible, except for those items that are directly related to your business. The biggest loss in this treatment is that you cannot deduct the cost of traveling to and from the location. Scheduling incidental business activities (or even conducting business remotely) during the trip will not change it from personal to business. There must be a significant and primary business reason for making the trip.

☞ **Example** Lance and his sister enjoyed being together so much that they decided he would come back in November to spend Thanksgiving with her. Lance took the week of Thanksgiving off from work and spent it in Iowa. However, while he was there he decided to make a quick trip to Omaha for a follow up visit with his client—using a full day to do so. The entire week-long trip cost Lance $1,500, of which $200 was for a car rental and food on the day he visited his client. Lance can deduct only $200 as a business expense for this trip because that is the portion directly related to business, while the rest was primarily personal.

Travel Outside of the United States

The rules for deducting business travel expenses become more complicated when the travel is outside the 50 states and Washington, D.C. There are a lot more "if's" and "or's" to consider. With careful planning, some of these rules can definitely be taken advantage of and result in a larger deduction then you might otherwise "deserve." On the other hand, they can quickly bite you and take away the deductions you would like to claim for your foreign travel expenses.

As was the case with travel within the United States, much of the determination comes down to whether the travel was entirely for business, primarily for business, or primarily for pleasure. In all cases, a pure, necessary and reasonable business expense is always deductible—regardless of the purpose of the travel. The greatest expense that is at stake when determining deductibility is the travel to and from the foreign location. In addition, some of the accommodations that you pay for during the travel may or may not be deductible.

Entirely for business. If the purpose of the travel is entirely for business, you may deduct the full amount of travel expenses to and from the location, plus any other travel-related expenses while there. "Entirely for business" generally means that you spend your entire time on the trip (during normal business hours) on business activities. With foreign travel, however, the rules that govern the definition of "entirely for business" are unique. It is possible for you to do things for pleasure while on the trip and have the purpose be "considered entirely for business" if you meet at least *one* of the following four exceptions:

1. You have no substantial control over the trip. This is the case if you are an employee and the employer pays for, or reimburses you for, the cost of the trip and you are not related to the employer or a managing executive or greater than 10% owner.

2. You are not outside the United States for more than one week, combining business and non-business activities. One week means seven consecutive days (*not* counting the day you leave the United States, but counting the day that you return). This is an intriguing exception. Could you go to Canada on a Monday, cross the border back into the United States on the following Monday, and then go back to Canada for another week beginning on Tuesday? It seems that the answer would be a technical "yes." Combined with some additional rules that I write about later in the chapter, this scenario could make for some interestingly deductible business travel plans.

3. You are outside the United States for more than one week but spend less than 25% of the total time you are outside the United States on non-business activities. For this rule you must count the day your trip began and the day it ended (different than in exception 2 above).

4. You can establish that a personal vacation was not a major consideration, even if you have substantial control over arranging the trip (such as being the owner of the business).

If one of the exceptions listed above applies to your travel, the expenses to and from the location are deductible (in addition to any business-related travel expenses while you are on the trip). Of course, personal expenses while traveling are not deductible.

Primarily business. If your foreign business travel is not entirely for business (or considered entirely for business because of one of the four exceptions), but is primarily for business, you will be able to deduct only a portion of your expenses for traveling to and from your destination. In this case the cost of travel will have to be pro-rated between business and non-business travel. You must count each day as business or non-business and divide the total number of business days by the total number of days outside the United States to determine the percentage of the expenses that can be deducted. (In this case, both of the days traveling to and from the location are counted in the total.)

The following list outlines what days may be counted as a business day:

- Transportation days. Any day that you spend traveling to or from a business destination is counted as a business day. However, if you do not take a direct route to the business location because you are making side trips for personal reasons, you may count only the number of days it would have taken if you had chosen a direct route.

- Your presence is required. Any day in which your presence is required at a particular place for a specific business purpose can be counted as a business day. This is the case even if you spend most of the day in non-business activities.

- You spend the day on business. If your main activity during working hours is focused on business, then it is a business day, regardless of what you do during the remaining hours of the day.

- Weekends and holidays. You can count weekends, holidays, and other necessary stand-by days as business days if they fall between business days. It is important to understand that it must be between two business days, not counting the travel-home day. For example, if you have a business day Friday, stay the weekend, and then travel home Monday the weekend does not count as business days.

Perhaps you noticed that these rules open up a lot of wiggle room as long as you carefully plan your travel. The following example and Table 18-1 illustrate how a business trip can contain a lot of personal time and still be deducted as a business expense.

Table 18-1. Walter's Travel Schedule and Business Purpose of Each Day

	Day	Activity	Business Purpose
1	Thursday	Travel from New York to London	Travel to destination
2	Friday	Meet with a customer in the morning; touring the rest of the day	Presence required
3	Saturday	Touring	Weekend rule
4	Sunday	Touring	Weekend rule
5	Monday	Meet with a customer in the morning; touring the rest of the day	Presence required
6	Tuesday	Travel to Scotland; touring	Travel to business

(continued)

Table 18-1. (*continued*)

Day		Activity	Business Purpose
7	Wednesday	Meet with a customer in the morning; touring the rest of the day	Presence required
8	Thursday	Travel to Ireland; touring	Travel to business
9	Friday	Meet with a customer in the morning; touring the rest of the day	Presence required
10	Saturday	Touring	Weekend rule
11	Sunday	Touring	Weekend rule
12	Monday	Travel to Paris; meet with a customer in the afternoon	Presence required
13	Tuesday	Meet with a customer in the morning; touring the rest of the day	Presence required
14	Wednesday	Travel to Belgium; touring	Travel to business
15	Thursday	Meet with a customer in the morning; touring the rest of the day	Presence required
16	Friday	Travel to Frankfurt, Germany; meet with a customer in the afternoon	Presence required
17	Saturday	Touring	Weekend rule
18	Sunday	Touring	Weekend rule
19	Monday	Meet with a customer in the morning; touring the rest of the day	Presence required
20	Tuesday	Travel to Munich, Germany; touring	Travel to business
21	Wednesday	Meet with a customer in the morning; touring the rest of the day	Presence required
22	Thursday	Travel to Switzerland; touring	Travel to business
23	Friday	Meet with a customer in the morning; touring the rest of the day	Presence required
24	Saturday	Touring	Weekend rule
25	Sunday	Touring	Weekend rule
26	Monday	Travel to London; meet with a customer in the afternoon	Travel to home
27	Tuesday	Return to New York	Travel to home

↪ **Example** Walter is an exporter of plastics. The majority of his customers are in Asia and Australia, but he wants to expand to Europe. His business model is to have one main distributer of his products in each country in which he sells his products and they, in turn, sell to others in their country. Walter has found the businesses in seven European countries that he thinks may be prime candidates to act as his distributors and is at the point where he needs to visit each one for final negotiations and inspection of their facilities.

Walter is also an avid traveler and well versed in the deductibility rules associated with foreign travel. With careful planning he has arranged for a four-week tour of Europe, where he will meet with 13 businesses. He expects each meeting to take an average of 4 hours, making his time spent in conducting business 52 hours. For Walter, 52 hours is a normal work week. However, he is able to spend four weeks in Europe and count the entire trip as a business expense. He does this by carefully placing his appointments with these businesses at just the right points in his schedule in order to count every day as a business day, per the IRS regulations. See Table 18-1 if you are interested in how he pulls this off.

In the example, is Walter's approach to applying the rules a little extreme? Perhaps. Could it be questioned by the IRS? Of course. Would he win the argument? I think he might. He would be able to establish that the primary purpose of the trip is for business, that there was good reason for him to travel to each destination, and that each day meets the rules that are established in order to be counted as a business day.

If he wanted to he could have extended his stay even further by inserting days, here and there, where he spent most of the working day catching up on business via computer and phone. Six or seven hours of office work, catching up on things that are happening during his absence, would count as a business day as well—and then he could spend the rest of that day touring too.

Most trips, however, are not planned so perfectly, or with the tax consequences as the top priority. In those cases, the expense of travel to and from the destination must be pro-rated proportionate to the amount of time spent conducting business. In addition, expenses for those days that are not spent doing business (such as hotels, meals, and transportation) are not deductible.

↪ **Example** Walter's friend, Andrew, thinks that Walter was brilliant for creating a month-long trip to Europe that was fully deductible. Andrew quickly threw together a 12-day business trip of his own, to Japan. Andrew flew to Japan one day, conducted business for four days, went on a tour of China for four days, conducted two more days of business, and then flew home.

Unfortunately for Andrew, he didn't pay as close attention to the tax rules as Walter did. The four-day tour did not meet any of the rules that would allow them to be counted as business days. Because of that, one third of the cost of the travel to and from Japan is considered personal (4 days personal ÷ 12 days total = 1/3 of the days) and is not deductible, as well as the lodging, food, and other expenses associated with those days.

Primarily personal. If the reason for the trip is primarily personal, then none of the expenses can be deducted except those that are directly related to doing business. All of the expenses of traveling to and from the destination would be non-deductible.

Luxury Water Travel

If you choose to travel to your foreign business destination by purchasing a ticket on a cruise ship, the cost of the travel that can be deducted is limited to twice the highest per-diem rate allowed for federal employee travel expenses. For example, if the highest per diem rate were $325 per day you could not deduct more than $650 per day ($325 highest per diem rate x 2 = $650 maximum deduction) as business travel expenses, even if it cost you significantly more. You can find the per-diem IRS Publication 1542 on the IRS website.

⌕ **Note**   The deduction is severely limited for conventions held on cruise ships. See the section on conventions, below, for more details.

If food and entertainment are separately itemized on your receipt for the cruise you may deduct only 50% of those costs. If they are not itemized you can deduct the entire amount, up to the daily limit.

➷ **Example**   Paul lives in California and ships his business products around the world. His largest customers are in Panama. Paul travels to see these customers in person at least once per year in order to maintain relationships and negotiate new contracts. This year Paul decides to travel to Panama and back on a cruise ship.

The cruise takes three days each way, and he stays in Panama for two days in the middle of the trip, which is plenty of time for Paul to conduct his business. The cruise costs $3,000 and includes all of his meals (which are not separately stated on his receipt.) The per-day cost of the cruise is $375 ($3,000 ÷ 8 days = $375), which is far below the limit of two times the per diem rate. Because of this, Paul's entire $3,000 travel expense is deductible.

Conventions, Seminars, and Conferences

Travel expenses for attending a convention (or seminar or conference) are deductible only if the convention benefits your trade or business. The convention agenda is what determines whether it is beneficial to your business, and it is the proof that you will need in case of an audit. The topics presented in the agenda must relate to your duties and responsibilities in your business.

For conventions held outside the of the North America area, you must also be able to show that it is as reasonable for this convention to be held outside of North America as it would be to hold it within that area. Things that might make it reasonable to hold it outside North America might include the purpose of the meeting, the purpose and locations of the sponsoring groups, and whether there are similar opportunities to attend such an event within the North America area.

For the purposes of this rule, the North America area is pretty broadly defined—making North America much larger than you might otherwise think. Here are the locations that are included in the allowable area:

American Samoa	Guam	Netherlands Antilles
Antigua and Barbuda	Guyana	Northern Mariana
Aruba	Honduras	Islands
Bahamas	Howland Island	Palau
Baker Island	Jamaica	Palmyra Atoll
Barbados	Jarvis Island	Puerto Rico
Bermuda	Johnston Island	Trinidad and Tobago
Canada	Kingman Reef	USA
Costa Rica	Marshall Islands	U.S. Virgin Islands
Dominica	Mexico	Wake Island
Dominican Republic	Micronesia	
Grenada	Midway Islands	

If the convention is held on a cruise ship, you have additional limitations placed on your deductions. First, you may not deduct more than $2,000 per year for conventions held on cruise ships. In addition, the convention must meet the following conditions:

1. The convention, seminar, or meeting is directly related to your trade or business.

2. The cruise ship is a vessel registered in the United States.

3. All of the cruise ship's ports of call are in the United States or in possessions of the United States.

4. You attach to your return a written statement signed by you that includes information about:

    a. The total days of the trip (not including the days of transportation to and from the cruise ship port),

    b. The number of hours each day that you devoted to scheduled business activities, and

    c. A program of the scheduled business activities of the meeting.

5. You attach to your return a written statement signed by an officer of the organization or group sponsoring the meeting that includes:

    a. A schedule of the business activities of each day of the meeting, and

    b. The number of hours you attended the scheduled business activities.

In reading the list of requirements that are in place in order to deduct the costs of a convention on a cruise ship, you get the idea that this is an area that can be easily abused and that the IRS wants none of it. Just be sure to put all of your records in place as they have outlined, and you will be in good shape.

Meals, Entertainment, and Gifts

Everyone Loves Getting a Tax Break for Doing Something Fun

There are many times when a meal, a gift, or entertainment is a very legitimate business expense—just as legitimate as advertising or other promotional expenses. However, there are also many times in which these "business" expenses are really just an excuse to have some fun and get a write-off in the process. Because it is not easy for the IRS to discern between legitimate expenses in these categories, and those that are not, there are strict rules imposed on the record-keeping requirements for these expenses. There are also significant limitations placed on the dollar value that you can deduct for these expenses. In many cases, 50% of the cost is taken right off the top of what you are allowed to deduct. I suppose this is Congress's way of dealing with—and limiting—the abuse of this deduction. Even so, there are some great opportunities available to save on your tax bill by properly deducting meals, entertainment, and gift expenses.

Meals

People seem to love deducting meals as a business expense. It must come down to the fact that they get a tax deduction for something they do every day: eat. Or maybe it gives them the excuse they need to eat out for lunch instead of brown-bagging it. Whatever the reasons people cherish this deduction, you'll want to understand the tax benefits and risks associated with deducting business meals before you plan your next "business" dinner.

Three categories of meals are deductible as a business expense:

- Meals while on a business trip (a travel expense)
- Meals with a business associate, such as a client, supplier, or vender (an entertainment expense)
- Meals to provide food for your employees

In the first two cases you are allowed to deduct 50% of the cost of the meal, within certain guidelines. However, the rules that determine the deductibility of the meal differ between "travel meals" and "entertainment meals." In the case of meals for employees, there are instances where the food is 100% deductible.

Meals as a Travel Expense

If the meal is for travel, you have two options for deducting the expense: you can choose to deduct your actual costs (what you paid for the meal), or you can choose to deduct a standard daily amount set by the IRS. With the actual-expense method, you must keep a record of the cost of each meal (including taxes and tips) during your travel. If you choose the standard daily amount, you can deduct one half of the per diem rate that federal employees are allowed to spend each day they travel. This amount differs each year, and it varies based on the city to which you are traveling. In general, the standard-rate for a day's worth of meals may range between $45 and $75, depending upon location. You can find the rates for each city in IRS Publication 1542 or on the IRS website.

If you are not a big spender on food you may get a bigger benefit from claiming the per diem rates and then spending less than the rate. In fact, if you manage to spend one half of the per diem rate you would actually be able to deduct 100% of your meals expense. If the per diem rate for the city you are in is $60, for example, you can deduct 50% of that ($30) as your standard-rate meal expense. If you actually spend only $30 on your food for the day you can effectively deduct 100% of your true expense. If you spend less than half of the standard rate the deal gets even better, allowing you to deduct more than you spent! If you go without food for the day, the government is actually paying you to fast! Maybe I'm going a little overboard here, but you get the idea.

On the other hand, many people will benefit more from the actual-expense method because they spend more on food than the per diem allowance. Check those per diem rates against your own spending habits and determine which method will bring you the best results.

☞ **Caution** If you use the standard per diem rates, you must use them for every trip during the year. You are not allowed to vary the methods for different trips.

When deducting a meal for business travel, the meal must occur during the time that you are actually conducting business. For example, if you travel out of state for two days of business, but then stay an extra day to sightsee, you can only deduct expenses for meals during those first two business days. In addition, if your trip includes a partial day (i.e., gone two full days and only the morning of the third day), then the per-diem rate for the partial day should be prorated to 75% of the normal per diem rate.

Finally, meals can be deducted for travel only when you are traveling out of town overnight. (The actual guidelines are that you are considered traveling if you are away from the general area of your home for a period substantially longer than an ordinary work day and it is reasonable to expect that during that time you would need sleep or rest.) If you are just away from the office only during a normal working day and buy lunch while you are there, it is considered a personal expense like any other food that you need. However, if you invite a business associate to eat with you, then you may be able to deduct that meal under the meals-as-entertainment rules described in the next sub-section.

Meals as an Entertainment Expense

When deducting a meal for entertainment purposes (such as taking a client to lunch), different rules need to be followed. First, your meal must have a business purpose—you must reasonably expect some benefit to come to your business as a result of the meal. (The benefit doesn't have to actually occur—you only need a reasonable expectation that it will.) This rule is most easily satisfied by having a business discussion of some significance (more than "So how's business?") before, during, or after the meal. In addition, you can deduct the expense only for people connected to your business. For example, you couldn't invite your client to a family reunion and then deduct the meal expense for your 10 cousins who joined you—only the cost of the meals for you and the client could be deducted.

○ **Tip**   An exception: You are allowed to deduct a meal for your spouse if you have brought him or her along to make the spouse of your business associate feel comfortable. This is considered a reasonable business expense.

🖝 **Caution**   You or your employee must be present at the meal in order to claim it as a business expenses. For example, you could not send a restaurant gift certificate to a client and deduct it as a business expense. Such an expense would fall under the gift rules instead, which are much more limited (as discussed at the end of this chapter).

The timing of the business discussion in relation to the meal (or entertainment) is important. If the "discussion" happens during a rock concert it won't count, because it would have been too loud for a serious business discussion. Also, if the discussion happened after a significant amount of alcohol is consumed it probably will not count either.

There is not a per diem alternative for meals-as-entertainment like there is for meals when traveling. You can deduct only the actual cost of the meal. In addition, the cost of the meal must be seen as reasonable under the circumstances (not lavish or extravagant) or the IRS can actually reduce it to a reasonable amount. (I think it would have to be pretty extreme for the IRS to challenge it. There is no exact number given, but I think common sense would rule in this case. Is it an ordinary and reasonable expense under the circumstance?)

🗐 **Note**   If food is provided as part of an event where attendees pay to participate (such as a trade show, conference, or entertainment), the meals are deductible as part of the cost of an event that generated revenue for the business.

Food provided freely to the public as part of a promotional event is fully deductible because it is more of an advertising expense than entertainment.

Record Keeping

Because of rampant abuse of the meals deduction, the IRS strictly enforces its record-keeping rules for these expenses. You must keep a record of the following five items for all meal expenses you deduct for entertainment purposes (when you pay for a meal for someone other than yourself):

- The date of the meal
- The cost of the meal, including taxes and tips.

- The place where the meal was purchased

- The business purpose of the meal—state whether the business conversation was held before, during, or after the meal, and what the conversation's business goal was.

- The business relationship you have with the people whose meals you paid for. List their names and any other information necessary to establish that they have a business relationship with you.

Interestingly, the IRS does *not* require any receipts for meals that cost less than $75. That said, you *do* need all of the information I listed, even if you don't keep a receipt. For practical purposes I recommend keeping receipts for all of these expenses. That way you are in the habit of doing this and you don't have to think about when to keep a receipt. Plus, three of the five record-keeping requirements are already on the receipt (date, cost, and place), so you can just write the purpose of the meal and the people involved on the back of the receipt, and you have a complete record.

For meals related to travel you only need the first two items on the list. If you use the per-diem rate you don't need any records of the items on the list. However, in both cases you do need proof that you were actually traveling for business purposes when those meals occurred.

Before you get too excited about this deduction and set up all kinds of business meals on your calendar, remember that the tax benefits of this deduction are pretty limited. First, the tax code eliminates half the cost of the meal right off the top by only allowing you to take a 50% deduction. Then the true benefit of the remaining 50% depends on your marginal tax bracket. If you are in the 15% bracket, your deduction equates to a 7.5% break on the total cost of your meal (the cost of the meal × 50% × 15% = 7.5% savings). In the best-case scenario, the highest amount that you might take off the cost of the bill through the tax savings is 34%. For that scenario to occur you would have to be self-employed, in the highest tax bracket, and living in a very-high tax state like California (15.3% self-employment tax + 39.6% federal tax + 3.8% additional Medicare tax + 9.3% state tax = 68% total tax bracket × 50% of the cost = 34% savings). Don't get caught in the mindset that a deduction for your meals means the government is footing the bill. You are still paying for most of it.

✎ **Caution**   I can't stress enough the importance of good recordkeeping when it comes to this deduction. Because of a long history of abuse in this area the IRS will heavily scrutinize your meal expenses if they audit your return. If you have the records they require, you will be in good shape. If you don't . . . well, it might spoil your dinner if I talk about it.

Meals for Employees

If a business provides meals to its employees for the employer's convenience, the meals may be 100% deductible and not included as additional pay to the employees. To be deductible the meals must fall into one of the following categories:

- *Employer Convenience.* This occurs when an employer needs the employee to remain on site for business reasons. If more than 50 of the employees are provided the meals for this reason it is considered that all the meals provided are for this purpose. Examples of this would be to attend a mandatory business meeting, meet with a client or customer, or to trade securities while the market is open. This could also occur to help the employees work late or on holidays, or if there are no available eating facilities within a reasonable distance where the employee could travel to and return within the allotted time frame for meals. (Meals provided to owners, 10% shareholders, officers, or directors are not deductible under the "employer's convenience" rules unless they are included in that individual's income, unless for a business meeting.)

- *Employer Events.* If the business is providing a recreational or social activity for employees where food is provided, these meals are generally fully deductible. Examples of this would be a company picnic or holiday party. However, the food costs must be reasonable. In some cases, such as high-end holiday parties, the cost of the food is extraordinary and would not qualify for the full deduction.

- *Employee Goodwill.* Nominal gifts of food to employees. Classic examples of this would be giving employees a turkey at Thanksgiving or ham at Easter.

- *Minimal, Hard-to-Track Items.* Food and drink items provided in the workplace that have a minimal value and are hard to trace to a specific employee are fully deductible. For example, if an employer provided free soft drinks and snacks, these items would be fully deductible.

- *Reimbursed by Client.* If a business tracks meal expenses and bills them to a client for reimbursement, those costs are deductible (and the reimbursement is included in income, so it is a wash).

- *Restaurants, Non-Luxury Water Vessels and Offshore or Alaskan Oil Rigs*. These employers are allowed to provide meals to their employees and fully deduct the costs.

To claim the full deduction of employee meals, the expense must be directly for food (i.e., no reimbursements or cash advances, etc.). Also, the food cannot be a reward or incentive (which would be considered compensation). In these cases the meals would be considered a form of payment and be included in the employee's W-2 form as compensation. (However, if the meals *are* included as employee income they are fully deductible to the employee.)

 Note   Food provided to spouses and children of employees at a company event is also deductible—the deduction is not exclusive to the employees only.

Entertainment

The rules governing entertainment expenses are almost identical to those governing "meals-as-entertainment" expenses. Entertainment would include such expenses as nightclubs, sporting events, theaters, and so on. To deduct such expenses the business must have *more than a general expectation* of deriving income or another specific business benefit to come from providing the entertainment, at some time in the future.

In addition, the entertainment must occur immediately before, after, or during a *substantial* business discussion. The business discussion must be the principal purpose of the business and entertainment and must represent an active effort by the business to obtain income or another specific business benefit. The entertainment can either be with a current client or customer or with a potential new business prospect.

There are a few types of entertainment expenses that are specifically *not* deductible. Some of the more common ones are:

- Entertainment facilities, such as yachts, swimming pools, hunting lodges, bowling alleys, etc.

- Club memberships, such as social, athletic, sporting, business, and other similar clubs. (Clubs that have a non-entertainment or social purpose, such as Kiwanis or Rotary, are deductible, as well as professional organizations with a business focus.)

Other than the specific differences that I have noted to this point, entertainment expenses are deductible at 50% of their reasonable cost and follow the rules noted in the meals-as-entertainment section. In addition, reasonable entertainment provided at an employee event (such as a picnic) is fully deductible, along the same lines as are mentioned in the section about employee meals.

The record-keeping requirements for entertainment expenses are stringent. They are identical to the meals-as-entertainment record-keeping requirements that are listed in the previous section. Take the time to keep these records so that the deductions will be upheld. Also take special note of the "Cautions" regarding timing listed in the meals section. The timing of the business discussion and the entertainment could end up countering the argument that the primary purpose was for business if the likelihood of a serious discussion happening is slim because of the circumstances, or if the business representative is not present during the entertainment.

Gifts

Business gifts are subject to very limiting rules regarding their deductibility. You cannot deduct more than $25 in gifts to any individual in a year, no matter how much you give them or how business-worthy the gift was. If you send a client a $500 gift you can deduct only $25. This doesn't mean you shouldn't give larger gifts—you just need to know that you cannot deduct that expense from your taxes.

The gift limitation applies whether the gift is given directly or indirectly. For example, if you give one gift to a client and another to his wife (or child, etc.), it is treated as if you gave the gift indirectly to the client (unless you have a clearly separate and independent business relationship with that family member). Likewise, if you give a gift to a business with the intent that a certain individual receive the benefit of that gift, it is counted as an indirect gift to that individual.

⮑ **Example**   Dillon's best client is Milton, a local business owner. At Christmas time, Dillon gave Milton a $100 gift certificate to his favorite restaurant and also gave a $50 silk scarf to Milton's wife. Dillon also sent a $120 gift basket full of food to Milton's business office, which Milton took home to his family. Dillon's total gifts to Milton were worth $270. All of them are treated as being given directly or indirectly to Milton, so Dillon will be allowed to deduct only $25 of that expense.

In addition, you and your spouse are counted as one giver of a gift (or gifts), so you cannot each give a gift to an individual and receive two deduction limits for those gifts. This is the case *even if* you and your spouse have separate businesses!

Inexpensive, incidental items are not included in the $25 limitation and are fully deductible. Incidental items would include such things as engraving, packaging, gift-wrapping, mailing, and insuring items. The key to being incidental is that it does not add substantial value to the gift.

Inexpensive items that are clearly promotional in nature are not considered gifts (such as a pen with your company logo on it). To qualify as a promotional item, its value must be less than $4 per item. The item must have your business name clearly printed on it, and it must be something that you distribute widely to many people.

Employee Benefits

And the Owner Benefits Too

Employee benefits are an additional expense that employers incur in order to attract and retain talented employees. Many of these benefits are tax-deductible to the employer, which can help reduce the true out-of-pocket cost to the employer. In some cases an owner is also eligible to take advantage of these "employee" benefits, which results in an even greater benefit to the employer by enabling him or her to transfer personal expenses to the business side of the equation. In this chapter we'll discuss three types of employee benefits:

- Fringe benefits
- Educational assistance programs
- Medical expenses and health insurance

Fringe Benefits

Fringe benefits are forms of payment to employees that are not given in the form of cash. Generally fringe benefits come in the form of the company paying for an item or service that benefits the employee. Most fringe benefits are taxable to the employee as wages. However, there are several that have been excluded from this treatment, allowing the bestowal of benefits to an employee, which are deductible to the employer but not taxable to the employee. This section will cover the following fringe benefits:

- Adoption assistance
- Athletic facilities
- *De minimis* benefits
- Employee discounts
- Life insurance
- No-additional-cost services

Adoption Assistance

Employers may help in the cost of an adoption made by an employee as long as there is a written plan for such a benefit that does not favor highly compensated employees, and that all employees are made aware of. The reimbursed adoption expenses must be substantiated by sufficient documentation. The reimbursement is excluded from income; however, it is included for purposes of payroll taxes.

No more than 5% of the total reimbursed adoption expenses during a year may be paid to a shareholder or owner (someone who owns more than 5% of the business on any given day of the year).

Athletic Facilities

The business can deduct the cost of an on-premises gym or other athletic facility, and not include it in employees' wages, if the facility is used primarily by employees, their spouses, and their children during the year. This is one of the more lenient allowances for fringe benefits (one of the easiest to deduct). An individual is considered an employee if he or she meets one of the following criteria:

- A current employee
- A former employee who left because of retirement or disability
- A widow or widower of a person who died while an employee
- A widow or widower of a person who left because of retirement or disability

- A partner who provides services to the partnership

- A leased employee who is under the supervision of the business and has performed full-time service to the business for at least one year

The gym or athletic facility must be located on premises that are owned or leased by the business (not necessarily the primary place of business).

De Minimis Benefits

De minimis benefits are those items or services that you provide to an employee that have so little value that accounting for it would be unreasonable or administratively impractical. Such benefits include:

- Personal use of an employer-provided cell phone that is provided primarily for business purposes

- Occasional personal use of a business copy machine, as long as 85% of the machine's use is for business purposes

- Non-cash holiday gifts with a low market value (such as a ham or turkey)

- Occasional tickets to theater or sporting events

- Snacks and drinks

✦ **Caution**   Cash and cash equivalents (such as a gift card), no matter how little, are never excludable: they must always be included in the employee's income.

Employee Discounts

Your business may offer discounts on your products or services, as long as the policy for discounts does not favor owners or highly compensated employees. For services the discount may be up to 20% off of the price normally charged to non-employees. For products the discount may be up to the average gross-profit percentage of all products as a whole. For example, if you average a 50% gross profit on your products, the employee discount may not be more than that amount for any individual product.

Life Insurance

You may provide up to $50,000 of group term life insurance per employee. Any excess amount that is provided will be included in the employee's wages based on the premiums paid. The plan must not discriminate between employees or favor highly compensated employees or owners.

No-Additional-Cost Services

Services provided to an employee that add no additional cost to the business may be excluded from income. Examples of this would include airline employees receiving free flights, free telephone service to a phone-company employee, or free use of tax software for an employee of a tax-preparation business. To be considered "no-additional cost," the service given must not have replaced the services that would have otherwise been given to a paying customer. For example, there must have been empty seats on a plane for an airline employee to use; they may not have used a seat that was needed by a paying customer.

As is the case with other fringe benefits, the services must not be provided in a way that favors highly compensated employees or owners. Also, services provided to employee family members are treated as if they were received by the employee.

Educational Assistance Programs

Your business may pay up to $5,250 per employee, per year, toward an employee's education expenses. Qualified expenses include tuition, fees, books, equipment, and supplies required for bachelor- and graduate-level courses. However, no courses involving sports, games, or hobbies may be paid for unless they are directly related to your business or are required to obtain a degree. In addition, no tools or supplies may be paid for if they are retained by the employee after the course is completed.

Education assistance program policies must be written and made known to all employees. The qualifications for the program must not favor owners or highly compensated employees. The program may also not provide more than 5% of its yearly benefits to those who own more than 5% of the business. Note that children of owners who are bonafide employees are not under the limitations of the 5% rule.

Medical Expenses and Health Insurance

There are a few ways in which a sole proprietor can benefit from medical and insurance expenses by running them through the business instead of through their personal expenses. As you offer these benefits to employees, a significant portion of the cost will be offset by the tax deductions that you are able to claim for them and for yourself. The three areas covered in this subsection are:

- The Self-Employed Health Insurance Deduction
- Health Reimbursement Arrangements
- The Health Care Tax Credit

Self-Employed Health Insurance

On one occasion I was asked to review a new client's personal tax return after his current accountant had filed it. As I looked at it, I realized that his Adjusted Gross Income (AGI) was only slightly higher than some key phase-outs that were having a significant effect on his return. I also noticed that he hadn't claimed the above-the-line deduction for self-employed health insurance premiums, even though he qualified to do so. In fact, the amount that he paid for health insurance premiums during the year was larger than the amount by which his AGI exceeded the phase-outs that were affecting him. By amending his tax return and claiming the Self-Employed Health Insurance Deduction, we were able to save him save him thousands of dollars in taxes because of the credits and deductions that became available as a result of his AGI falling below the phase-outs.

Generally, health insurance premiums are considered a personal expense that can be deducted as part of the medical expenses deduction on Schedule A with all of the other itemized deductions. Claiming the deduction in this way makes the expense subject to the 7.5% or 10% AGI limitation, which often eliminates much (if not all) of the benefit of the deduction. It also means that the deduction has no benefit unless all of your itemized deductions combined together are greater than the standard deduction. These factors make it so that many people receive very little benefit from medical insurance expenses as a tax deduction.

However, if you own a business you can claim health insurance expenses as an above-the-line deduction instead of using them as an itemized deduction. To be eligible, you must be a sole proprietor, an active member of a partnership, or at least a 2% shareholder in an S-corporation to qualify. You must also have no employer-sponsored health insurance plan available to you (through your own employment or through your spouse's employment). For example, if you are an employee of a business but also run your own business on the side, you could not claim this deduction if you are eligible as an employee to be covered under your employer's insurance plan. However, if your spouse is eligible for insurance through her employer, but you are not, you can claim the cost of premiums for your own insurance.

The deduction cannot exceed your net earned income from the business, minus one half of your self-employment tax and minus any retirement plan contributions. For owners of S-corporations, the premiums must be paid by the corporation or reimbursed by the corporation and be reflected as income in the owner's W-2 form.

☞ **Example**   Jill owns a bakery as a sole proprietor. Her net income from the business this year was $35,000. Her personal health insurance premiums were $5,000 for the year. She also made a $6,000 contribution to her IRA. Given these circumstances, Jill can claim the self-employed health insurance deduction because she has sufficient net income ($35,000 net income − $6,000 IRA contribution − $2,473 [one half of self-employment tax] = $26,527, which is greater than the $5,000 in health insurance premiums).

Health Reimbursement Arrangements (HRAs)

There is an IRS-approved conduit for deducting medical expenses as business expenses, which is known as a *Health Reimbursement Arrangement* (HRA). An HRA is a system in which the business reimburses its employees for medical expenses. The employer sets the terms of what will be reimbursed and is fully responsible for its funding (no employee contributions are allowed). Any reimbursements made for qualified medical expenses are deductible expenses for the business.

A self-employed business owner (sole proprietor) is not allowed to participate in an HRA program—at least directly. However, if the business owner's spouse is employed by the business he or she *would be* allowed to participate. This strategy is explored further in Chapter 21. There are two major tax benefits to using an HRA program. First, medical expenses are deductible from the first dollar spent and not limited by the 7.5% or 10% of AGI floor normally placed on medical expenses claimed as an itemized deduction. Second, for self-employed individuals the deduction reduces income taxes *and* self-employment taxes, whereas the itemized deduction would not reduce the self-employment tax.

✦ **Caution**   As it currently stands, the Affordable Care Act (a.k.a. ObamaCare) puts severe limitations on HRAs beginning in 2014. It will be important to watch for any changes to this law to determine whether this will be a viable tax strategy in 2014 and beyond.

Health Care Tax Credit

To help cover the cost of insurance coverage, a credit is available to small businesses during the first five years of the Affordable Care Act. For businesses with 10 or fewer employees and an average employee salary of less than $25,000, the credit is 50% of the cost of premiums (or of the average cost in the state, if lower) for the coverage of employees (but not for the cost of covering the owners). The credit is only available to those businesses which buy their insurance through the government exchanges. It is quickly reduced for companies that have more than 10 employees, as well as for businesses that pay their employees better wages. The credit completely disappears if the average employee wages are higher than $50,000 or if the company employs more than 25 people. The owners and family members of owners are not counted in the employee number or in the average wages.

To qualify for the credit, the employer must pay at least 50% of employee premiums. The credit can be used against the Alternative Minimum Tax (AMT), but it is nonrefundable, so the employer will receive no help in paying for the insurance if he owes no taxes.

○ **Tip**   This credit is not as beneficial as other credits. This is because the credit takes the place of the health insurance costs the business could have deducted if it had claimed no credit. This increases the company's taxable income and thus reduces some of the credit's benefit—at times making it not worth taking the credit at all.

Employing Family Members

These "Child Labor Laws" Can Really Lower Your Taxes

One of the greatest tax benefits of owning your own business is finding ways to transform personal, non-deductible expenses into deductible business expenses. A great non-tax benefit of owning your own business is that you are the boss and get to decide how you run that business— including whom you hire as an employee. In this chapter these two benefits meet and combine to form a powerful tax-saving strategy. Hiring family members as legitimate employees of your business can bring significant savings on your tax return. The tax available to you will depend mostly on what member of your family you employ, and as such, the strategies in this chapter are broken up into three main categories:

- Employing children
- Employing your spouse
- Employing your parents

Employing Children

Does little Johnny need to learn how to work? Does Suzie need something to do with her time? Do you need a way to reduce your taxes? If so, these needs could be combined for a match made in tax heaven. Employing your children in your business can save money in both income taxes and payroll taxes.

At the foundation of this strategy is something known as income shifting—taking income from an individual in a higher tax bracket and moving it to someone in a low tax bracket. This is especially effective for immediate family members who would already be sharing in each other's income. Used wisely, this strategy can save a lot of money.

⮑ **Example** Martha has a bookkeeping business based out of her home. While some of the work she does requires a high level of skill and training, much of it is mundane, such as filing, opening mail, and shredding and shredding documents. Martha has a 12-year-old daughter, Ruby, who needs to earn money for extracurricular activities and who could easily perform the mundane activities of Martha's business, freeing Martha up to do more work that she can bill for.

Martha and her husband are in the 28% federal tax bracket. If Martha hires Ruby to work for her 10 hours per week, at $12 per hour, Ruby will earn about $6,000 per year. By shifting this income to Ruby it would save Martha $1,680 in federal income taxes per year. (If you add to that the average state tax of around 5% she will have saved around $2,000 in total income taxes.) What is more, Ruby would not have to pay any income tax on that money either (more on that later).

The savings of this strategy do not stop with federal and state income taxes. Sole proprietors, as well as husband–wife partnerships (not other partnerships or business entities), who employ their own children who are younger than 18 years old are not required to pay any Social Security, Medicare, or unemployment taxes on those wages! This is an additional savings of up to 15.3% on that shifted income. To realize the full savings, the business-owner-parent's income needs to be below the cap for the Social Security tax, which is $113,700 in 2013.

⮑ **Example** Martha's net income from her bookkeeping business is around $80,000 per year. If Martha pays Ruby $6,000 per year, that amount will be deducted from Martha's income, saving her $918 in self-employment taxes. In addition, since Ruby is Martha's daughter, she will not have to pay payroll taxes on those wages, so the $918 is a true savings. When added to the income tax savings in the previous example, Martha will save almost $3,000 in taxes by hiring her daughter and paying Ruby $6,000 in wages. In essence it is costing Martha only $3,000 to give her daughter $6,000 (while giving her work experience to boot).

This strategy has its maximum benefit when the child owes no tax on the income that he or she receives. A dependent child cannot claim a personal exemption on a tax return, but *is* able to claim the standard deduction.

Because of this, the first $6,100 of income to the child (the amount equal to the standard deduction in 2013) is completely tax-free.

If you would like to shift more tax-free income to your child, you could do so by having him or her make contributions to an IRA. If the child contributes the maximum $5,500 to a traditional IRA during the year, she could earn $11,600 before paying any tax. If you have even more money available to pay your child you can use a 401(k) instead of an IRA and pay your child as much as $23,600 ($6,100 in take-home pay plus $17,500 in 401(k) contributions) before she pays a penny in tax! You could also make employer matches for those contributions and profit sharing contributions—all of which are deductible business expenses. If you have two or three children, the potential tax savings becomes very significant.

⤳ **Example**   After two years of being able to focus solely on the income-generating aspects of the business, Martha's income and workload have increased significantly. Martha decides to train Ruby (who is now 14) to perform bookkeeping tasks so that Martha can keep up with the workload of the business. As she performs higher-level skilled work Martha can legitimately pay her higher wages for the work that she does. Ruby works 18 hours per week (2 hours per weekday and 8 hours on Saturday) and earns $25 per hour for her work, for a total of $22,500 per year. Ruby keeps $6,100 to pay for her activities and puts the remaining $16,400 into her 401(k).

Martha also hires her son, Tommy, to do the administrative office work that was previously done by his sister Ruby. Because the business has grown, Martha needs him to work 15 hours per week at $12 per hour, for a total of $9,000 per year. Tommy keeps $6,100 to pay for his activities and puts the remaining $9,900 in his 401(k).

By hiring her two children, Martha has shifted $31,500 ($22,500 for Ruby and $9,000 for Tommy) of her highly taxed income to her children, who pay zero tax. In doing so, she has saved $15,215 in taxes (28% federal, 5% state, and 15.3% payroll).

As you read these examples you may have some concern about putting so much money into an IRA or 401(k) for children who will not be able to touch that money for 40–50 years (when they are 59½). Never fear! When the children turn 18 and head off to college they will leave their employment with your business and at that point can roll the 401(k) funds into an IRA, and then use the money, penalty-free, for some of their most important early-adulthood expenses.

There are several opportunities for them to use the IRA money without paying a penalty tax. First, they can use the money for their education expenses. Second, they can use the money to pay for their medical expenses. Third, they can use some of the money (up to $10,000) to buy their first house. In all of these cases they will be able to withdraw funds from the IRA without penalty. They will pay income tax on the money withdrawn, but that will likely be at a very low tax rate during their college and early working years. Using this strategy you can permanently shift income to a significantly lower tax and use that income to pay for things, such as college, that you needed to save for anyway. In fact, even if the child uses the money for other reasons, the penalty tax is only 10%, which is less than the payroll taxes you would have otherwise paid.

Another concern that may have crossed your mind is that you don't have that kind of disposable income available to pay your children. Never fear! You can work out an agreement with your children that they need to use a portion (or all) of the income to pay for things that you would have spent money on anyway, such as clothing, school supplies, and extracurricular activities. In that way you are not really using any money that you wouldn't have already spent, and you are saving taxes in the process. Perhaps you could pass on the tax savings to the children as their compensation—giving them money to for what they need and being in the same position financially as you were before. It is a win—win situation.

✒ **Caution**　If your child is using the income to pay for things that would have otherwise been your responsibility to pay for as a parent, there is one thing to be careful of. You must be sure that the things the child pays for do not add up to more than half of his/her support. If that happens you could lose your ability to claim the child as a dependent, which would certainly have a negative impact on your taxes and possibly leave you worse off than if you had not employed the strategy at all. However, if you are paying them a lot of money and most of it goes into a retirement account, you do not need to worry about losing your claim on them as a dependent.

For the IRS and the tax courts to honor this strategy, the child must do legitimate work and be paid a competitive wage. You can't pay a child $50 to empty the trash and expect such a payment to be upheld in court. As long as the child is doing work that you would legitimately pay someone else to do, at a rate that is common in the marketplace for that type of work, you will be safe in claiming the wages as a deduction.

One more consideration is the age of your child compared to the work that you are claiming that he/she performs. If you are paying your five-year-old to do your filing or answer phones, it will probably be met with some skepticism. Tax courts have upheld wages for children as young as seven years old doing menial tasks, such as cleaning. Just be sure that what you are claiming makes sense. It is also wise to keep good records of the time spent each day and the tasks that were performed.

Employing Your Spouse

Employing your spouse in your business does not bring the same level of tax benefits as employing a child. Your spouse's income will join with your income on your tax return, so there is no advantage for income taxes. In addition, you must pay the payroll taxes on your spouse's income as well. However, there are two key areas where employing your spouse can save a significant amount of money.

❥ **Caution** While there are potentially significant tax savings to be found in the following two strategies, both require the spouse to be treated as a legitimate employee. This means that the spouse must be paid wages similar to those be found in the marketplace for similar work. It also requires the spouse to be paid through a payroll system and receive a W-2. In doing so, the spouse will be subject to payroll taxes, which may reduce the overall benefit of the strategies (especially if the business-owner-spouse's income is above the $113,700 Social Security tax cap). These factors may be outweighed by the total tax savings of the strategies, but they must be considered in the decision.

Health Reimbursement Arrangements

The first opportunity for significant tax savings is with medical expenses. There is an IRS-approved conduit for medical expenses known as a Health Reimbursement Arrangement (HRA). An HRA is a system in which the business reimburses its employees for medical expenses. The employer sets the terms of what will be reimbursed and is fully responsible for its funding (no employee contributions are allowed). Any reimbursements made for qualified medical expenses are deductible expenses for the business.

A self-employed business owner (sole proprietor) is not allowed to participate in an HRA program—at least directly. However, if the business owner's spouse is employed by the business, he or she *would be* allowed to participate. If the terms of the program (set by the employer) dictate that reimbursements can be made for the employee, the employee's spouse, and the employee's children then, voila! the business owner is now covered by the program as the spouse of an employee!

There are two major tax benefits to using an HRA program. First, medical expenses are deductible from the first dollar spent and not limited by the 7.5% or 10% of Adjusted Gross Income (AGI) floor normally placed on medical expenses claimed as an itemized deduction. Second, for self-employed individuals the deduction reduces income taxes *and* self-employment taxes, whereas the itemized deduction would not reduce the self-employment tax.

🔥 **Caution** As it currently stands, the Affordable Care Act (aka ObamaCare) puts severe limitations on HRAs beginning in 2014. It will be important to watch for any changes to this law to determine whether this will be a viable tax strategy in 2014 and beyond.

Retirement Account Contributions

The second opportunity for tax savings that comes from employing a spouse in your business is through retirement account contributions. This strategy is really for those individuals who already contribute the maximum $51,000 to an employer-sponsored plan but would like to contribute more if they could. By employing a spouse you open up the opportunity for additional tax savings by having a new account available to contribute additional amounts—up to an additional $51,000 if the spouse's wages are high enough.

Employing Your Parents

Of all the family members whom you can employ to garner tax benefits, employing your parents is the least tax-beneficial strategy of the three. Even so, there are a few opportunities to save money by hiring your parents.

The first and potentially best opportunity comes about if you are already paying to support your parents. Perhaps they have medical needs or housing issues that they cannot afford and you have agreed to help them out. If you pay for these things out-of-pocket you will probably receive no tax benefit for it. However, if you can hire them to do something for your business, you will receive a tax deduction for their wages. This is a great way to deduct expenses that would have otherwise been non-deductible.

The second opportunity is in a situation in which parents are in the opposite circumstances—those who have all the money that they need for their retirement and are in a low tax bracket (while you are in a higher one). In this circumstance, where your parents don't need any additional money, you could hire them to do something in your business and they could set the money aside (net of their taxes) in a separate account and never use it. Then, in the future they can give the money to you and your spouse and children in yearly amounts that do not exceed the annual gift-tax exclusion. Or, alternatively, they could leave the amount to you as a tax-free inheritance. In this way you will have shifted income to a family member in a lower tax bracket and then recover the money at a later date with no additional tax.

The third opportunity is rather insignificant, but perhaps still worth pointing out. As an employer you must pay a payroll tax known as unemployment tax. It is 6% of the first $7,000 of an employee's wages, for a maximum $420 tax per employee (the tax is known as FUTA). If you are a sole proprietor and employ your parents, you do not have to pay that tax on their wages. Again, it is not a significant amount—but at the same time, who wouldn't want an extra $420 in their pocket? (Incidentally, this tax also does not need to be paid on wages for a spouse or children either).

As is the case with spouses and children, the parent must perform legitimate work and receive reasonable pay for the work that they do. However, in some cases it may be easier to justify a high pay for a parent doing limited work than it would be for a paying a child. For example, if your parent's profession before retirement was of a nature that his or her knowledge would benefit your business, that parent could be paid as a consultant or advisor to the business. Such work does not require a significant amount of labor or time, but generally demands a higher wage. Just be sure that the fee you pay will be deemed reasonable if it is looked at by a tax court.

Depreciation

Very Complex Tax Rules Boiled Down into Fairly Simple Terms

The rules governing depreciation are very complex, complicated, and convoluted. To give you an idea of how complex they really are, one of the premier guides on depreciation written for tax professionals, the *U.S. Master Depreciation Guide,* by CCH, is more than 1,000 pages long! Because of the vast number of details and nuances regarding depreciation, I am not going to attempt to give you 1,000 pages worth of information summed up into a 10-page chapter. Instead, this chapter will help you understand the general concept of depreciation and then focus on three key things that you will need to understand as you pursue your tax strategy. The subjects covered in this chapter will be:

- What depreciation is and how it works
- Bonus depreciation
- The Section 179 Deduction
- What happens when you sell a depreciated item

What Depreciation Is and How It Works

My hope in this section is to give you an overarching idea of how depreciation works in the tax code. I will try to make it as simple and general as possible, but that still may not be enough. If you begin to go cross-eyed or feel like your brain is going to burst, just skip to the remaining three sections of this chapter. They are very important for you to understand and I don't want you to just give up on this chapter before you even get to them. With that said, let's begin.

There is a general principle in accounting that states that expenses and income should be recognized in the year in which they bring benefit to the business. For example, if you rented a warehouse for a five-year period, but decided to pay the entire rent the day you moved in, this principle dictates that you should recognize only one year's worth of rent each year for five years (even though the entire amount was paid in one year). The reason for this treatment is that the true benefit of the total expense is enjoyed over five years, and so it is a more accurate reflection of what is really happening in the business to spread the recognition of the expenses over the period of time that is benefited, regardless of the actual cash outflow that occurred, in order to match the expenses with the income that is generated over that same period.

You will find that, most of the time, the tax code follows this principle. To be more accurate, tax laws almost always follow this principle when it benefits the government to do so, and the laws stray from the principle when doing so brings in tax revenue at a more rapid pace. Depreciation is one example of the tax laws following this general principle.

Anytime you purchase an item for your business that has lasting value (of more than a year), that item is most likely subject to the rules of depreciation. Examples of such things are computers, vehicles, furniture, and equipment. If you buy a truck, for example, you would expect it to benefit your business for several years, and so does the IRS.

Every item that you might buy falls under a predefined category for its expected lifespan. All of the items within a certain range of expected lifespans are then assigned a set number of years over which the depreciation should be taken (in other words, a set number of years over which the expense can be recognized). For example, all assets with an expected useful lifetime between four and nine years will be depreciated over a five-year period. Some of the items that fall in this category are cars, most trucks, technology equipment, and office machinery. If you purchased a computer for $1,000 you would recognize one fifth of that cost ($200) each year for five years (assuming a basic, "straight-line" depreciation method is used).

To keep accountants and attorneys in business, Congress has made the depreciation methods a little more complicated than the preceding scenario. The tax code does not simply divide the cost evenly over the stated number of years. Instead, it uses an "accelerated" method of depreciation.

An example of accelerated depreciation is the *200% declining balance* method. In this method, 200% of one year's portion of depreciation is taken each year, based on the value of the item that has yet to be depreciated. For example, if you purchased a $1,000 computer it would be depreciated over five years. Under the simple version of depreciation you would recognize one-fifth of the cost each year, or $200. Under the accelerated method you would recognize 200% of that amount in the first year, or $400. The next year you would divide the remaining un-depreciated balance, or $600 ($1,000 original cost – $400 first-year depreciation = $600 remaining un-depreciated) by the number of years left in the asset's lifetime—in this case four years (5-year depreciation – the first year = 4 years remaining). The $600 remaining value divided by the four years remaining equals $150 per year. Then, 200% of the year's amount is taken, or $300. This process continues until the entire value of the asset has been depreciated to $0.

The tax law then adds in one more wrinkle, just to make it interesting. With the accelerated depreciation method you do not actually deduct a full year's worth of depreciation in the first year. Depending on the type of item that you purchase and the overall timing of all of your purchases during the year, you may need to deduct one-half of the yearly amount, or another amount based on the month or quarter in which it is purchased.

If the computer used in the example above were depreciated using the half-year method of accelerated depreciation, the first year's depreciation would actually be $200 (200% value was $400, then divided in half for the half-year method). Because of this, the second year would actually be $320 ($1,000 cost – $200 = $800 remaining, $800 × 20% = $160 depreciation × 200% = $320).

The IRS has published official charts that show the amount of the original cost that should be depreciated each year. As an example I have included one of these charts, Table 22-1 below, which shows the depreciation that should be taken on 3-, 5-, 7-, and 10-year items under the half-year convention of the Modified Accelerated Cost Recovery (MACRS) system of depreciation that is commonly used on a tax return.

Table 22-1. Depreciation Table for 3-, 5-, 7-, and 10-Year Recovery Periods—Half-Year Convention

	3-Year	5-Year	7-Year	10-Year
1	33.33	20.00	14.29	10.00
2	44.45	32.00	24.49	18.00
3	14.81	19.20	17.49	14.40
4	7.41	11.52	12.49	11.52
5		11.52	8.93	9.22
6		5.76	8.92	7.37
7			8.93	6.55
8			4.46	6.55
9				6.56
10				6.55
11				3.28

The take-away from all of this is that many things that you purchase in your business will have to be depreciated, meaning that you will not be allowed to use the full cost of the item as an expense against your income in the year you buy it. It is important to know this because it can dramatically affect your expected taxable income. Based on the item you bought, and the timing of your purchase, varying amounts will be deducted each year until the full cost of the item has been recovered.

However, there are two opportunities within the tax code for you to take a much larger portion of that expense as a current-year deduction: bonus depreciation and the Section 179 deduction. Each of these is described in detail in the following two sections of this chapter.

Bonus Depreciation

Bonus depreciation is a measure that Congress will use occasionally as a way to stimulate the economy by encouraging businesses to buy assets in the current year that they may have otherwise waited to purchase. Bonus depreciation allows business owners to depreciate a significant portion of the purchased price of an asset in the year they buy it, instead of spreading the cost out over many years. In 2013, the tax code allows for 50% bonus depreciation, which means that 50% of the cost of the asset is depreciated in the first year and the remaining 50% will be subject to the normal depreciation schedules.

There is no limit on the total dollar amount of assets that can receive this special treatment. The assets must be tangible but have a normal depreciable life of 20 years or less, or be computer software (an exception to the "tangible" rule). The asset must also be new (the buyer is the first to use it), and it must be purchased *and placed in service* by the last day of the year.

To receive bonus depreciation, the asset must be used primarily (more than 50%) for business purposes. If a portion of its use is for non-business purposes then only the pro-rated ratio of business use can be deducted. For example, an item that costs $1,000 and is used 75% for business purposes can receive only a $375 bonus depreciation ($1,000 × 75% business use = $750 is depreciable, $750 depreciable × 50% = $375 bonus depreciation). If during the lifetime of the asset its business use ever drops below 50%, a portion of the asset's value will be recaptured and treated as income in that year.

○ **Tip** Bonus depreciation is often allowed during difficult economic times. However, during these same times many businesses are not very profitable. If your business is in a slump but you expect it to improve in the future, it may be wise to elect out of bonus depreciation. If your income is low, then your tax bracket is low also, which means that the bonus depreciation may not bring much benefit. If you choose normal depreciation methods instead there will be larger amounts of depreciation available from those items to offset income in years when you are in a higher tax bracket.

The Section 179 Deduction

There is a provision in the tax code that allows businesses to treat certain assets to be expensed in the year they are purchased instead of requiring them to be depreciated over time. This provision is commonly known as a Section 179 Deduction (so named because it is found in Section 179 of the Internal Revenue Code—accountants aren't very creative with such things). It can make a very significant difference on your tax liability in a given year if you make a large purchase and can write the entire amount off in that year, rather than depreciating the item over a number of years.

Of course, there are certain limitations attached to the use of this deduction. First, it can be used only by individuals and business entities (not estates or trusts, or certain lessors). Second, in 2013 it can only be used for up to $500,000 of assets purchased during the year. Any additional assets must be subjected to the other depreciation rules. Third, the Section 179 Deduction can be used only if you have purchased less than $2,000,000 of new assets during the year. If you have exceeded that limit the amount of assets that can be expensed is reduced, dollar for dollar, by the amount that your purchases exceeded $2,000,000. If you have purchased more than $2,500,000 then you would not be able to use the deduction and *all* assets would fall under regular depreciation guidelines.

↪ **Example** Vince purchased $2,040,000 in new equipment for his construction company during the year. Vince would be able to use the Section 179 Deduction for $1,960,000 of that equipment because the total equipment purchase of $2,040,000 exceeded the purchase limit of $2,000,000 by $40,000. That $40,000 excess in purchases reduces the $2,000,000 maximum 179 Deduction dollar for dollar, making Vince's maximum available deduction $1,960,000 ($2,000,000 max deduction − $40,000 over spending limit = $1,960,000 available deduction for Vince).

○ **Tip** Under current law the Section 179 deduction is set to return to lower, pre-2003 rates. As it now stands, beginning in 2014 you will not be able to expense more than $25,000 using this deduction, and you cannot use it if you have purchased more than $200,000 of equipment during the year.

An additional limitation placed on the Section 179 Deduction is that it cannot exceed the total taxable income for the business or individual from all business sources (including employment income) during that tax year. Any additional amount would be carried forward to a future year.

⇒ **Example** Duncan is a software engineer for a startup tech company and receives an annual salary of $80,000. He also runs a side business that offers off-site backup systems for computer data, which nets an annual profit of $20,000. This year Duncan purchased a new set of servers for the side business to expand his capacity for growth in clientele. The new servers cost $120,000. Duncan will be able to use the Section 179 deduction for $100,000 of that expense, but the remaining $20,000 will have to be carried over to future years because the total deduction cannot exceed the combined net income from all of his business and employment income sources [($80,000 salary + $20,000 business income = $100,000 total net income, which would also be the maximum deduction).

○ **Tip** If your total Section 179 Deduction will be limited to a smaller amount that you spent on asset purchases during the year, take care in deciding which assets to use the deduction for because the normal depreciable life of each asset will affect the overall outcome of your return. For example, if you purchased an asset that requires seven-year depreciation and another that requires three-year depreciation, use the seven-year asset for the 179 Deduction so that you can expense it immediately and the other asset will depreciate fairly quickly as well (three years) so that the total deductions taken in the first and subsequent years will be higher and use up the depreciation faster.

To be expensed under the Section 179 rules, the asset must be used primarily (more than 50%) for business purposes. If a portion of its use is for non-business purposes then only the pro-rated ratio of business use can be deducted (e.g., an item that costs $1,000 and is used 75% for business purposes can receive only a $750 Section 179 deduction). If during the lifetime of the asset its business use ever drops below 50%, a portion of the asset's value will be recaptured and treated as income in that year. If you think there is a likelihood of an asset being used more than 50% for personal reasons it may be best not to use this deduction on the asset.

Nearly every depreciable asset that you would buy for your business is eligible for the Section 179 Deduction. Unlike bonus depreciation, the 179 Deduction is allowed for both new and used assets (bonus depreciation can only be taken for new items). However, to qualify for the deduction, the asset must be tangible (meaning you can touch it) and used in the United States. In addition, there are certain items such as heaters and air conditioners, as well as items purchased for long-term dwelling buildings (such as apartments), that cannot be expensed. There are also special limitations placed on the purchase of vehicles. The specific rules in this regard are too complex for the purposes of this book, but if you will be making a substantial purchase and are counting on this deduction, it would be worthwhile to check with a professional to know whether the item qualifies.

○ **Tip**   Under current law, the Section 179 Deduction will not allow intangible items, such as software, to be expensed, unless Congress acts to modify the 2013 law to match the way it has been from 2003 through 2012.

What Happens When You Sell a Depreciated Item

Every item, or asset, that you purchase has something called a tax basis. The "basis" is a way of tracking the value of the item for tax purposes so that when you sell or dispose of the item it can be determined whether you have done so for a gain or a loss. The basis is nothing more than a running total of all of the money you have actually spent on the item netted against the amount that you have taken as an expense on your tax return.

⇨ **Example**   Frank purchased a box trailer for his landscaping business. He paid the dealer $20,000 for the trailer, plus $1,000 in taxes. At that point the tax basis of Frank's trailer is $21,000—the total amount that he had to spend to buy the trailer.

Frank immediately drove the trailer to a neighboring business where it was outfitted with an array of tool boxes and racks for all of his landscaping equipment. The cost of this upgrade was $4,000, bringing his total cost for the trailer (as well as his tax basis) to $25,000.

At the end of the year, Frank's accountant reported $5,000 of depreciation on the trailer on his tax return. The new tax basis of the trailer, after taking depreciation, is $20,000 ($25,000 basis − $5,000 depreciation = $20,000 new basis).

When you sell a depreciated asset you will be required to report the net-sales revenue that you received from the asset on your tax return. The sales price is compared to the basis of the asset to determine whether you have sold it for a gain or a loss. If you sell the item for more than its basis, you will have to "recapture" some, or all, of the depreciation that you have taken. The depreciation tables are intended to follow the decline in value of the item as it ages. If you sell the item for more than its depreciated basis it means that it was depreciated more than it should have been (which means that you have paid less tax than you should have because of the excess depreciation). The government wants that tax back, so you must recapture (or give back) the excess depreciation on your return.

↪ **Example** Soon after Frank purchased the new trailer, he lost one of his biggest clients. Because of the significant decrease in his workload, Frank didn't need to use the new trailer—the work could be handled comfortably with his other equipment. Frank parked the trailer in his garage so that it would be protected from damage until such time that he needed to use it. After three years, it became apparent to Frank that he was not gaining new clients very quickly and would not need the trailer any time soon. He decided to sell the trailer to raise some much-needed cash.

Because the trailer was in near-perfect condition Frank was able to sell it for a pretty good price for a used, customized trailer—$20,000. During the three years that he owned the trailer Frank's accountant had reported depreciated (according to the schedules) of $17,800, making the tax basis of the trailer $7,200 ($25,000 original basis − $17,800 depreciation taken = $7,200 remaining basis).

Frank will have to recapture $12,800 of the previous depreciation because of the $20,000 he received on the sale ($20,000 sales price − $7,200 tax basis = $12,800 depreciation recapture).

For non–real estate assets, depreciation recapture is treated as ordinary income (since this was the type of income that was offset when the depreciation was taken). There's a potential catch in this scenario if the recapture is significant enough to push you into a higher tax bracket. In this case you could actually end up paying more for the recapture than you saved from the depreciation.

The possibility of a large recapture is much greater when you have used the Section 179 Deduction or bonus depreciation. In these cases the asset has likely been depreciated at a much faster rate than the asset has actually gone down in value. Selling an asset within a few years of taking one of these special deductions could result in a significant recapture (and tax) in the year you sell it.

If you actually sell an asset for more than the price you originally paid for it (a true gain), you must first recapture all of the depreciation that you have claimed on the asset, and then any remaining gain is treated as a capital gain and taxed at capital-gains rates. If you sell an asset for less than its tax basis you can claim the difference between the sale price and the basis as a loss.

Real estate that is used in a business (including business use of a home) has one additional recapture rule. For any asset that has been appreciated at accelerated rates you must calculate the difference between straight-line depreciation and the accelerated depreciation. The amount of depreciation that would have been taken under the straight-line method is taxed under its own brackets, with a maximum rate of 25%. The remaining depreciation that was taken is taxed at ordinary rates and any remaining gain falls under the capital-gains rules.

✦ **Caution**   I have spoken with clients who want to avoid the possibility of recapturing depreciation. Often it is because they intend to sell the asset within a few years and would rather forgo the yearly benefit to avoid the big hit from the recapture in the year that they sell. For some this strategy makes even more sense because their overall tax picture receives no benefit from claiming the depreciation (because they already have an overall loss, or they are not allowed to claim it because of the passive loss rules). This is a great idea.

However, the tax laws are heartless when it comes to this strategy. When an asset is sold you must recapture all of the depreciation that you *could have claimed*, regardless of whether you actually claimed it. So, you might as well claim the depreciation and get what benefit you can from it so that you are not hit with a double-whammy in the end.

Real Estate Income and Deductions

For many, many years, real estate has been one of the great bastions of tax planning. Real estate offers many of the same tax benefits as owning a business. It also offers the opportunity for tax-deferred growth—often for decades at a time and with no requirements that would force you to recognize the gain. Under current tax law, real estate also offers the opportunity to report losses on a tax return while maintaining a positive cash flow to the owner.

There are also many nuances in the tax law related to real estate, which can make it confusing and difficult to get your tax planning and reporting right. However, once you understand the strategies contained in the chapters of Part V, you will be well on your way to fully harnessing the tax-saving potential of real estate ventures.

Real Estate Losses

Your Loss Is Your Gain

Real estate has long been the traditional safe haven for taxes. It provides an opportunity for tax-free (deferred) cash flow. It also offers tax-deferred appreciation, or growth in the value of the investment. It even offers the opportunity to sell assets and purchase others without incurring any tax on the realized gains. Combining these tax benefits with the ability to use high amounts of leverage in the purchase of real estate makes for an ideal way to produce tax-favored income for the short- and long-term future. In fact, real estate is the most commonly used investment for those seeking tax incentives. Illustrating the point, after some modifications to the real estate tax laws in 1986, a committee member—Fortney H. (Pete) Stark, (D-CA)—on the House Ways and Means Committee famously stated: "It'd take a genius to invest in real estate and pay taxes."

Of all of the tax-reduction strategies that real estate offers, one of the more complicated and lucrative strategies is the ability to use losses from the real estate to offset income from other areas of the tax return. In the case of most income sources (such as investment income or business income), losses are not that beneficial because, by definition, you always lose more money than you save in taxes. In real estate, however, this is not always the case. Because of the depreciation that is taken on the real estate, it is possible—even common—to have a positive cash flow from a property while at the same time reporting a loss on your tax return.

⇨ **Example**   Olivia owns a townhome that she uses as a rental property. She purchased the townhome for $200,000 and made $50,000 in improvements, bringing her total cost for the home to $250,000. She rents the home for $1,000 per month, bringing a total gross income of $12,000 per year. Her annual expenses (including mortgage interest, property taxes, and maintenance) are about $5,000 per year. This leaves Olivia with a positive net cash flow of $7,000 per year ($12,000 income – $5,000 expenses = $7,000 net positive cash flow).

In addition to the real, out-of-pocket expenses, Olivia is also able to claim $7,250 of depreciation expense on her tax return. Doing so creates a reported loss of $250 on her tax return, which offsets her other sources of income. Even though she had a cash flow income of $7,000, on her tax return it appears as if she had a loss.

Depreciation is taken on real estate to account for an assumed loss of value over time as the property ages. However, this assumption of real estate values going down is rarely true. In reality the value of real estate usually goes up over time. With real estate you receive the simultaneous benefit of tax deferral on the true increase of the property's value and annual tax deductions from the depreciation of the property. It's like earning wages from your employer but reporting the income on your tax return as a deductible expense.

Because of the tremendous benefits that can be gained from this phenomenon, some rules have been set in place in an effort to limit the benefits of this strategy. There are three important facets of this limitation that you need to understand to plan properly for the effects of real estate income on your return. These three items are:

- Treatment of passive losses
- Active participation rules
- The real estate professional designation

Treatment of Passive Losses

Passive income comes from ownership in real estate or businesses in which a person does not actively participate. For example, if you gave $10,000 to a friend to help him start a business, but did not actually perform labor in the running of the business, that $10,000 investment would be considered passive and any income would be considered passive income. In general, passive losses can be deducted only from passive income. Losses that exceed income in a given year must be carried forward to a future year to be deducted against future passive income.

Real estate rental activities are automatically presumed to be passive invest-ments. As such, losses in real estate cannot be deducted from other income (such as wages, investments, or business income) in order to reduce your Adjusted Gross Income (AGI). There are several exceptions to this auto-matic assumption, most of which are very narrow and uncommon. One of the exceptions worth noting is that rentals in which the average stay is seven days or less (such as hotels) are not considered passive income, but are instead considered an active business (as long as you materially participate in the busi-ness and are not just a passive investor).

Even if your rental activities fall into the passive-loss rules, there are two important instances in which some or all of your passive losses are allowed as deductions against other sources of income. The first is when you actively participate in the rental real estate activity and the second is when you meet the guidelines that classify you as a real estate professional. Each of these two exceptions is described in the sections that follow.

Active Participation Rules

If you actively participate in real estate rental activities you may qualify to deduct up to $25,000 of passive real estate losses each year. To be considered an active participant in real estate you must:

- Own at least 10% of the property that has a loss.

- Actively participate in management decisions. You are allowed to hire a property manager, but must do more than simply ratify the manager's decisions. Such activities might include approving new tenants, determining rental terms, and approving expenditures.

In addition, the $25,000 allowable loss may be limited by your Modified AGI (MAGI). The full loss is allowable for taxpayers with an MAGI up to $100,000. The allowable loss is reduced by $0.50 for every $1 of MAGI over the $100,000 limit, with the allowable loss being reduced to $0 when AGI is $150,000 or greater. Modified AGI is calculated as follows:

+	Adjusted Gross Income (AGI)
–	Social Security or Railroad Income included in AGI
+	Deductions Taken for Passive Activity Losses
–	Income from Passive Activities
+	Loss Allowed for Real Estate Professionals
+	Deductions Taken for Traditional IRA Contributions
+	Deductions Taken for Student Loan and Tuition Expenses
+	Deduction for Half of Self-Employment Tax
+	Excluded Interest from Education Bonds
+	Employer-paid Adoption Expenses
+	Deductions Taken for Domestic Production Activities
–	Income from a Roth IRA Conversion
=	Modified Adjusted Gross Income (MAGI)

To determine the allowable loss you must first combine all income and losses from all of the real estate activities in which you actively participate. The net loss is then applied to the net income from any other passive activities. Any remaining amount can then be used against other types of income on your return.

✒ **Caution** The rental income (or loss) from a personal residence is disregarded in the calculation of the allowable loss. The property is considered a residence for these purposes if your personal use of the property exceeds the greater of 14 days or 10% of the days that the home is rented at fair market value.

The Real Estate Professional Designation

Real estate rental activities will not be considered passive—allowing you to avoid the limits on losses—if you qualify as a *Real Estate Professional*. There are several tests that must be met to qualify as a Real Estate Professional. The first requirement is that you must materially participate in the management of the property for which you are making the claim. You are considered to materially participate if you meet *at least one* of the following criteria:

- You work 500 hours or more per year on the property.
- You perform substantially all of the work that is required for the property.
- You work more than 100 hours per year on the activity and no one else works more than you do on the property.
- You materially participated in the property in any 5 of the previous 10 years.

Material participation is determined for each property individually. If you have multiple properties, it can become very difficult to meet those tests, even if you spend all of your time working on those properties. Because of this, there is an option available that allows you to elect to aggregate all of your real estate properties into one overall activity. By doing so, the cumulative number of hours spent on all of the properties can add up to meet the material participation rule.

Caution While electing to aggregate all of your real estate properties into one overall activity has its advantages (such as being able to deduct your losses against ordinary income, regardless of AGI), it also comes with significant disadvantages. First, once you have made the election you must continue with that election in all future years in which you qualify for it. You may not revoke the election without permission from the IRS.

Second, once you have made this election you cannot claim carried-over losses on a property when you sell it, until you have sold *all* of your properties, since they are treated as one activity.

Before electing to aggregate your activities for the purposes of qualifying for material participation I strongly recommend speaking with a qualified tax professional to fully understand and analyze all of the future implications of doing so.

In addition to the material participation test, you must also meet *each* of the following tests to qualify as a Real Estate Professional:

- More than 50% of your personal service in all of your business activities is performed in real property businesses in which you materially participate. Time spent as an employee does not count toward the 50% threshold unless you are a more-than-5%-owner in the business in which you are employed.

- You spend more than 750 hours of your personal service time in real property business in which you materially participate.

- For married couples, the tests above must be met by one spouse (you cannot combine the time spent by both spouses in order to meet the test).

If you are truly in the real estate business, have a high AGI, and have significant rental losses, using this designation may bring a real benefit.

Real Estate Income and Deductions

A Uniquely Taxed Business

In many ways, the taxation of real estate is just like the taxation of any other business. In fact, if you are involved in the real estate business, Chapters 18, 19, 21, and 22 in Part 4 of this book are required reading. The same rules that apply to a business regarding travel expenses, meals, depreciation, and so on apply also to the real estate business.

With that said, there are also many ways in which real estate businesses are taxed that are unique. These nuances bring with them tax strategies geared toward the real estate business. Several of these unique features are focused on in this chapter, including:

- Rent recognition rules
- Allowable expenses
- Repairs vs. improvements
- Depreciation
- Travel
- Self-renting

Rent Recognition Rules

There are a few things to be aware of regarding the recognition of income for rental property. First, if you receive a payment for rent in advance, you must recognize that payment as rental income in the year that you receive it, *no matter which* method of accounting (cash or accrual) you use. This can occur when a tenant pays several months of rent at a time, pays "first and last month's rent," or even with the payment of a security deposit. Even though a security deposit may be paid specifically toward the possibility of future repairs, not rent, and is refundable, it is counted as rental income when received. The only way that this tax treatment of a deposit can be avoided is if the owner has no control over the money in any way, such as a deposit in a third-party escrow account. Another example of a payment that must be recognized in the current year is if a tenant pays a fee to get out of a lease early—even if the fee is for a rent commitment in a future year.

Second, if a tenant provides services or property in trade for rent, the fair market value of those services or property must be recognized as rental income. Generally, if you agree on a price for those items, the price will be recognized as the fair market value (unless the price is unreasonably different than what would be paid on the market). For example, if a tenant agrees to maintain the landscaping of the rental in trade for a $150 reduction in rent each month, the $150 difference must be recognized as income.

Third, if a tenant makes improvements to the property you *do not* recognize income for the value of those improvements, *unless* the improvements are done in trade for rent. For example, an acquaintance of mine recently replaced a fence on the property of the home he rents in order to keep his dog contained in the yard without being on a leash. The landlord was willing to let him put up the fence, but didn't reduce his rent as a trade for the service. Because of this, the landlord does not need to recognize any rental income for the fence. However, the landlord's basis in the fence is $0 and he is not able to claim any depreciation on the new fence as an asset.

Fourth, if a tenant pays your expenses directly, such as making payments for repairs, mortgage payments, property tax payments, insurance payments, or utility bills that are in your name, you must recognize those payments as income. The good news is that you can also recognize the expenses to offset the income on the return.

Finally, if you receive insurance proceeds for a loss of rental income, those proceeds are counted as rent.

Allowable Expenses

As with any business, expenses that are directly related to the rental property and that are considered "ordinary and customary" are generally allowable as deductions from rental income on your tax return. There are, however, two important exceptions to this rule.

First, to deduct expenses for a rental, the property must be actively held out for rent. If you do not have tenants for a given time period you must be able to show that you were actively seeking to have tenants during that time— otherwise you cannot deduct expenses during that period. The easiest way to show that you were actively seeking tenants would be to provide proof of advertising the property for rent. If you have recently purchased the property and need to upgrade it before renting, the expenses you incur before putting it up for rent must generally be included in the overall cost of purchasing and buying the house (subjecting those expenses to depreciation).

Second, if the property has multiple uses or dwellings you must split the expenses between those uses or dwellings as best as you possibly can. For example, if you own a duplex and live in half of it and rent out the other half, you would deduct only half of your mortgage interest and property taxes and so on.

If an expense is not directly related to a specific portion of the property (such as repairing a broken window on the rented portion) then you can divide up the cost in the way that most accurately reflects the correct allocation. Often the best way to divide up general expenses is by square footage. For example, if the rented portion of a property is 400 square feet and the non-rented portion is 600 square feet, then 40% of the general expense would be assigned to the rental. At other times the percentage-of-square-feet method may not be appropriate. For example, if a portion of the space is occupied by a welding shop and the remaining space is used as a warehouse, it is likely that the majority of the electricity used in the building belongs to the welding-shop space.

Though there are too many possibilities to list all deductible rental expenses, the following list provides a glance at many of the common expenses that are incurred in the rental business:

Advertising	Insurance	Pest Control
Association Dues	Legal Fees	Property Taxes
Bank Fees	Licenses	Repairs
Bookkeeping	Maintenance	Supplies
Cleaning	Management Fees	Tax Accounting
Commissions	Mortgage Interest	Telephone
Decorating	Painting	Travel Costs
Gardening	Permits	Utilities

If you rent the property for less than fair market value (e.g., to help a friend), you cannot deduct more expenses than the rent (i.e., there is no loss available, not even as a carryover). However, there is an exception that allows you to rent a property to a family member for below-market rates, up to as much as 20% lower than market value.

Repairs vs. Improvements

Whenever possible (and accurate), it is best to categorize changes to the physical aspects of the property as repairs instead of improvements. The reason for this is that repair expenses can be deducted in the year they occur, whereas improvements must be depreciated over a number of years (as much as 39 years, depending on the type of property and the improvement).

The main distinction between the two is that repairs are made to keep your property in good operating condition, whereas improvements are those made to add value to the property, prolong the life of the property, or change its use. Repairs that are made as part of an overall improvement program may not be deducted as repair expenses, but must be included in the overall cost of the improvements. The following list illustrates the difference between some common repairs and improvements:

Repair	Improvement
Fix a broken window	Upgrade a window
Paint a wall	Add a wall and paint it
Reseal an asphalt driveway	Pave a driveway
Repair a leaky gutter	Install a new gutter
Replace a damaged carpet	Replace carpet with hardwood
Fix a broken lock	Install dead bolts
Repair a broken fence	Completely replace a fence
Repair a leaky roof	A new roof before leaks arise

Depreciation

Depreciation for rental properties follows the same basic rules as other depreciable items as outlined in Chapter 22. However, there are two important things to be aware of when considering depreciation of real estate. First, land cannot be depreciated. For every property you must allocate an appropriate amount of the purchase price to the value of the land, and only the remaining amount may be depreciated. Use the appraisal of the property as the source for the land's value. If you did not get an appraisal, most property tax statements from the county show an estimated value for the land. While the county's value is usually not as accurate, it will be close enough and likely acceptable to the IRS. A third method is to assign a percentage of the property value to the land based on surrounding properties, but this method should be used as a last resort.

Second, when making improvements to a property, it can be very valuable to itemize the labor and materials costs of each facet of the improvement. Individual improvements are subject to a wide variance in the number of years of depreciation that is required, and by separating out each individual expense you would likely be able to depreciate the overall cost at a much faster rate, resulting in lower taxes in the near term. In contrast, if all of the expenses are lumped into one large improvement, the depreciation must be spread out over the life time of the property. If the costs of improvements are significant, the difference between itemization and lump sum depreciation can really add up.

↬ **Example**   A new carpet installed in a residential property can be depreciated over a five-year period. However, if many improvements are made to the property at the same time and the cost of the new carpet is included in the overall total cost of the improvements, it will have to be depreciated over a period of 27½ years. Depreciating a $2,000 carpet over five years allows for $400 of depreciation each year, whereas depreciating it over 27½ years would allow only $73 of depreciation per year.

Travel

To understand fully all of the rules that govern travel expenses, be sure to read Chapter 18. With that in mind, one popular strategy that real estate owners employ is to purchase rental properties in places where they already travel with their families, in order to be able to write off those travel expenses on their tax return. For example, if your parents live out of state and you normally visit them twice each year, you could buy a rental property near their home and use those trips to also check on the property and make any needed repairs or maintenance while you are there. If you follow all of the rules governing travel costs, this could be a very effective way to transfer a non-deductible, personal expense over to a deductible expense on your tax return.

✒ **Caution**   This strategy must be weighed against the non-tax issues that landlords face when owning property that is far from your home. The expense that comes with hiring a property manager (assuming you wouldn't if the property were nearby) may outweigh the tax benefits of writing off the occasional travel expenses.

Also, if you want to employ this strategy by purchasing a rental property that you will actually use for vacations, be sure to read the additional rules that apply to such situations that are outlined in Chapter 25.

Self-Renting

One interesting tax reduction strategy that some individuals employ is to rent their property to a business that they own. Doing so allows business income to be changed into passive income, potentially reducing taxes. By renting to your business you create an expense for the business, which reduces earned income and, for sole proprietors, the self-employment tax. In turn, the rent increases passive income. However, this increased income is not subject to the self-employment tax. In addition, the increased passive income could be used to offset additional passive losses from other properties that might otherwise have to be carried over to future years.

Second Homes and Vacation Rentals

Be Sure You Get This Right

Chapters 23 and 24 focused on all of the rules related to rental real estate that is solely dedicated to that purpose. In many cases, however, individuals own real estate that they rent during part of the year and use for personal benefit during another part of the year. In these cases, there are a few additional rules that come into play that determine the expenses that you are allowed to claim as deductions on your tax return. At times these rules can make a significant difference in the tax you will owe, so it is important to understand how they work. It is possible that something as simple as staying one extra day in your rental in a given year could really cost you a lot of money. The following items will be discussed in this chapter:

- Tax-free income and home swapping
- Personal use vs. fair market rents
- Pro-rated deductions

Tax-Free Income and Home Swapping

Though it may seem like a strange idea to some, I have known people who trade their homes with another person for a week or two each year to vacation in a faraway place and stay in a nice home at little cost. In fact, there are exchanges on the Internet where you can enter the dates and destination that you desire and the business will try to match you up with another person who would like to visit your home town at the same time. Then you swap homes with that person and save each other a lot of money. Each year you can pick a different location and try to match up with a different person to make a swap again.

I have known others who live in ideal locations for certain events who rent their house out for the event and just go away for a little while. The first time I heard of this was when I lived in Utah and people around us were planning to rent their homes out during the 2002 Winter Olympics. By leaving and renting their homes out for a couple of weeks they were able to earn enough money to pay for a vacation and a couple of months of their mortgage payments. I have heard of others who live near college football stadiums and rent their homes out on the weekends of home games each year.

If you are okay with strangers' living in your home while you are temporarily gone, this could be a great way to earn some extra money. In fact, as long as you do not rent your home out for more than 15 days during a year, the income that you earn is **tax-free**! You can't take any deductions for the home (beyond those available as personal deductions), but you don't have to recognize any income either. I didn't include this idea in the tax-free income chapter, but it is pretty intriguing.

⯊ **Note**   Home swaps are considered rents. If you swap homes for more than 15 days during the year you are actually supposed to recognize the fair market value of that swap as rental income, subject to the rules for personal use outlined in the next sections.

Personal Use vs. Fair Market Rents

If you do own a home that you rent out more than 15 days in the year, as well as use for personal reasons, you must account for the income and expenses on that home by using a special formula. This formula determines whether you can claim a loss from the rental of the home. This is the case regardless of whether the home is your primary residence, a second home, or a vacation rental—in any case you must fall in line with the following rules.

First, you must calculate the number of days that you use the home for personal use. Personal use days include:

- Each day, or portion of a day, that you use the home for personal reasons. Even if you use the home for personal purposes on a day that it is rented out at fair-market value, you must count that day as a day of personal use for this part of the equation. However, do not count days where you used the home and the day was primarily spent making repairs or getting it ready for tenants (this is an important loophole).

- Each day in which the home is used by your spouse, children, grandchildren, parents, brothers, sisters, or grandparents. This is the case, regardless of whether or not they pay you fair-market value for rent, if the home is a vacation rental. However, if the home is being used as their primary residence and they pay you fair-market rent, you do not have to count those days as personal-use days.

Next, you must count the number of days that the home was rented at fair-market value to individuals not included in the preceding list. Then you must determine whether your personal-use days exceeded the greater of 14 days or 10% of all days that the property was used. The formula for the second factor would look like:

[Were the total personal days > (10% × total days used by anyone)?]

If your personal-use days were more than the greater of 14 days or 10% of all the days used, then you are only allowed to deduct expenses to the extent of income—you cannot claim a loss from the rental of the home. (However, you can still claim the personal portions of the expenses as itemized deductions on your return.)

Regardless of whether you are allowed a loss on the home, all expenses for the home must be pro-rated according to the steps outlined in the section below.

Note The terms "home" or "residence" are broadly defined in this rule. Any place may qualify under these rules as long as it has minimum living accommodations, such as a bathroom, a place to sleep, and a place to prepare food. Under these guidelines many nontraditional homes come into consideration, such as motor homes, trailers, and boats.

If you use a residence for more than 14 days or more than 10% of the total days it is used, you can count the property as a second home and deduct the personal portion of interest expense and property taxes as itemized deductions on Schedule A of your return.

Pro-rated Deductions

If you have used a home for both personal and rental purposes during the year (regardless of how many personal days), you must allocate all of the expenses in pro-rated amounts between personal and rental use. Expenses are allocated as deductions taken against rental income based on this formula:

[Days rented at fair market value ÷ Total days of rental and personal use]

The days that the property is held out for rent, but not actually rented, are not counted as rental days. However, contrary to the rules in the previous section (determining the ability to claim a loss), any day that you rent the property to a family member at fair-market rates counts toward the days-rented-at-fair-market-value portion of the formula. In addition, in this formula you do not need to count as a personal day any days in which you use the property for personal use and also rent it a fair-market value.

Once you have determined the ratio from the formula above, you must apply that ratio to each deductible expense to determine how much you may deduct from rental income on your return. As an example, if you rented a property at full market value 90 days during the year, and also used it for personal purposes an additional 10 days, the ratio of expenses that you could deduct would be 90% [90 days fair-market value ÷ (90 market value days + 10 personal days = 100 total days) = 90% business use]. In this example you would deduct expenses as outlined below:

	Full Cost	90% Deductible
Association Dues	$ 600	$ 540
Maintenance	$ 461	$ 415
Mortgage Interest	$ 5,000	$ 4,500
Property Taxes	$ 1,300	$ 1,170
Repairs	$ 250	$ 225
Supplies	$ 300	$ 270
Utilities	$ 1,200	$ 1,080
Total	$ 9,111	$ 8,200

þ **Note** You are not considered to have made any personal use of a residence that you rent or try to rent at fair market value before selling it if you actually sell the home within 12 months. For example, if you lived in a home from January 1 to April 15, then rent the home from May 1 to September 30, and then sell the home on November 15, your use of the house from January through April is *not* considered personal use. This means that the deductions for the rental are not subject to the rental income limitation.

Personal Expenses, Deductions, and Credits

The vast majority of personal expenses are not allowed as tax deductions. The reason for this is clear: If we were allowed to deduct all of our personal expenses from our income there would be very little left to tax. However, Congress has deemed certain personal expenses important enough (for a variety of reasons) to subsidize and encourage those expenses through deductions and credits in the tax code.

Each of these deductions and credits has varying levels of benefit, based on the way the tax code is written. These variations are also due, in part, to your personal circumstances and the way that they play out on your tax return. Carefully study the chapters in Part VI to learn which of these strategies will bring worthwhile results.

Medical and Dental Expenses

There's Never a Good Time for These Expenses, but at Least You Can Deduct Them

I have found that most itemized deductions remain about the same from year to year for most of my clients. Their mortgage interest and property taxes usually don't fluctuate very much. They donate about the same amount to charities each year. However, one deduction that changes significantly from year to year is medical expenses. Expenses for doctors, dentists, hospitals, health insurance, and other related items can be deducted from your taxable income as an itemized deduction and sometimes can add up to a significant break on your tax bill.

There are two significant types of personal medical deductions that can be taken on an individual's return (for the business deductions see Chapter 20), as well as one new tax and credit that applies to those who don't have health insurance. The three topics covered in this chapter are:

- Itemized medical deductions
- Health Savings Accounts
- Health Care Coverage Tax and Credit

Itemized Medical Deductions

Medical expenses are one of the best-known itemized deductions. The only solace that people can find in paying high fees to their doctors and dentists is in the hope that they can claim it as a write-off come tax time. For some people, medical expenses end up being the greatest reducer of their tax bill. However, for many this is not the case because the laws governing this deduction have several things in place that can limit or even eliminate your ability to claim those expenses.

To claim medical expenses as an itemized deduction you must first be able to cross a few tax-law hurdles. First, medical expenses must "qualify" as *deductible* medical expenses. This hurdle is not very high, in my opinion, as the list of qualified expenses is very long and fairly generous. However, there are many things that you could conceivably argue are medical expenses that will not be accepted. For example, a perennial favorite that shows up in the tax court is a person claiming that a tropical vacation was a necessary medical expense. It well may be that a vacation is necessary and good for your health . . . but it's definitely *not* a deductible expense.

The second, more difficult hurdle is that only those qualified expenses that exceed a certain percentage of your Adjusted Gross Income (AGI) can be taken as a deduction. In 2013 that hurdle is 7.5% of AGI if you are over 65 years old, and 10% for everyone else. If you are subject to the Alternative Minimum Tax (AMT) it's even worse—you can deduct only those expenses in excess of 10% of your AGI, regardless of your age.

↪ **Example**   Lucy is 68 years old, her AGI is $60,000, and her total medical expenses for the year were $6,000. She is allowed to deduct $1,500 in medical expenses as an itemized deduction, which are the amount of expenses that were in excess of the 7.5% floor, or $4,500 ($60,000 × 7.5% = $4,500). If she were subject to the AMT, however, she would not be able to deduct any of her medical expenses for the year because they do not add up to more than 10% of her AGI.

In 2013 a new rule came into effect that increased the AGI to 10% for all tax-payers under 65, regardless of whether they are subject to the AMT. This tax increase is a result of the Affordable Care Act (a.k.a. ObamaCare). This is one of the many adjustments that were made to the tax laws to pay for this new program. This higher floor will affect a significant number of people when they file their returns—eliminating the deduction for a large number of people, and limiting it for many others.

↦ **Example** Mary and Jon have an AGI of $80,000. Their total medical expenses for the year add up to $7,800. Under 2012 law they could have taken an itemized deduction of $1,800, the amount of expenses that exceed the 7.5% floor, which in their case is $6,000 ($80,000 × 0.075 = $6,000). Beginning in 2013, under the same circumstances, Mary and Jon cannot deduct any medical expenses because their new floor is $8,000 (10% of AGI), which is greater than their $7,800 of expenses. If their combined federal and state marginal tax brackets equaled 35%, they will end up paying an additional $540 in taxes (0.30 × $1,800 that they could no longer deduct = $540).

The third hurdle that you must cross to claim medical expenses as an itemized deduction is that all of your itemized deductions, added together, must be greater than the standard deduction in order to receive any benefit. Otherwise, it would be more beneficial to take the standard deduction and the medical and other deductions become inconsequential. These three hurdles combine to make it so that a surprisingly small portion of the average person's total medical expenses are actually deductible.

○ **Tip** If you are in a position to control when you pay for your medical expenses, you can plan those expenses in a way that will help you reap the greatest benefit. Aim to delay procedures until late enough in the year that you can pay for them in the following year. Then, in the following year be sure to pay for all new expenses before the year's end. In that way you can increase the amount of medical expenses that are deductible in one year (above 7.5 or 10%) and get more deductions out of those expenses than you otherwise would have by spreading them out over the two years.

✒ **Caution** While the timing of payments is a legitimate strategy for maximizing your medical expense deduction, it is not possible to utilize this strategy by pre-paying your medical bills. Pre-payments for services not yet rendered are not deductible until the service is received.

One key to making the most of this strategy is being aware of all of the expenses that qualify for the deduction. There are many expenses that are not covered by health insurance companies (such as chiropractic care and acupuncture) but are actually considered deductible expenses in the tax code. In addition to the obvious out-of-pocket medical expenses, tracking and claiming some frequently overlooked medical expenses often can get you over the

7.5% or 10% hurdle and allow you to take some of your medical expenses as deductions. Here are some examples:

- The mileage that you put on your car for medical purposes is a deductible expense. All travel necessary to visit a doctor, hospital, or pharmacy can be deducted at a standard rate of $0.24 per mile in 2013, plus parking and tolls. If you are going to claim a mileage deduction, keep accurate records of starting and ending odometer readings, the reason for the travel, and the dates. Also get a third-party record of your vehicle's mileage at the beginning of each year (such as a receipt from an oil change). These things will help you keep the deductions you claimed if you are faced with an audit.

- Meals eaten during medical trips away from home can be claimed as a medical expense, as well as $50 per night, per person for lodging if you are an outpatient of a hospital or clinic and there is no significant element of pleasure involved in the travel (i.e., you are there for treatment and not sightseeing or other such things during that time). Notice that it is a per-person amount, so a parent taking a child to a clinic, for example, would allow for $100 per night in deductions (and, no, a family of six does not mean a $300 deduction—only one additional person and only if necessary).

- Health and dental insurance premiums are deductible. Many do not think of insurance as a medical expense, but it is deductible as long as you haven't used the self-employed health insurance deduction. The cost of Medicare Part A and Part D is considered a deductible health insurance expense, so be sure to include it in the calculation if you participate in those programs.

- If you have long-term care insurance, a portion of the premiums may be deductible.

- The expense of home improvements or additions that are primarily for medical care are deductible to the extent that they cost more than the value they add to the property. For example, if a wheelchair ramp costs $3,000 to install and increases the value of the home by $1,000, then $2,000 is deductible as a medical expense. If the improvement adds no value to the home, the entire expense is deductible.

A more comprehensive list of qualified medical expenses is included at the end of this chapter, as is a list of those items that are not deductible.

○ **Tip** The self-employed health insurance deduction often produces a better tax result than counting your premiums toward the itemized deduction, even if you are unable to cross the 7.5% (or 10%) hurdle without the premiums. If you are a business owner, look first to that deduction, if you qualify. See Chapter 20 for more details.

Your medical expenses include those paid for you, your spouse, your dependents, and anyone you could have claimed as a dependent (e.g., "dependents" whose income level was too high for you to claim them). You cannot claim a deduction for expenses you paid for anyone else.

You must keep good records and have receipts for all of your medical expenses. Expenses that are reimbursed by a health insurance plan or an employer are not deductible. Expenses paid for with funds from a Health Savings Account (HSA) are also not deductible.

Health Savings Accounts (HSAs)

Health Savings Accounts (HSAs) are special savings accounts, much like IRAs, are set aside specifically for medical expenses. To encourage people to save for medical expenses (and reduce the overall burden on the government), lawmakers allow individuals to claim a tax deduction from their income when they contribute funds to an HSA. Every dollar contributed to the HSA directly reduces your AGI and taxable income by one dollar as well.

Money in an HSA can be withdrawn tax-free at any time, as long as it is used for qualified medical expenses. This tax treatment is significant— you receive a deduction for the contribution and you are not taxed when the money is withdrawn, meaning that the money contributed to an HSA is *never* taxed. There is *no other arrangement* treated so favorably in the tax code. HSAs are the most beneficial thing that Congress has created for the American taxpayer in decades.

As discussed in the previous section, medical expenses can be deducted from your taxable income only if you itemize deductions and if those expenses exceed the 7.5% or 10% of AGI floor. Otherwise you receive no tax benefit from those medical expenses (and even if you do, a significant portion of those expenses remain un-deductible).

⇌ **Example**   James is a 66-year-old professional fisherman in Louisiana. This year he had an AGI of $80,000 and $6,500 in medical expenses. He can deduct only $500 of those expenses (7.5% × $80,000 AGI = $6,000 nondeductible expense → $6,500 expenses − $6,000 nondeductible = $500 deductible). If James were subject to the AMT, he would get no deduction because his expenses would not exceed the nondeductible amount (10% × $80,000 = $8,000 nondeductible).

With an HSA you are able to circumvent these rules. Even if you only contributed to an HSA the amount of money that you owe for medical expenses and you turn right around and pay the money out of the account, you would be better off on your taxes because you would circumvent the itemization requirement for deductible expenses and avoid the 7.5% or 10% of AGI floor that limits those deductions. In this way you can deduct every dollar that you spend on medical costs, not just those that exceed the AGI floor.

An additional benefit to HSA contributions is that the AMT has no effect on your ability to claim the deduction, as it does when you're itemizing. In fact, the AMT is *reduced* when you claim the HSA deduction because it directly reduces your AGI and your taxable income.

HSAs offer a tax planning option that is close to a rare "double-dipping" opportunity in the tax code. To achieve the maximum benefit of an HSA, follow these steps:

1.   Contribute the full amount allowable to your HSA in order to get the maximum deduction.

2.   Withdraw no money from the HSA for medical expenses you incur—just leave all of the funds in the HSA.

3.   Allow the contributions to grow tax-free for the future.

4.   Pay all of your current medical expenses out of pocket. Included in those expenses is the cost of your health insurance premiums (which cannot be paid from the HSA).

By following these steps you will not only get a tax deduction for the HSA contribution, but you will also get an additional deduction for expenses over 7.5% (or 10%) of AGI (including premiums) if you itemize. On top of that you will receive tax-free growth on the money invested in your HSA. Isn't that beautiful?

If your budget is really tight and you can't afford to contribute the maximum amount to an HSA, at a minimum you should put money into the account as you pay your medical bills. If a doctor bills you for $150, send the $150 to your HSA first and then pay the doctor from the account. Doing so will usually bring a greater tax benefit than paying the doctor from funds outside the HSA.

In this way you ensure that each dollar you pay in medical expenses becomes a deduction. If you pay with funds outside the HSA, your medical expenses will be limited by the itemization thresholds.

Once you make a contribution you can withdraw the funds at any time. While the money is in the HSA, it can be invested and grow tax-free. When you need the money, you can withdraw it tax-free, as long as you use it for medical expenses. If you don't use the money in the savings account for medical expenses, you can use it for any expenses once you reach retirement age (59½). If you use the money for non-medical expenses after that point, the amount withdrawn will be subject to income taxes, in the same way all non-Roth retirement accounts are taxed, but would not be subject to any penalties.

○ **Tip**   Contributions to an IRA or 401(k) do not limit your ability to contribute to an HSA. If you have made the maximum contribution to an IRA, an HSA could be a great way to significantly increase the contribution you can make to an IRA-like account. In addition, HSA contributions have no high-income cap. High-income earners who might not be allowed to make contributions to an IRA can contribute to HSAs. See Chapter 15 for more details.

◆ **Caution**   Don't use HSA funds for unqualified medical expenses before you are 59½. If you do, you will pay taxes on the amounts used, as well as a 20% penalty.

Contributions to an HSA are limited to a maximum amount each year (determined by the IRS). If you are older than the age of 55, you can contribute an additional $1,000 over the annual limits as a "catch-up" contribution. Contributions for a given year can be made up to April 15 of the following year. The maximum contributions to an HSA that are allowed each year increase annually, based on inflation. Table 26-1 show where the annual contribution limits are currently set.

Table 26-1. Maximum Allowable HSA Contributions in 2013

	Younger than 50 Years Old	Age 50 or Older
Individual	$3,250	$4,250
Family	$6,450	$7,450

✐ **Caution**   Contribute no more than the maximum allowable for an HSA—you'll pay fairly steep penalties if you do.

To take advantage of the opportunities that HSA accounts provide, you must first ensure that you have a qualifying high-deductible health insurance plan. The best way to find out whether your plan qualifies is to contact your insurance company or your Human Resources Department if it is through your employer. Once you have the right plan, you must set up an HSA with a provider (the insurance plan and the savings account are completely separate from each other). Many large banks offer HSAs. They usually give you a special debit card for the account, which makes it very easy to access the funds when you need to pay a bill. Once you have the right plan and the account, contribute as much as you can up to the maximum allowed for the year.

🗎 **Note**   If you need to switch insurance plans to qualify for an HSA, there is a very good chance that the money you save in premiums will add up to a large portion of the maximum HSA contribution. Contribute at least the amount you save in premiums each month.

With the money that you are able to save in premiums (and deposit in the HSA) you will probably be able to cover and expenses that you have to pay because of the higher deductible. If you don't have many expenses, then you have truly saved money that you would have otherwise spent on premiums.

There are just a few other items to be aware of before opening up your HSA account. First, you could be ineligible for an HSA because of an employer-sponsored health plan, unless it is an HSA plan. Be sure to check with your human resource department if you receive your insurance through an employer. Second, you can purchase over-the-counter medications with HSA funds only if they are prescribed by a doctor. And finally, as with all great tax strategies, keep good records of the medical expenses you pay for using funds from your HSA.

Health Care Coverage Tax and Credit

All insurance programs need a mix of healthy individuals along with the sick ones in order to spread out the cost of coverage over more people. For this reason, the creators of this bill needed a way to encourage those who don't need insurance to buy it anyway—or at least to pay into the system if they refuse.

Beginning in 2014, if you're not insured at the minimum level of coverage dictated by the government, you will pay a penalty tax. In 2014 the penalty equals 1% of all income in excess of the filing thresholds (which in 2012 were $9,750 for single individuals, $19,500 for married couples). The uninsured pay a minimum penalty of $95 per adult and $47.50 per child under age 18, if the 1%-of-income calculation comes out to be less than those amounts. The maximum penalty is $285 per person, no matter how high their income.

The penalty increases dramatically over the following two years (2015 and 2016). In 2015 the penalty is 2% of income, with a minimum penalty of $325 and a maximum penalty of $975. In 2016 the maximum penalty increases to $2,085, and it is indexed to increase with inflation each year thereafter.

Insurers will send 1099 forms to the IRS to prove coverage of those with individually purchased plans. If your insurance is provided by an employer, the value of your insurance will be reported on your W-2. Using these two methods the IRS can verify that each person is covered by a qualifying health insurance plan so that it can in turn charge the penalty to those who are not.

○ **Tip**   If the penalty goes unpaid, the IRS cannot charge additional penalties or interest on the original penalty. Nor can the IRS file a levy or lien to collect the penalty. Their only means of collection is to withhold the amounts owed from future refunds. This nuance will make for some interesting tax planning for a few people out there, I am sure.

The bill includes a refundable credit to low-income households to help them fund the purchase of insurance through the government "health exchanges." The value of the credit will be based on a percentage of the household's income. The credit will be sent directly from the Treasury to the Exchange, so it will not come in the form of money to the individual.

To qualify for the credit your income will need to be between 100% and 400% of the federal poverty level. In 2012 a family of four would qualify for the credit if their income fell between $23,550 and $94,200 (between $11,490 and $45,960 for a single individual). Families with incomes *below* these levels do not qualify for the credit because they would qualify for other government assistance for their health care needs.

Qualified Medical Expenses

Although not exhaustive, the following list gives you an idea of allowable medical expenses. Some of the items on this list may surprise you:

- Abortion (where legal)
- Acupuncture
- Adoption (medical costs for the child but not the birth mother)
- Air conditioner (for allergy relief and cystic fibrosis)
- Alcoholism treatment
- Ambulance
- Animals (seeing eye dog, hearing dog or animal, and other medical-assistance animals)
- Attendant for blind or deaf student
- Braille literature (only the excess over the regular cost)
- Car (equipment to accommodate wheelchair or special controls)
- Childbirth preparation classes for the mother
- Chiropractors
- Christian Science treatments
- Computer data storage of medical records
- Contact lenses
- Contraceptive prescriptions
- Cosmetic surgery for deformities (not for unnecessary reasons)
- Crutches
- Deafness aids (hearing aid, animal, lip reading, special telephones and televisions)
- Dental expenses
- Dentures
- Diagnostics
- Diapers needed for a severe neurological disease
- Doctors

- Domestic aid given by a nurse
- Drug-addiction recovery
- Dyslexia training
- Eye exams
- Fertility treatments
- Glasses
- Health club (only if prescribed by a doctor for a medical condition)
- Hospital care
- Native American medicine man
- Insulin
- Insurance (accident, health, medical, dental, contact replacement, Medicare Part A & D)
- Lab fees
- Laser eye surgery
- Lead-paint removal
- Lifetime medical care (prepaid)
- Limbs (artificial)
- Lodging (limited to $50 per night)
- Long-term care expenses
- Mattress (prescribed for arthritis)
- Nursing home
- Nursing services
- Obstetrics
- Operations (only legal ones)
- Optometrists
- Orthodontia
- Orthopedic shoes
- Oxygen equipment
- Special plumbing for the handicapped
- Prescription drugs

- Psychiatric care
- Psychologists
- Psychotherapists
- Reconstructive surgery
- Sexual dysfunction treatment
- Smoking cessation
- Sterilization operation
- Swimming pool for polio or arthritis treatment
- Taxicab to medical care
- Transplants (donor's cost)
- Transportation for medical care
- Vasectomy
- Weight-loss program for a specific disease
- Wheelchair
- Wig (when related to a disease)
- X-rays

Here is a list of some of the expenses that are *not* allowed as deductions. I enjoy looking at this list to see the creative things that people have tried to claim as a medical expense. This list is not exhaustive, but should give you a good idea of what not to claim:

- Adoption (medical expenses for natural mother)
- Child care while parent sees doctor
- Chauffeur
- Clothing
- Cosmetic surgery (when unnecessary)
- Dancing lessons
- Deprogramming
- Diaper service
- Drugs (when illegal under federal law, even if prescribed)
- Dust elimination
- Ear piercing

- Electrolysis
- Funeral expenses
- Furnace
- Gravestone
- Hair transplants
- Health club dues, not prescribed for a specific condition
- Hygienic supplies
- Life insurance
- Marriage counseling
- Scientology audits and processing
- Self-help medical remedies
- Spiritual guidance
- Tattoos
- Teeth whitening
- Vacations
- Weight-loss programs for appearance, even if prescribed

Your Residence

After Taxes, Your Home May Be Your Biggest Expense—It May Also Be a Great Tax Deduction

As a general principle, the tax code allows you to take a deduction for expenses that you incur in an effort to create income. The allowance of these deductions encourages people to invest in things that increase their income—increasing taxes as a result. That is why most expenses related to a business are allowed as deductions, when those same items are not deductible when used for personal reasons.

The opposite of this principle is true as well. In most cases the tax code does *not* allow you to take a deduction for personal expenses—for things that are intended for your personal benefit and not for the purpose of generating income. However, Congress makes exceptions to this rule when it wants to encourage specific behaviors. This is the case with the home mortgage interest deduction and other deductions and credits related to money that you spend on your home. Home ownership has been shown to be a positive factor in society and so Congress has done things through the tax code to make it financially easier to own a home (or at least that is the intent). Seven home-related tax issues are discussed in this chapter:

- The Mortgage Interest Deduction
- The Property Tax Deduction
- Credits related to energy efficiency
- Deductions for home improvements for the disabled
- Home Sale Exemption from Capital Gains
- Foreclosures and short sales

The Mortgage Interest Deduction

To encourage home ownership, the tax code allows for deductions on mortgage interest. Two types of mortgage interest are deductible: acquisition-debt interest and home-equity debt interest.

Acquisition debt is debt used to purchase, build, or substantially improve a qualified residence. Qualified acquisition debt also includes the refinancing of original acquisition debt, as long as the refinancing amount is less than the amount of acquisition debt that existed immediately before the refinance. Only the interest on acquisition debt up to $1 million can be deducted—any additional amount is not deductible under the current rules.

☞ **Example** Greg purchased his home for $250,000, using $50,000 from his savings for a down payment and using a loan for the rest. All of the interest paid on the $200,000 in acquisition debt is allowed as an itemized deduction because the entire loan was used to purchase the home.

A few years later, Greg decided to make improvements to his home. He borrowed an additional $100,000 from the bank and used $75,000 of it to improve his home (the rest he used to buy a car). He then refinanced his first and second loans to consolidate them into one loan. That brought the total debt on his principal residence to $300,000 ($200,000 original loan + $100,000 new loan). However, he can deduct only the interest that he pays on $275,000 of the loan as acquisition debt ($200,000 for the purchase and $75,000 for substantial improvements).

Bruce, Greg's wealthy brother, bought his home around the same time as Greg. Bruce's home cost $2.5 million. Bruce used $1 million of his savings as a down payment on the home and secured a loan for the remaining $1.5 million. Although the entire $1.5 million is considered acquisition debt, only the interest paid on the first $1 million of the loan is deductible as acquisition debt interest because of the limitations placed on the mortgage interest deduction.

Cindy, Bruce and Greg's prudent sister, also purchased a home. Her home cost $300,000, which she paid for entirely with cash. If Cindy later had an emergency and needed to take out a home equity loan of $200,000 to pay for medical bills, none of the interest on the loan would be deductible as acquisition debt because it was not used to purchase, build, or substantially improve her home. Had she originally used a $200,000 loan to purchase the house and kept her savings in the bank for such an emergency, the interest on that loan would have been deductible.

Mortgage interest is deductible only for the taxpayer's residence. However, the term "residence" is defined fairly liberally for this deduction. A "residence" could be an RV or boat, as long as the vehicle includes a bathroom and cooking and sleeping accommodations. A qualified residence is also not confined to one home. The tax code actually allows for two residences to be used for this deduction: your principal residence and one other residence (such as a vacation home that is not rented out during the year). Actually, the second residence can be rented out and still qualify for the deduction if you use it for the greater of either 14 days per year, or 10% of the days that it is rented at fair market value.

🖐 **Caution**   If you are subject to the Alternative Minimum Tax (AMT), you don't qualify to deduct a boat (with living quarters) or an RV as a second home—you can deduct interest on a second home only if it is a traditional residence.

The second type of deductible mortgage interest is from loans known as home equity debt. Home equity debt is any debt borrowed for an amount greater than the unpaid principal from the original acquisition debt (or new improvement debt).

↪ **Example**   Jim and Angela purchased a home 10 years ago for $150,000, of which $120,000 was paid for using a loan. They have devoted all of their extra income to pay the loan off quickly and they have only $20,000 left to pay on the loan's principal. If they were to take out a new loan on the house for $120,000, only $20,000 of the new loan would be considered acquisition debt, and the remainder would be considered a home equity loan because $20,000 was the amount of principal that remained on the acquisition debt just before the refinance.

One significant difference in the rules for home equity debt versus acquisition debt is that the loan can be used to purchase *anything* and still be deductible. In the earlier example of Greg, the interest from the $25,000 of the loan that he used to buy a car could be deducted as home equity interest, even though it could not be deducted under the rules of acquisition debt.

The amount of home equity debt that is deductible is limited in two ways. First, the home equity debt, combined with the acquisition debt, cannot be greater than the value of the home. If home values drop substantially from their purchase price, this rule can eliminate your ability to claim the deduction for home equity loan interest. The second limitation on the home equity loan deduction is that you can deduct interest only on a maximum of $100,000 of home equity debt.

○ **Tip**   If you have a loan greater than $1 million, you can treat up to $100,000 of the additional loan value as a home equity loan and deduct it (even if the entire amount was acquisition debt). In the earlier example of Bruce, even though his deduction was limited to the interest from the first $1 million of his loan, he could have taken an additional home equity debt deduction for another $100,000. You can deduct even more interest than the $1.1 million rule allows if part of the home is used for business purposes. See Chapter 17 for more details on this strategy.

The most important thing you can do in cultivating mortgage interest deductions is to keep good records. This is especially important if you refinance your house or take out home equity lines of credit. Track carefully how you use the funds so you can take the proper deduction and back it up in the event of an audit.

You'll want to keep a couple of other things in mind when planning for these interest deductions as well. First, as is the case with all itemized deductions, the mortgage interest deduction is of no value to you if the standard deduction is greater than all of your itemized deductions combined. Many people receive *no* benefit from their mortgage interest deduction because they do not have enough deductions to itemize. It is frustrating to me when people in the real estate or mortgage industry tell clients that their mortgage interest will be deductible when it is often not enough of a deduction for them to itemize.

Second, if you are paying the interest on a home for someone else (such as a child or elderly parent), you may not take the deduction for that interest, unless the mortgage is in your name. If you pay the interest but the home is not in your name, the payment is only a gift.

Finally, if you own multiple homes, you can deduct the interest for only two of the homes—your principal residence and one other. The second home you choose for the mortgage interest deduction can be changed on a yearly basis.

✦ **Caution**   Although many advocate remaining in debt in order to retain the interest deduction, I am not one of them. If you have a mortgage and you don't have the financial ability to pay it off, then you should take full advantage of this deduction. However, if you have the money available to pay off your mortgage, I think you'll find many more benefits to being debt-free and to owning a home than you will have by retaining the tax deduction. Remember, to get a deduction, you must always spend more money than you will save in taxes—significantly more. If you are in the 25% tax bracket and pay $12,000 in interest, you will save only $3,000 in taxes from the deductions. Even with the deduction you are still $9,000 poorer than you would be had you not had a mortgage.

Points Treated as Interest

At the closing of a loan, an extra fee can be paid to the lender to secure a lower interest rate. This payment is usually referred to as a "point." The IRS considers points to be the equivalent of interest, and as such they are deductible. In most cases, the deduction must be spread over the life of the loan. For example, if you paid $3,000 in points on a 30-year loan, you could deduct $100 per year as mortgage interest ($3,000 in points ÷ 30 years = $100 per year). However, you can deduct the entire amount paid in the first year if you meet the following conditions:

- The fees are designated as points on the settlement statement.

- The fees are based on a percentage of the loan value.

- The fees are for the *purchase* of your *principal* residence (not a refinance or for a second home).

- The fees are paid directly by you (not rolled into the loan).

- It is normal practice in your area to pay the amount of points you paid (you didn't pay significantly more than most people in order to take advantage of the larger deduction).

- The points are not in lieu of other fees, such as appraisals, title fees, and so on (they are used only to reduce the interest rate).

Mortgage Insurance

For a limited time, one other mortgage expense can be deducted. If you purchased your primary residence between January 1, 2007 and December 31, 2013, any mortgage insurance premiums paid during that time are deductible. It is possible that this deduction will be renewed for 2014, but had not yet been at the time that this book went to production. The insurance premiums must apply to the year you paid them, so a prepayment of the insurance for future years would not count. In addition, your ability to take this deduction is phased out if your Adjusted Gross Income (AGI) is between $100,000 and $110,000, and is eliminated thereafter.

The Property Tax Deduction

The tax code also allows you to deduct real estate taxes charged by any state, local, or foreign government. Only the portion of the tax that is based on the assessed value of the property is deductible. Many states and counties also impose local benefit taxes for improvements to property, such as assessments for streets, sidewalks, and sewer lines. These taxes cannot be deducted. However, you can increase the cost basis of your property by the amount of the other non-deductible taxes. Local benefits taxes *are* deductible if they are for maintenance or repair, or interest charges related to those benefits.

If a portion of your monthly mortgage payment goes into an escrow account from which the lender pays your real estate taxes, you cannot deduct the amount paid into the escrow account. Instead you must deduct the amount actually paid out of the escrow account during the year, which will be listed on the 1098 tax form that the lender sends you at the beginning of each year.

The property tax deduction is not limited by the rules that apply to the mortgage interest deduction. For example, you can claim the deduction for as many properties as you own and pay taxes on (as opposed to the two-residence rule for mortgage interest). In addition, the property tax deduction is not limited by the value of the property. Unlike the $1.1 million limitation placed on mortgage interest, you could own real estate worth $100 million or more and still deduct the entire amount that you pay in real estate tax.

Credits Related to Energy Efficiency

There are two credits available for individuals who make improvements to their homes with items that improve energy efficiency. The first is known as the Residential Energy Efficient Property Credit. This is a non-refundable tax credit intended to encourage the installation of alternative energy equipment in their homes. Equipment that qualifies for the credit includes solar water heaters, solar electricity equipment, fuel cell plants, small wind energy equipment, and geothermal heat pumps. The property must be installed in the taxpayer's residence and must be located in the United States.

The credit is equal to 30% of the cost of the equipment (however, the credit is limited for fuel cells to a maximum of $500 per half kilowatt hour). If the credit exceeds the amount of tax owed by the individual, the remainder is carried over to the following year. This credit is currently set to expire on December 31, 2016 (the equipment must be *installed* before that date to qualify for the credit).

✦ **Caution** Solar water heaters that are used to heat a swimming pool or hot tub do not qualify for the credit. If the water heater heats water for the house and a pool, the cost must be pro-rated and only the portion allocated to the house may be used for the credit.

The second credit for energy efficient property is known as the Nonbusiness Energy Property Credit. This credit is set to expire at the end of 2013, but may be reinstated. The credit has two parts. First, there is a credit of 10% (up to a maximum dollar amount) of the cost of installing energy-efficient improvements that are designed to prevent heat loss or gain, such as insulation, exterior windows, skylights, exterior doors, and metal roofs with special energy-efficient properties.

Second, there is a credit of 100% (up to a maximum dollar amount) of the cost of installation of energy efficient equipment such as water heaters, heat pumps, air conditioners, and biomass fuel stoves as long as they meet certain energy-efficient specifications.

The energy-efficient property credit is severely limited by maximum dollar caps. The maximum credit allowed for windows and skylights is $200. The maximum for heaters is $150. For all other items the maximum is $300. All credits taken for these items *combined* cannot exceed $500 in the taxpayer's *lifetime*.

✦ **Caution** I have spoken with a lot of people who have fallen prey to salespeople who tout the wonders of this credit. These sellers may say something like, "There is a tax credit for 100% of the cost of this heater, so you can buy it now and get your money back when you file your taxes!" What they neglect to mention is that the credit is 100% of the cost, *up to a maximum of* $150. The rest of the cost is not eligible for the credit. In addition, some people don't have taxable income after their deductions are taken into account. This credit is non-refundable, so it will do no good for a person who owes no tax. Whenever you hear a salesperson (or advertisement) spouting tax benefits, be careful. Far too often they are only telling part of the story.

Deductions for Home Improvements for the Disabled

The expense of home improvements or additions that are primarily for medical care or for the disabled are deductible to the extent that they cost more than the value they add to the property. Such improvements may include a wheelchair ramp, handrails in the bathroom, or a powered lift for stairways.

They could also include ventilation systems designed to remove harmful particles from the air. There are too many possibilities to list, but the important part is that, if it is necessary for medical purposes, it is deductible on your return to the extent that it does not increase the property's value. If the improvement adds no value to the home, the entire expense is deductible.

⇨ **Example**   Maggie recently had a stroke that left her without full movement in her legs. She is able to care for herself, but is not able to lift her legs over obstacles. For this reason she needed to remodel her bathroom so that the shower does not require her to step into a bath tub. The remodel cost $2,000 and her realtor estimates that the work increased the value of the home by $500. Maggie can deduct $1,500 of the cost as a medical expense ($2,000 total cost – $500 increase in the home's value = $1,500 deductible expense. (The remaining $500 would be added to the cost basis of her home.

This deduction is actually taken as part of the medical expense deduction and subject to limitations based on AGI. See Chapter 26 to learn more about the limitations imposed on the medical expense deduction.

Home Sale Exemption from Capital Gains

Generally, any time that you purchase an asset for a given price, and then later sell it for a greater price, taxes are levied on that gain (the difference between the purchase and sale price). The tax code provides an important exception (or exclusion) to this rule when it comes to your personal residence. If you meet certain guidelines the gain that you receive when selling your home can be tax-free. Many people have used this exclusion to periodically capture a tax-free gain from selling their home and, over time, use those gains to eventually pay for their new home entirely out of their tax-free gains, resulting in a huge cumulative tax savings.

There are three main guidelines that must be met to achieve tax-free status on the sale of your residence. First, you must have lived in the home as your principal residence for two of the previous five years (from the date of the sale). Second, you must have owned the home for two of the previous five years (which may seem redundant, but it's not). Third, you cannot claim this exclusion more than once in a two-year period.

The maximum gain exclusion per individual is **$250,000**, which translates to $500,000 for a married couple. Any gain on the home greater than the maximum exclusion amount would be taxed. The exclusion applies only to the use of the home as a personal residence.

There are many nuances and additional details in this exemption. Most of these are discussed in much greater detail in Chapter 10, which you should definitely read if you plan to sell, or have recently sold, your home.

Foreclosures and Short Sales

The tax code treats a forgiven debt as income—it is essentially the same thing as receiving income that you use to pay off the debt. Nowhere can this fact be more painful than in the foreclosure or short-sale of your home. Not only does it add insult to injury (you lose your home because you are having a hard time financially and then the IRS sends you a big bill), but the tax burden that comes from the debt forgiveness can be extremely high. The difference between the amount of money that you owed and the amount that the lender can sell the home for is treated as ordinary income on your tax return.

⮑ **Example**   Damon purchased a home for $450,000 with 100% financing. Soon after he purchased the home there was a collapse in the economy that led to a 50% decrease in home values, as well as a significant decrease in Damon's income. Damon did his best to hang on to the home, using up much of his savings, before he decided that he would have to let it go into foreclosure. The bank repossessed the home and eventually sold it for $200,000. The following year the bank reported to the IRS that Damon had a "discharge of indebtedness" of $250,000 ($450,000 original debt – $200,00 sale price = $250,000 in debt forgiveness). Barring any exclusions that may apply, Damon will have to report the $250,000 debt forgiveness as income on his tax return for that year.

Fortunately, there are several exceptions to this rule that can help to reduce or eliminate this tax burden. The first exclusion is known as Qualified Principal Residence Indebtedness. This is a temporary exclusion that was enacted in the wake of the 2008 economic crisis. The rule makes it so that any debt forgiveness for a home that occurs between January 1, 2007 and December 31, 2013 is not subject to income tax or included in an individual's income. To qualify for this exclusion, the debt must be acquisition debt (only the portion of the loan used to purchase the home) for the individual's principal residence and is available for only up to $2,000,000 of debt forgiven. This exclusion is not expected to be extended beyond 2013.

In addition to the temporary exclusion, there is another permanent exclusion that may apply. The taxpayer need not recognize income if he or she is in bankruptcy or is insolvent. (*Insolvent* means that the taxpayer's debts exceed the market value of his or her assets immediately before the forgiveness of the debt). However, the exclusion for insolvency is applicable only to the extent that of the insolvency.

⇝ **Example** Damon stopped making payments on the home when he realized that there was no way he would be able to keep it, which was a few months before he would have completely wiped out his savings. At the time the bank foreclosed on the home Damon had $10,000 left in the bank and a car that he owned free and clear, which was worth about $5,000. Damon had no other assets debts. At the time of the foreclosure Damon was insolvent by $235,000 ($450,000 debt – $200,000 home value - $10,000 in savings – $5,000 value of car = $235,000 insolvent).

The bank charged Damon with $250,000 of debt forgiveness; however Damon will have to report only $15,000 of that as income on his tax return because that is the extent to which the debt forgiveness exceeded his insolvency.

With each of these exclusions, the basis of the home is reduced by the amount of debt forgiveness that was excluded from income, which determines any gain that is captured when the home later sold.

Your Children

Kids Aren't as Taxing as People Claim—In Fact, They'll Lower Your Taxes Quite a Bit

People seem a little shocked when they learn that I have eight children. Sometimes I joke that I have a lot of kids because they are such a great tax write-off. Although there is no truth in the joke in regard to why I have eight children, it is true that kids provide some great tax benefits.

The first tax benefit that comes from having dependent children in the home is that you receive an additional exemption for each child, which automatically reduces your taxable income by $3,900 per child (see Chapter 4 for details). Then the Child Tax Credit and any other applicable credits kick in to bring you even greater tax savings. With all of these tax-saving opportunities it is conceivable that the cost of supporting a child's basic needs could be offset by the tax savings of these laws. Here is a list of the child-related tax credits that are covered in this chapter:

- The Child Tax Credit (Refundable)
- The Additional Child Tax Credit (Non-Refundable)
- The Child Care Credit
- The Adoption Credit

In addition to the strategies discussed in this chapter, be sure to also read about how to reduce your taxes by employing children in your business, discussed in Chapter 21.

The Child Tax Credit (Non-Refundable)

The child tax credit is one of the best tax benefits available. It is a dollar-for-dollar credit against your tax for as much as $1,000 per child. This credit is available to you if you have a "qualifying" child. To qualify, your child must:

- Be your son, daughter, stepson or stepdaughter, or a descendant of those children, or a brother, sister, step-brother or stepsister, or a descendant of those persons. These children include foster and adopted children.

- Be 16 years old or younger at the year's end.

- Live in the same principal residence as you do, for more than half of the year (including children born at the end of the year, as long as their residence was the same as yours).

- Not provide more than half of his or her own support during the year.

If the child meets all four criteria, he or she qualifies to be claimed for the credit. The only other thing that could stand in the way of claiming the credit is your Adjusted Gross Income (AGI). The $1,000 credit begins to be reduced at an AGI of $110,000 if you are married, or $75,000 if you are single. The credit is completely phased out by the time your AGI reaches $130,000 or $95,000, respectively. If your income is close to the phase-out range for this credit it is worth careful planning to reduce your AGI below the phase-out as much as possible.

The child tax credit is nonrefundable, meaning that it can be used to reduce your tax liability only to $0. Once the credit brings your tax liability to $0, the remainder of the credit is forfeited and is not carried forward into future years.

⇝ **Example** Ted and Vickie own a daycare service and have two children who qualify for the child tax credit. Because they have two qualifying children and an AGI of $90,000, they have a total potential credit of $2,000. However, their total tax liability is only $1,200, so the credit will eliminate the entire $1,200 of income taxes they would have owed, but $800 of the credit will go unused.

If you share responsibility for caring for a child with another taxpayer (besides your spouse), specific rules determine which person can claim the credit. Consult an advisor in this situation, or study the pertinent IRS documents.

The Additional Child Tax Credit (Refundable)

In contrast to the child tax credit, the *additional* child tax credit is *refundable*. This means that even if your tax liability has been reduced to $0, you can receive a "refund" for the amount of credit that wasn't used in that year. The refundable additional child tax credit is equal to the lesser of:

- The unused portion of the child tax credit

  or

- Your total *earned* income, minus $3,000, multiplied by 15%

⇨ **Example** Ted and Vickie's earned income was $90,000. This means they could claim a refundable credit of $800. This is because the unused portion of their child tax credit of $800 is less than the alternate calculation of $13,050 ($90,000 – $3,000 = $87,000; $87,000 × 15% = $13,050).

A significant benefit that comes from the Additional Child Tax Credit is that it reduces the self-employment tax, as well as any tax penalties that you might owe, whereas the non-refundable tax credit reduces only income tax and Alternative Minimum Tax (AMT). This can really help those who run their own business and have little to no income tax, but have a hefty self-employment tax. This credit is set to expire at the end of 2017.

○ **Tip** If you are expecting a child to be born very close to the end of the year and the delivery will be induced, the potentially large tax ramifications of this credit and the dependency exemption may be one factor (of many) worth considering when you determine the birth date. It isn't the most important factor, obviously, but all else being equal it would be worth considering.

The Child Care Credit

A non-refundable credit is available for child care expenses that are incurred to enable a taxpayer to earn an income. For the expenses to qualify, the person receiving care must be a dependent of the taxpayer and no older than 12 years old. (The child can be older than 12 if he or she is mentally or physically unable to care for him/herself.)

Expenses that qualify for this credit include household services (such as cleaning and cooking), in-home child care and services outside the home as long as the child is normally in the home at least eight hours per day. The payments can be made to a family member of the taxpayer, as long as the caregiver is not a dependent of the taxpayer and is not a child of the taxpayer younger than the age of 19.

✎ **Caution**   I am often given receipts for overnight summer camps as expenses that my clients want to claim for this credit. However, none of the cost of an overnight camp qualifies for the child care credit. On the other hand, day camps (where the child returns home each night) do qualify for this credit.

To claim the credit the child care must be for the purpose of allowing the taxpayer to go to work, or to seek employment. If married, both spouses must work in order to claim this credit. If one spouse does not work then no credit can be claimed. An exception to this is if one spouse is a full-time student or is mentally or physically incapable of self-care.

The maximum amount of child care expenses that can be claimed is $3,000 per year for one child, or $6,000 for two or more children. The credit is 35% of allowable expenses for taxpayers with an AGI of $15,000 or less. The credit is reduced by 1% for every $2,000 of AGI (or fraction thereof) over the $15,000 threshold, until it reaches the minimum credit of 20% of allowable expenses for anyone with an AGI greater than $43,000 per year.

⮑ **Example**   Lynne is a single mother of two children, ages 8 and 10. She spends $6,500 per year on child care, evenly split between the kids, so that she can be at work during some of the time that her children are not in school. Lynne's AGI is $40,000 per year. Lynne would be able to claim a Child Care Credit of $1,320 [($40,000 AGI – $15,000 threshold = $25,000 over the threshold) → ($25,000 over brings a 13% reduction from the maximum credit of 35% by reducing it 1% for every $2,000 over the threshold, 35% – 13% = 22% credit) → ($6,000 maximum expenses allowed × 22% = $1,320)].

The maximum credit that a person could claim would be $2,100 for two children with $6,000 of expenses and less than $15,000 of income, making it pretty unlikely that the full amount of the credit will be claimed. Making matters worse, an individual with less than $15,000 of AGI and two children would owe no tax (because the exemptions and standard deduction would eliminate his/her taxable income), and since the credit is non-refundable, it would do the person no good. I have a hard time understanding how they came up with the phase-outs for this law; they really don't make sense. Regardless, individuals with a higher tax liability may be able to benefit from this credit by as much as $600 fewer taxes if they have one eligible child, or $1,200 for two (or more) children.

The allowable child care expenses cannot exceed the individual's earned income for the year. In the case of a married couple, the expenses cannot exceed the earned income of the spouse with the lower income. In the case of a spouse who is a full-time student or unable to care for him- or herself, the law assumes an earned income amount for each month of school attendance or disability in the amount of $250 per month for one child or $500 per month for two.

📖 **Note** You will be required to put the Social Security number (or employer tax ID) and other identifying information of the child care provider on your tax return, as well as the Social Security number of the child who is being claimed. Depending on the person you have arranged with for care, this could pose an obstacle to claiming the credit.

The Adoption Credit

Adopting a child can be extremely expensive. I have been surprised recently by clients who have had to pay as much as $35,000 for an adoption (and I'm sure there are more expensive stories out there). Of course, you can't put a price on the joy and blessings that come to the family from the adoption.

Congress views adoption as a good thing to encourage in our society. For this reason they have instilled a significant credit for adoption expenses in the tax code. Unlike other credits that are usually based on a percentage of the money you spent, the adoption credit brings a dollar-for-dollar benefit for all of your costs, up to a maximum amount of $12,970. Every dollar that you spend up to that amount will come back to you in tax benefits—assuming you have enough of a tax liability to be offset by the credit (since it is non-refundable). Unused credits can be carried forward to the following year.

Of course, the credit is phased out for high-income taxpayers. In 2013 the phase-out begins at $194,580 AGI and the credit is completely eliminated once AGI reaches $234,580.

📖 **Note** In 2010 and 2011, the Adoption Credit was refundable and allowed for a higher amount of qualified expenses. If you are filing a return for one of those years please be sure to speak with a tax preparer or to understand the significant implications of the refundable credit. There is no indication at this point in time that the refundable nature of this credit will be reinstated for future years.

Charitable Contributions

It Pays to Be Kind

Congress wants to encourage charitable giving because it benefits the country in so many ways. To that end, the tax code allows contributions to qualified charities to be deducted from your tax return as an itemized deduction. In fact, the tax code is so encouraging of charitable giving that it provides a rare "double-dip" opportunity in which you can get two tax reductions for the price of one.

There are many ways to support and donate to charitable organizations: You can give money directly to the organization; you can volunteer your time; or you can give items of value in order to further an organization's work. With nearly every type of gift there is also a way to deduct the value of that gift from your tax return.

As is the case with all tax deductions, no one should give to charity for the sole purpose of getting a deduction—it doesn't make financial sense. However, you probably contribute to charitable organizations more often than you realize. Each time you take items to Good Will, give money in church collections, or drive a group of kids on a Boy Scout trip, you are making a deductible charitable contribution. The key to capturing the tax benefits of these everyday events is to recognize them as such and then to record them.

It is important to know, however, that not every charitable act is deductible. There are many good things that you can do for people and organizations that don't fall within the guidelines of the tax code. For example, if you help an individual in need by giving him/her money for food, clothing, or shelter, you cannot deduct those gifts. To be deductible, the contributions must be given to a charitable organization recognized by the IRS, not to an individual or non-recognized organization. (In fact, the organization should be able to show proof that it is recognized by the IRS.) This is probably because there would not be a viable way for the IRS to verify the gifts that you claim if they were given directly to people. Charitable organizations, on the other hand, are registered with the IRS and have an incentive to report your gifts accurately (so that they don't lose their status as a non-taxable entity). This helps ensure that people aren't just giving each other money and claiming large deductions for "donations" of charitable gifts.

In this chapter I cover five key areas related to the charitable giving deduction:

- Gifts of money
- Non-money gifts
- Gifts of service
- Gifts of appreciated assets—the best way to give
- Maximizing the tax benefit of your gifts

Gifts of Money

Contributions of money are deductible on a dollar-for-dollar basis. You should avoid using cash for your contributions. Instead, use checks so that you have a verifiable record of payment. When you claim charitable contributions as a deduction on your tax return, you must keep good records of each donation, the organization it was given to, and the date and value of the donation. If you donate more than $250 to any organization during the year, be sure to get a receipt or letter from the organization. Without this proof of your donation, the deductions will not be allowed.

If you receive anything in return for your donation, you must subtract the value of that item from your deduction. For example, if you buy a ticket to a fundraising dinner for $200 and the value of the dinner is $50, your deduction for the charitable contribution would be only $150. Most charitable organizations make the value of any gift or service you receive very clear on the receipt they give you so that you can claim the appropriate amount for your deduction. Also be sure to note that contributions to political organizations or campaigns are *not* deductible.

The maximum deduction allowed to be taken in one year is limited to 50% of your Adjustable Gross Income (AGI). Anything more than that can be carried forward for future use for up to five years. Contributions to certain organizations are limited to 30% of AGI.

⮑ **Example**   Collin is retired. He doesn't require a very significant income to live on. In fact, he is very comfortable with an income of $40,000 per year (with an AGI of $30,000). Collin has a favorite charity that he has donated to for decades. The charity recently approached him for a substantial donation to help build a new facility that they need to expand their work. Collin agreed to donate $50,000 to the building of the facility.

Collin will reap a benefit on his tax return for the donation. In fact, that benefit will come over a span of four years. Collin's AGI is $30,000, so the maximum charitable contribution deduction that he can claim per year is $15,000 ($30,000 AGI × 50% of AGI limitation = $15,000). The remaining charitable contribution that he cannot deduct in the first year will roll forward each year until it is used up completely, or for five years, whichever comes first. He will be able to claim $15,000 each year for the first three years (totaling $45,000) and then use the remaining $5,000 in the fourth year.

Non-Money Gifts

In addition to the contributions you make in money, you probably also make contributions "in kind." When you clean out your garage or attic and donate things to a local charitable thrift store, you can take a deduction for those non-cash donations. The value of the deduction you can claim is the fair-market value of the item you donated. This value is usually determined by the price a thrift store could sell the item for (and is almost never close to what you paid for it). The donated item must also be in good condition. There are a few special rules that come into play regarding in-kind donations:

- If you donate a single non-cash item worth more than $5,000, you must get an independent appraisal of its value.

- Art, jewelry, or collectables must be appraised before you can deduct them, even if they are worth less than $5,000.

- Donations of food are not deductible.

- Vehicle donations have additional rules that you should be familiar with before making such a donation.

📄 **Note**   If you claim a significant amount of non-cash contributions, your records should include, first and foremost, a detailed list of what you donated and of the thrift-store value of each item. It is also advisable to take pictures of the things you will donate. Finally, be sure to get receipts from the charitable organization for the items you donated.

○ **Tip** Many thrift stores offer a list that shows the value of items that are commonly contributed. In addition, software programs are available that give you national averages of the thrift store value for thousands of items. The key is to be generous in your giving, but not overly generous in the value that you place on those gifts on your tax return.

Gifts of Service

One type of charitable contribution that is not deductible, even when given to recognized organizations, is the giving of your time. Many people assume that they can deduct their time given to a charity at the rate that they would otherwise charge in their profession. For example, an attorney may give free advice to the local Good Will when he would have charged another person or business $500 for that advice. He may not deduct the $500 as a contribution. The reason for this seems to come down to verifiability, as well as the risk of arbitrary values being applied to a person's time in order to juice the deductible amount.

Though time and personal service are not deductible, travel expenses incurred in order to give that service may be, if no significant element of personal pleasure, recreation, or vacation is involved. The most common deduction for charitable travel is for the mileage put on your vehicle while traveling to, from, and during the service for the charity. Charitable mileage can be deducted at the standard rate of $0.14 per mile, plus parking and tolls. Incidentally, the $0.14 per mile rate is *not* indexed for inflation and would literally take an act of Congress to be changed. You may also deduct actual travel expenses instead of the standard mileage rate, as well as any other actual costs incurred in giving the service.

✦ **Caution** If you are going to claim a mileage deduction, keep accurate records of starting and ending odometer readings, reasons for the travel, and dates. Also get a third-party record of your vehicle's mileage at the beginning of each year (such as the receipt from an oil change).

I have heard about a lot of organizations lately that bring people to exotic locations in order to perform a service, such as helping a local orphanage. If you pay for travel to such a location in order to perform service for a recognized charity, your out-of-pocket costs are deductible *only if* there is no substantial pleasure involved in the trip. If you go sightseeing for a few days and stay at a resort, there is a really good chance that your deduction will be denied.

Gifts of Appreciated Assets—the Best Way to Give (from a Tax Perspective)

The charitable contribution deduction has one of my favorite opportunities for "double-dipping" in the tax code. That opportunity comes when you contribute appreciated assets, such as investments, to a recognized charitable organization. When you make a contribution of an appreciated asset, you can take a deduction in the same way you would if you had written a check to the organization at the asset's current market value. The bonus for contributing an appreciated asset, though, is that you will not have to pay capital gains taxes on that asset. You get a deduction for the full market value without ever recognizing (and paying taxes on) the gain. That's two benefits for the price of one—a very rare treat in the tax code.

↪ **Example** Nicole purchased 10 shares of stock in August of Year 1 for $100 per share (for a total cost of $1,000). In September of Year 2 she sold the stock at a price of $300 per share, or $3,000. This transaction resulted in a long-term gain of $2,000. Her tax bracket for long-term capital gains was 15%, so she had to pay $300 in tax on the gain.

In Year 2 Nicole also donated $3,000 to the Red Cross, her favorite charity. She did so by writing a check. This donation gave her a $3,000 deduction, resulting in a tax savings of $840 (she's in the 28% marginal income tax bracket).

As an alternative, Nicole could have donated the $3,000 to the American Red Cross in the form of her shares of Google stock, instead of selling the shares and writing a check to the Red Cross. If she had done so, she would not have had to pay the $300 capital gains tax and would still have received the $840 in tax savings from the deduction. This would have brought a combined $1,140 tax savings, or 38% of the value of the contribution.

This special tax treatment is available only for assets that have *long-term* gain. Donations of assets that have been held for a year or less (short-term gains), or of an asset that would bring ordinary income when sold (such as inventory) are not given this special tax treatment.

The total value (of deductions) that comes from donations of appreciated assets cannot exceed 30% of your AGI for the year. Any deductions of appreciated assets that are more than 30% of AGI can be carried forward for up to five years for future deductions. After five years the carry-forward disappears.

○ **Tip**   Do not use this strategy for assets that would sell at a loss. In that case it would be more beneficial to sell the position, capture the loss so that you can use it on your tax return, and then donate the cash to charity for the deduction. It is exactly opposite to the strategy for donating positions with capital gains.

Maximizing the Tax Benefit of Your Gifts

Careful planning can help you make the most of your charitable deductions, especially in certain situations. One of those is when your taxable income is very close to the threshold between tax brackets. Another is when your total itemized deductions are close to the same value as the standard deduction. In both of these situations, you may benefit by carefully planning the timing of a contribution.

⮑ **Example**   Sarah is a sales manager for a phone book company. She gives 10% of her income to her church each year as a tithing contribution. She knows that she will receive an especially large bonus in January for the success the company has had this year. As she plans her taxes, she realizes the bonus will bump her from her usual 15% tax bracket up to the 25% tax bracket next year. She decides to hold off on making this year's contribution to her church until January 1, so that she can have two years' worth of charitable contribution deductions next year, when they will save her 25% in taxes instead of 15%.

To get the greatest charitable contribution deduction possible for you, you'll need to have a method to properly record what you give. If you already track your expenses, just add the "Charity" category to your system. If you don't normally track your expenses ... start! At least do so for tax-deductible items. Keep a list of your contributions in the place where you pay your bills. If you do a fair amount of driving for charitable organizations, keep a mileage log book in your car. In short, find a way to capture and record each occasion in which you give charitably in your everyday life.

Education Expenses

You'll Pay Dearly if You Play Hooky on This Chapter

You may ask why the government gives tax deductions and credits for higher-education expenses. One reason may be that a well-educated society is generally more prosperous, competitive, and successful. A more cynical rationalization might be that higher education generally leads to higher income, which leads to higher tax revenue—so the deductions and credits are a down payment on higher tax revenue for that person's lifetime. Whatever the reason may be, the result is that there are some great tax benefits available for those who pay for higher education.

If you have had expenses related to higher education during the year, you can likely use those expenses to reduce your tax bill. You can claim your qualified education expenses in a variety of ways, including three deductions, two credits, and a potential tax-free income source. You should consider the value of each of the possibilities *every year*, because many of the nuances between them can make one option better in a given year and another option better in the next. Compare the benefit of each option on your return by running the calculations for each option before deciding where to claim your expenses. The opportunities that are discussed in this chapter are:

- The Tuition and Fees Deduction
- Education as a Business Deduction

- The American Opportunity Credit
- The Lifetime Learning Credit
- The Student Loan Interest Deduction
- Student loan debt forgiveness

🗏 **Note**   With all of these deductions and credits there is no double-dipping allowed. You cannot claim the same expenses under multiple credits. All expenses that you claim must also be net of any tax-exempt assistance (such as a scholarship) as well as net of any withdrawals from qualified tuition savings programs (such as Coverdell or 529 plans).

The Tuition and Fees Deduction

The first way you can utilize your education expenses for tuition and fees is by taking them as an above-the-line deduction, which directly reduces your Adjusted Gross Income (AGI). For some people, the reduction in AGI that comes from taking this deduction is very beneficial because it can have a domino effect on other deductions and credits that would otherwise be reduced or eliminated by phase-outs. In these cases, using the deduction may actually be more beneficial than claiming the education credits (you can't claim both the Tuition and Fees Deduction and an education credit on the same tax return; you must choose one or the other). It is wise to prepare your tax return using both methods in order to determine the best option.

🗏 **Note**   As it currently stands, the Tuition and Fees Deduction will expire at the end of 2013. It is uncertain whether it will be reinstated by Congress after that. Be sure to verify the details (and existence) of the deduction beginning in 2014 before making decisions based on your ability to claim it.

The deduction is limited to a maximum of $4,000 of qualified expenses *per tax return* (not per student) for those with an AGI of $65,000 or less ($130,000 or less for couples). If your AGI is between $65,000 and $80,000 ($130,000 and $160,000 for couples) the maximum deduction was $2,000. If your AGI is above that range, the deduction is not available to you.

The income stair-step limitations that are placed on this deduction create some dramatic results on a tax return for those who cross over the threshold amounts. Unlike most phase-outs, which have a gradual reduction in their benefit, this deduction is reduced dramatically as soon as your AGI is $1 higher than the phase-out limits. This type of limitation can have a significant effect on your tax planning because just a dollar or two of excess AGI could reduce your deduction by $2,000! If it appears that your AGI will be close to the phase-out levels, it would be worth looking into a broad variety of measures to reduce your AGI to an amount lower than the threshold.

⇨ **Example**   Nelson spent $4,000 on tuition for night school while he continued to work full time during the day. Nelson's current salary is $66,000 per year, his AGI is $65,100, and he is in the 15% tax bracket. Since his AGI is $100 over the income limit for the Tuition and Fees Deduction, his allowable deduction is reduced by $2,000.

It would be extremely beneficial to Nelson if he found a way to reduce his AGI by $100, such as by making a $100 contribution to an IRA. Doing so would restore an additional $2,000 in deductions for his tuition *and* reduce his AGI by $100 for the IRA contribution. By putting $100 in an IRA he will have saved $315 in taxes! [($100 IRA deduction + $2,000 additional tuition deduction = $2,100) × 15% tax bracket = $315.]

👉 **Caution**   You cannot claim the American Opportunity Credit if the student is married and filing separately from his or her spouse, or if the student is claimed as a dependent on another person's tax return, if he or she were a non-resident alien for part of the year or if you claimed one of the education credits for that student on your tax return.

Education as a Business Deduction

Another way of deducting your education expenses is as a business expense. Recognizing these costs as a business expense will reduce your AGI as well as your self-employment tax. The added benefit of a lower self-employment tax can make this option very attractive.

Education expenses can be deducted as a business expense if the education *maintains or improves* the skills *required* in your business. The expenses cannot be deducted if the education is needed so you can meet the *minimum* education necessary to qualify for the trade or business based on laws, regulations, or standards of the profession. If the education qualifies as a deduction, all related expenses (including books, fees, and so on) can be deducted as well.

⇌ **Example** Leo is an attorney. To practice law in his state, he is required to have a law degree from a qualified institution and pass the bar exam. In addition, he must take continuing education courses each year to maintain his license. The cost of his law degree would not qualify as a business expense because it is necessary to meet the minimum requirements to qualify for his profession. However, the continuing education does qualify as a business expense because it helps him maintain or improve the skills required for his profession.

There are other ways to deduct education expenses through a business as well, such as with education assistance programs and scholarships. See Chapter 20 for more details.

The American Opportunity Credit

A third possible way to claim a tax benefit from your educational expenses is through the American Opportunity Credit (a modified version of the HOPE Scholarship Credit), which is set to expire (and revert to the HOPE Credit) after 2017. The maximum amount available for this credit is $2,500 *per student*, per year. (Note that this is different than the Tuition and Fees Deduction, which has a maximum deduction *per return*).

The credit can be claimed only for expenses incurred during the first four years of a student's post-secondary education (meaning after high school). Students who "extend" their college education to five or six years are out of luck. However, this is much better that the original HOPE Credit, which covered only the first two years of college education. The expenses that qualify for this credit are tuition, fees, books, supplies, and equipment that are necessary in order to obtain a degree. This is a much broader list of expenses than is available for the other education deductions and credits, in which only tuition and fees are allowable expenses.

The credit is calculated in the following way: 100% of the first $2,000 of qualified expenses, plus 25% of the next $2,000 in expenses.

⇌ **Example** Marcus is a part-time student and has an AGI of $40,000 (well below the phase-out limit for the credit). He spent $3,000 on tuition during the year. Marcus will be able to claim a credit of $2,250 [(100% of $2,000) + (25% of 1,000) = $2,250].

Up to 40% of the credit is refundable, meaning that it can be paid to you in the form of a refund even if you owe no taxes. The credit phases out when your AGI is greater than $80,000 if you're single, or $160,000 if you're married.

↩ **Example**   Shannon is in her second year of college. She has paid $12,000 in qualified education expenses during the year. Her income for the year was $25,000—well below the phase-out thresholds. Based on this information, Shannon can claim the maximum credit of $2,500.

In addition, her taxable income is only $8,000, which results in a tax liability of $800. The tax credit will eliminate the $800 in taxes, with $1,700 of the credit left unused. As much as 40% of the credit is refundable, or $1,000 in Shannon's case, so she will receive $1,000 in additional refunds because of this credit. The remaining $700 of the credit will go unused and will not carry over into future years.

If the American Opportunity Credit is claimed for a student on a tax return, the Lifetime Learning Credit may not be claimed for that same student and the Tuition and Fees Deduction may not be claimed for anyone on that same return in a given year.

You cannot claim the American Opportunity Credit if the student is married and filing separately from his or her spouse, or if the student is claimed as a dependent on another person's tax return. The student must have not been convicted of a felony drug possession or distribution offense. Finally, the student must also be enrolled at least half-time in a program that leads to a degree, certificate, or other recognized educational credentials.

○ **Tip**   If parents do not qualify to claim the American Opportunity Credit because their income is too high, they may choose to waive claiming the child as a dependent in order for the child to claim the credit. However, the child is still unable to claim herself as a dependent on her own return. In a narrow set of circumstances, this strategy could result in a lower overall tax burden.

The Lifetime Learning Credit

The fourth option for reducing your tax bill through qualified education expenses is found in the Lifetime Learning Credit. This is a non-refundable credit of up to a maximum of $2,000 *per tax return*, per year. Unlike the American Opportunity Credit, which is calculated on a per-student basis, the lifetime learning credit is calculated per tax return, no matter how many students you claim. The calculation for this credit is very simple: 20% of the first $10,000 of tuition paid during the year. The $10,000 limit is for all the students claimed on the tax return, added together.

○ **Tip**   If you have more than one student in your household, it is okay to claim some students under the American Opportunity Credit and others under the Lifetime Learning Credit. However, you *cannot* claim the same student under both credits.

This credit is much easier to qualify for than the American Opportunity Credit, because the student need only be enrolled in one class per year at a qualified educational institution, and the credit can be claimed for as many years as the student has tuition expenses (as opposed to the four-year limit for the American Opportunity Credit). The classes that are paid for do not even need to lead to a degree.

The lifetime learning credit is phased out when the taxpayer's AGI is between $50,000 and $60,000 for singles and between $100,000 and $120,000 for married couples.

○ **Tip**   Because of the income limits, high-income parents who can't claim the credits and whose income results in the phase-out of the dependency exemptions may consider waiving that exemption so the child can claim the credit. This would be a benefit only if the child has sufficient income tax liability that can be offset by the credit.

The Student Loan Interest Deduction

The interest paid on student loans is deductible as an above-the-line deduction, up to $2,500 per year. The loan must have been used solely for the purpose of paying for higher education expenses (not for doing other things, such as buying stock, as I once did as a risk-taking college student).

The deduction is subject to AGI-based phase-outs. The phase-out occurs when the Modified AGI (MAGI) is between $60,000 and $75,000 for single taxpayers, and is completely eliminated thereafter. For married couples the phase-out is between $125,000 and $155,000 MAGI.

In 2013 the law is also set to revert to a previous rule that allows the deduction to be taken only during the first 60 months of repayment.

✐ **Caution**   In case your tax brain was working overtime and you had come up with a great scheme of dodging taxes through interfamily loans, you need to know that the student loan interest deduction cannot be taken for loans made to the student by family members.

Student Loan Debt Forgiveness

In general, the tax code treats a forgiven debt as income—it is essentially the same thing as receiving income that you use to pay off the debt. However, there is an exception to this rule for the forgiveness of student loan debt in certain circumstances. As an incentive to induce students preparing for certain professions to work in underserved areas, the government has established a program of debt forgiveness in trade for a predetermined number of years in that underserved area. For example, if a medical student agrees to work as a doctor for a certain number of years in an underserved rural community, the government will, in turn, discharge that student's debt. In these specific, qualified situations the debt forgiveness is not counted as income and is not taxable.

Other Important Things to Know

Beyond the taxation of income, deductions, and credits, there are a few more important things that you should know. First, the Alternative Minimum Tax is always lurking in the shadows of your tax world. Be sure to know how it works and whether you are in danger of its wrath.

Second, be sure to understand the penalties and interest the IRS can hit you with, and how to avoid them. Third, it is important to know when to get help. There are times when professional advice can make a very big difference. And last, the Affordable Care Act reaches into nearly every aspect of your tax return. Be sure to understand how it will affect your return. Part VII has a chapter devoted to each of these topics, which you won't want to miss.

The Alternative Minimum Tax

Let the Fear and Trembling Begin

Every year more people are becoming aware of the existence of the Alternative Minimum Tax (AMT). Some of this awareness is the result of the media's focus on it. Unfortunately, though, many people become aware of this tax only because it has shown up on their tax return unexpectedly. Every year more middle-income Americans find themselves caught by the AMT, and it is painful when it catches you.

The AMT is like that kid in school who said he would share his candy with you if you did something for him and then, after you did it, he just laughed as he ran away. In the same way, the AMT reneges on the promise that certain deductions will reduce your taxes. After you sacrifice and plan for all of the tax-reduction strategies available to you and triumphantly get to the line on your tax return that shows your lowered tax liability, the AMT comes in and tells you that your tax is not high enough and takes away some of your deductions to increase your tax. Are you angry yet?

The AMT was first levied in 1970. It was originally designed to target *155* ultra-high-income households that had little to no tax liability because of how they had structured their deductions. The tax has been modified several times over the last four decades, but the income thresholds that trigger the tax have *not* been indexed for inflation. As a result, millions of not-so-high-income households are now affected by the tax. If it were not for the one-year patches that Congress enacts each year, many millions more would be affected.

⇨ **Example** Spencer is a single man who works on a road crew for a living. He makes $23 per hour, or about $48,000 per year. Even though his income is far from "high," he is subject to the AMT.

The AMT was originally designed to make wealthy individuals who had found a way to pay no income tax begin to pay their "fair share." It is a complicated system of taxation that has its own separate formula, independent of the normal income tax calculation.

Many of the itemized deductions allowed in the calculation of regular income tax are eliminated in the AMT calculations. State income taxes, sales tax, and real-estate taxes are not deductible. Interest on loans for boats or RVs, as well as some home equity interest, is not deductible. All miscellaneous itemized deductions subject to the 2% Adjusted Gross Income (AGI) floor are taken away for the AMT as well. The medical-expense limitation is increased to 10% of AGI instead of 7.5%. Income from certain municipal bonds that is not taxed in the regular tax is added back for the AMT. And so it goes down the line. In short, many of the things that taxpayers rely on to reduce their tax liability are omitted in the calculation of the AMT.

If you use the standard deduction, you will need to be concerned with the AMT if you are single and have an AGI above $51,900, or if you are married and have an AGI over $80,800 in 2013. After many years of annual bickering over these thresholds, Congress has finally indexed them to increase every year, based on inflation. If you itemize your deductions, you will be affected by the AMT if your AGI, minus the *allowable* AMT itemized deductions, is above the previously listed numbers. As you can see, these AGI numbers apply to many who are not exactly "high-income" taxpayers.

The tax is a flat tax of 26% or 28%, depending on your income. If the calculation of the AMT turns out to be higher than the calculation of your regular income tax, you will owe the higher amount. To make matters worse, some tax credits can't offset the AMT—compounding the difference between the AMT and the regular tax.

If your AGI will subject you to the AMT, you should consider several things in your tax planning. First, ensure that any "tax-free" municipal bond or bond fund that you purchase includes no "special activity" bonds. The interest from those bonds will be included in the AMT calculation—meaning that these "tax-free bonds" will not be tax-free. The investment company you use to buy the bonds can tell you whether the individual bonds, or those held in your bond fund, are AMT-free.

The second thing you should be aware of in your tax planning is that the very deductions you claim when itemizing deductions on Schedule A (such as state taxes) may be what trigger the AMT. Shifting where you claim these deductions, or when you incur the expenses, can affect the amount of AMT you will owe.

Third, be aware of the deductions that *are* allowed under the AMT. Home mortgage interest and charitable-giving deductions are fully allowed against the AMT. Above-the-line deductions are also allowed and will reduce this tax. Focus on increasing deductions that minimize the AMT and reducing those that don't, and you may find that you have a better result in the end.

Here are some specific strategies to reduce your AMT:

- Pay medical expenses on a pretax basis. You can do this by using a medical reimbursement plan, Health Reimbursement Arrangement (HRA), or Flexible Spending Account (FSA). You can also do this by contributing to a Health Savings Account (HSA), as discussed in Chapter 26. In this way you can deduct medical expenses that are less than the 10%-of-AGI floor that the AMT requires. You can also thus reduce your AGI, thereby reducing your tax.

- Ask your employer to set up an "accountable" employee expense reimbursement plan. The "unreimbursed employee expenses" deduction is not allowed under the AMT. Even if your employer is unwilling to reimburse those expenses, see if the company will reduce your income by that amount and then reimburse you. In this way the employer will save money in employment taxes, and you will save money in employment taxes, income taxes, and AMT taxes.

- In certain situations you should take the standard deduction instead of itemizing, even when the itemized deductions are larger. This is because some of those deductions are eliminated when the AMT is calculated. Run the numbers both ways to see which brings the better result.

- Take as many business-expense deductions as you legiti-mately can. They are fully deductible this way, and with them you avoid losing the deductions under the AMT. You could do this, for example, by deducting a portion of your real-estate tax as an expense when you claim a business use of your home.

- Minimize any overpayment of state taxes. If you paid additional state taxes in order to reduce your federal tax and then receive a state refund on the extra, this strategy will backfire if you are subject to the AMT.

- The preferred tax rates on capital gains and qualified dividends are not changed by the AMT calculations. These sources of income become even more beneficial in the context of the AMT. Increasing these sources of income and reducing others will reduce your AMT.

- Time your income and expenses with the AMT in mind. This can prove very helpful if you're at risk of being subject to the AMT. If you can postpone income and accelerate specific deductions in a particular year, you could avoid the AMT in that year, and even if you end up paying the AMT in the next year, the net effect over two years may be better.

The AMT is a very complicated tax. It has so many moving parts and variables that it is hard to fully understand even for many tax *professionals*, much less other people who don't devote their life's work to taxes. The thorns are so numerous that I cannot fully list them here. If you are at risk of being significantly affected by the AMT, I highly recommend professional advice.

Penalties and Interest

Be Careful—They Carry a Punch

Ignore them long enough and they will go away, right? Not if you're talking about talking about the IRS or the penalties and interest that they can levy. The longer you ignore them, the worse it gets and the worse they get. I have had several new clients come to me who are at the point of receiving serious threats from the IRS because they have not filed tax returns for a few years. Once we compile all of their missing returns it is often the case that they owe more money from penalties and interest than they owed in taxes!

Not all penalties are equal either. Certain penalties can be relatively benign, while others are downright vicious. It is good to understand the consequences of each of these penalties so that you can make informed decisions in your dealings with the IRS. This chapter covers the following topics:

- Failure to File Penalty
- Failure to Pay Penalty
- Underpayment of Estimated Tax Penalty
- Interest
- Early withdrawal from retirement accounts
- Unqualified withdrawal from a Health Savings Account (HSA)

- Excess contribution to retirement accounts
- Penalty abatement

Failure to File Penalty

One thing I try to make very clear to people is that even when you don't have money to pay your taxes *you should still file a return.* Not filing a return is a terrible mistake. One reason is that once you file a return the IRS's clock starts ticking on the amount of time it has to audit or adjust your return. Once you file the return the IRS has only three years from the date of filing, or the due date (whichever is later) to audit your return (assuming you have not made serious omissions or committed fraud). If you do not file a return, the IRS has until the day you die (actually, a little longer) to assess the taxes it believes you owe!

The second reason to file a return is that the Failure to File Penalty is very steep. The penalty is 5% of the taxes due for *every month* (or portion thereof) that the return is late. The maximum penalty is 25%, so if you are more than five months late you will receive the maximum 25% penalty.

The best defense against incurring this penalty is to file for an automatic six-month extension of time to prepare and file your return *before* the original due date of the return, which is April 15. This extension gives you up to October 15 to pull everything together. Be sure to file a return by that extended date, though, because if you file after it the extension becomes void and the failure to file penalty time line reverts back to the original due date of the return.

The penalties for not paying the taxes you owe are much smaller than the penalty for not filing (and you will eventually pay for both whether you file or not). For this reason you should always file the return before the extended due date and save yourself an automatic 25% increase in the amount you owe (plus interest).

If you are owed a refund on your tax return there is no Failure to File Penalty, since the penalty is based on the amount that you owe. However, you must file within three years of the due date for the return in order to receive the refund; otherwise the IRS gets to keep it (and is still able to come after you to file a return). While you may wonder why someone would not file a return if he/she is owed a refund, I have actually seen it a surprising number of times.

Failure to Pay Penalty

If you are unable to pay the taxes that you owe by April 15 you will be subject to the Failure to Pay Penalty. This penalty is 0.5% of the tax that you owe, charged every month (or portion thereof) on the outstanding balance until the tax is paid in full. There is no maximum amount that can be charged for this penalty—it will continue to accumulate indefinitely until you pay the tax.

✔ Caution There is a common misunderstanding that filing for an extension of time to prepare your tax return also gives you an extension of time to pay your taxes. This is not true. Any taxes that you owe at the time of filing (after the original due date) will be subject to the Failure to Pay Penalty. For this reason you should always make your best guess about the amount of tax you will owe and pay that amount by April 15, even if you will file your tax return at a later date.

Underpayment of Estimated Tax Penalty

The tax code calls for a pay-as-you-go system. You are required to pay taxes throughout the year based on what your total tax bill will be at the end of the year. If your estimate is wrong and you pay too little, you will pay a penalty on the difference.

➥ Example Max's total tax obligation is $12,000 at the end of the year, which means he should have paid $1,000 per month (or really $3,000 per quarter) in estimated payments as he went through the year. Max underestimated his tax obligation and only paid $8,000, so he will pay penalties on the $4,000 shortfall.

The penalty is essentially an interest payment. The penalty rate is set each quarter and is based on the going interest rate for treasury bills. Your penalty is calculated against the total quarterly shortfall. The quarterly payments are due on April 15, June 15, September 15, and January 15. The late date of April 15 allows you to complete your previous year's tax return so that you have a number to base your payments on. The late date of January 15 allows you time to figure out your actual total income for the year. The other two dates (June and September) fall on the last month of each quarter. Why don't they just use April, July, October, and January to make it every three months? Who knows? Maybe it would make things too simple.

➥ Example Max underpaid his estimated payments by $1,000 per quarter. He will have to calculate the penalty on each quarterly payment separately, based on the number of days between the due date of that payment and the day that the payment was actually made (i.e., 365 days between the first underpayment of $1,000 that was due on April 15 and the actual payment date of April 15 the following year; 304 days between June 15 and April 15; 212 days between September 15 and April 15; 90 days between January 15 and April 15). Each of these numbers of days would be used to calculate the pro-rated penalty that should be charged on each under payment. If the penalty rate were 4% during this time, Max's total late penalty would be $106.

As you can see from the example, this penalty is not tremendously punitive. If you are making estimated payments that are fairly close to the real amount you will owe, not having certainty is nothing to lose sleep over. In fact, I know some people who feel like they can earn more money from their investments than the IRS will charge them for penalties, so they just wait to pay their taxes each year and pay whatever penalty comes. I don't necessarily recommend that, but I can see why they do it.

If trying to estimate what your tax payments should be each quarter sounds like too much work, the good news is that the IRS has provided a safe harbor. As long as your estimated payments equal at least 90% of what you actually owe, there is no penalty. As an alternative, you can pay 100% of your tax obligation from the previous year, which will eliminate estimated payment penalties for you—no matter what your actual bill ends up being. If your Adjusted Gross Income (AGI) was over $150,000 you must pay 110% of the previous year's tab in order to take advantage of this safe harbor.

Another time in which no penalties are charged is if the amount you owe after estimated payments is less than $1,000. This is the case regardless of whether you have paid 90% of your total bill, or 100%/110% of last year's bill.

These estimated payments can be made through withholdings from your paycheck, or through making quarterly payments directly to the IRS. An important note is that the IRS considers all withholdings to have been paid evenly throughout the year, regardless of when they were actually paid. It is especially important for business owners to know that they could conceivably make no estimated payments during the year, then pay themselves through payroll at the end of the year, withholding a sufficient amount to cover the estimated payments. In doing so the IRS would treat the payments as if they had been made on time and not calculate penalties on the first three quarterly payments.

Finally, if you own a business and your income is highly variable, you are not required to make payments of equal amounts each quarter. What you may do instead is use your year-to-date income numbers each quarter and annualize them to estimate what your tax payment should be, based on those annualized numbers.

Interest

On top of all of the other potential penalties and interest that may be levied on you, the IRS will also charge you interest on the tax you owe. The interest will compound and accumulate until your entire bill is paid. The interest rate is based on the rates of current treasury bills and is set on a quarterly basis.

Early Withdrawal from Retirement Accounts

The government does not want you to take money out of your qualified retirement accounts before you reach retirement age (meaning, you remove money from the account before you reach the age of 59½). If they did not prevent you from removing funds from your retirement account you would be able to manipulate your tax return by claiming deductions for contributions in a high-tax year and then withdrawing those contributions in a lower-tax year. For this reason the IRS has imposed a 10% penalty tax for withdrawing money early from a qualified account.

✦ **Caution**   In the case of the Savings Incentive Match Plan for Employees (SIMPLE) IRA, the 10% early withdrawal penalty is actually increased to 25% if the money is moved out of the plan in the first two years.

📖 **Note**   457(b) plans are the only type of qualified retirement account that does not have a 10% penalty for early withdrawals.

The tax code does provide opportunities to make penalty-free withdrawals in certain circumstances. These exceptions available for employer-sponsored retirement plans are:

- Withdrawals that are rolled into another retirement plan within 60 days (this may be done only once per year)

- Distributions upon the death or permanent disability of the account owner

- Distributions upon separation of employment if the account owner is 55 years old (or older)

- Distributions to a spouse by a court order in a divorce

- Distributions up to the amount of deductible medical expenses during the year (whether or not deductions are itemized on the return)

- Distributions due to an IRS levy (at least they don't *penalize* you when they take your retirement money)

- Distributions made as substantially equal periodic payments over the expected lifetime of the owner

> ✎ **Caution** The exception which allows for "substantially equal" withdrawals of the owner's expected lifetime can be very tricky to orchestrate and carries significant financial risk. If you plan to withdraw funds under this rule, be sure to hire a very competent professional to help you.

For non-employer–sponsored, traditional IRA accounts, all of the aforementioned exceptions apply, except the one regarding separation from service after age 55. In addition to that list there are a few other times when you can remove money from a traditional IRA without incurring the penalty. They include:

- Insurance premiums for unemployed individuals

- First-time home buyer's expenses. (The exception is for withdrawals up to a maximum of $10,000, and only once in an individual's lifetime. It is also worth noting that a "first-time" home buyer is one who has not owned a home in the previous two years—not necessarily limited to the truly first-time buyer.)

- Education expenses (discussed more in Chapter 13)

> ○ **Tip** If you need to withdraw money from an employer-sponsored plan, such as a 401(k), but do not qualify for the exceptions, you may still have another option. If you are no longer working for the employer who sponsored the plan you can first roll the money into an IRA and then withdraw the money under one of the IRA penalty exceptions.

If you *are* still employed with the company, check with the Human Resources Department to see if the retirement plan allows for loans to be taken from the funds. Many plans do allow for loans, which gives you the opportunity to withdraw funds without incurring taxes or penalties.

To qualify as a first-time home buyer, you can purchase the home for yourself, your spouse, your children, your grandchildren, or a living ancestor of you or your spouse. The "first-time" status is based on the *purchaser*, not the resident or owner.

The first-time home buyer exception is for a principal residence. You could own a rental property and not own a principal residence, and you would still qualify for the exception when you buy a new home.

When withdrawing money from a retirement account, be sure to withhold enough taxes from the withdrawal to cover your additional tax liability at the end of the year, in order to avoid penalties and interest that are imposed on late payments of taxes. Also, If you take an early distribution be sure to pay for all your medical bills and other "exceptions" before the year's end to ensure that you utilize as much of the exemption as possible.

Unqualified Withdrawal from a Health Savings Account (HSA)

If you remove money from an HSA account for something other than qualified medical expenses before you are 59½, you will pay a 20% penalty on that withdrawal. However, it is important to note that the IRS only asks you to report your total qualified medical expenses and your total withdrawals during the year. So, if you accidentally use your HSA debit card at the gas station, just be sure that you pay for an equal amount of qualified medical expenses during the year using non-HSA money. If you do so, the two expenses will cancel out and you will not need to pay the penalty. Of course, I don't recommend this be your standard operating procedure. For information on what medical expenses qualify, see Chapter 26.

Excess Contribution to Retirement Accounts

If you accidentally contribute more than the maximum amount allowed to an IRA or employer-sponsored retirement plan, be sure to correct that mistake as soon as possible. If you correct the error by April 15 of the following year you will not owe any penalties.

⌕ **Note** When removing excess contributions from a qualified retirement account you must also remove any gains that are attributable to those contributions. This eliminates the temptation to overfund an account at the beginning of each year and keep the gains in the account.

Penalty Abatement

The IRS is allowed to waive or reduce some of the penalties but not others. They key to getting penalties abated is having a really good reason—one that shows you had reasonable cause and that your reason for being penalized was not caused by willful neglect. The IRS considers requests for penalty abatement on a case-by-case basis, but a few things will play in your favor:

- There was a specific incident or event that *prevented* you from complying with the rules (a great example would be that you were in a coma from April 1 to May 1 and unable to file your return).

- You complied with the rules as soon as you were able to, or once the error was discovered.

- You have a good history of complying with the tax laws.

- For an accuracy-related penalty, you can show that you had good cause for your original position and that you were acting in good faith.

If your penalties are significant and you believe that you have a good reason for them to be abated, it may be worthwhile to hire a professional who is experienced in penalty abatements to help you.

Do It Yourself, or Hire a Professional?

Either Way, This Chapter Will Help You Get the Best Results

As you have read through this book, you have followed me into the brambles of your taxberry bush as I've held up the branches and showed you some of the available fruit. There are surely more berries available in your unique situation, but you are now, I hope, much more familiar with some of the better clusters and how to pick them without getting caught by the thorns.

As you read you may have felt the stirrings of a newfound passion for taxberry picking. Or perhaps what I have done is help you recognize the need to hire a professional picker. Whether you choose to prepare your taxes yourself or to hire a professional, the knowledge you acquire from this book will help you nurture and develop your taxberries and thus enjoy the fruits of a more plentiful harvest.

No exact formula will determine whether you need to hire a professional or do it yourself. I can say, though, that certain tax situations can become very complicated, very quickly. For these, you would probably benefit from professional help. You should seriously consider hiring a professional picker if:

- You own a business.

- Your Adjusted Gross Income (AGI) is near some of the thresholds that limit or eliminate deductions and credits.

- You are (or are close to being) subject to the Alternative Minimum Tax (AMT).

- You are able to take advantage of some of the strategies in this book but are uncertain of how they work or don't have time to learn more about them.

- You itemized deductions and they are very close to the standard deduction.

- You have multiple sources of income (this is especially significant if you have several business-related sources of income).

The greater the number of items in this list that apply to you, the greater the likelihood that you would benefit from the help of a professional tax preparer.

If you decide to hire a professional, you'll want to maximize your return on investment. To do so, it is critical that you understand your professional preparer's work circumstances.

The Limits of the Harvest

One of my family's frustrations during berry-picking season is the scarcity of time. The best berries can be picked only during three to four weeks in a season. This means we must either devote all of our spare time to getting as many berries as possible or sacrifice the number of berries we pick in order to have a life apart from the harvest. This decision becomes difficult because we know that to harvest enough berries to make jam, syrup, and frozen fruit for the year will take a tremendous amount of time—but we really do want those results.

The professional taxberry picker faces the same obstacle: the amount of time available for the harvest. Tax preparers have a very narrow window of time to harvest all of the fruit they can. In most cases that window comes in a 10-week period between February 1 and April 15. It is in this window of time that they have to pick berries for all of their clients. It is also the window of time in which many professional tax preparers make between 80% and 90% of their income.

Because many tax preparers are paid a set price per return, or per hour, and they have two and a half months to prepare as many returns as they can, they have a great incentive to turn their tax preparation business into a well-oiled assembly line of tax returns. They work as many hours as humanly possible in those 10 weeks, and by the end of the season they are physically, mentally, and emotionally exhausted—unable to look at another taxberry bush for weeks. They have picked *a lot* of bushes, but they have likely missed some of the hidden berries along the way.

The sincere desire of most tax preparers is to do the best job they can for each client. But in the heat of the season they simply don't have time to "dig deep into the thorny bush." Because they're experienced, they will almost certainly harvest more berries and avoid more thorns than you would doing it alone, but unless you climb into the brambles yourself, and know where to look, there is no way for you to know if they have gotten everything or if they have cleaned off only the visible fruit. This is a significant problem, but I offer a solution.

Step One: Know Your Taxberry Bush

Study this book and others to become as knowledgeable as you can about your personal taxberry bush. Become familiar with the main components of your tax return so you can understand the relative benefit of each strategy. Then, familiarize yourself with each of the strategies and determine which ones apply to you.

Taking this first step will help you recognize the berries on your own bush and know which will be of greatest worth. This will help you better prepare and cultivate your harvest in coming years since you can enhance so many tax strategies by paying close attention to them *throughout* the year. Your knowledge will also help you point out those berries to the picker *before* the harvest season.

Step Two: Use the Off Season

Work with your tax preparer in the *off season*. Ask for an analysis of your individual situation and a search for the hidden fruit. Bring up ideas you have gathered from studying this book, and let your tax preparer crunch the numbers. If you don't expect a large refund (or need it soon), ask your preparer to file an extension so he/she can spend more time preparing your return carefully. Great things can come from this.

To continue with the berry bush analogy, an expert in blackberry plants can do many things in the off-harvest season to improve the quantity and quality of the fruit on the bush. He can ask questions about your habits and practices.

He can show you where to prune, which branches to lift or tie, and how and when to water. What is more, as he is doing this, he will become very familiar with *your* taxberry bush. Yours will no longer be one of many that all look the same. He will have studied your taxberry bush and seen exactly where the berries are growing and be ready to quickly gather all of them at harvest time.

So it is with taxes. When I have had the opportunity to analyze and plan for an individual's tax situation, I know exactly what to do when I prepare the return. During the year I am able to spend all of the necessary time to find and cultivate the hidden fruit. I can make recommendations on how to structure financial affairs in a way that will make a significant difference at harvest time.

Enjoying Your Harvest's Bounty

In summary, study this book to understand your taxberry bush better. If you decide to hire a professional, consult with him or her in the off season on how to prepare and cultivate your fruit. Then, when the harvest comes it will be plentiful. It will be worth far more than the price paid for the advice, and the fruit will be very sweet. Happy picking!

Tax Implications of Health Care Reform

Everything You Need to Know

Many people are wondering how new taxes created in the Affordable Care Act (a.k.a. ObamaCare) will affect them. In one way or another, this new bill will touch everyone. For some, the impact will be significant. Although some pieces of this chapter are scattered throughout this book in areas that the new law affects (while other parts are found only in this chapter), it is important to put the whole picture together in one chapter because of the broad impact the ACA and its provisions will have on so many people.

Before getting into the details, you should understand that the most significant tax changes that come from this new law begin to take effect in 2013 and later. I have organized this chapter into three main sections, based on who is affected by various parts of the law. The three sections focus on:

- The effect on individuals
- The effect on businesses
- The effect on health insurance plans

The Effect on Individuals

The key revenue raiser in the bill is the Medicare surtax (surtax is a tax added to another tax). There are actually *two* surtaxes. The first is an additional 0.9% tax on all wages and self-employment income ("earned income") over a certain threshold. The second is a 3.8% tax on "unearned income."

➥ **Example**   Archie is a single, self-employed investment advisor. He spends a lot of his free time working on his personal investment portfolio. His total income for the year is $300,000, of which $250,000 came from his business and $50,000 from his investments. Because of the new law, Archie will pay:

- ✓   A $450 surtax on his self-employment earnings, because they exceeded the threshold.

- ✓   A $1,900 surtax on his "unearned" investment income.

The 0.9% surtax of *earned* income will be assessed on all earned income above $200,000 for single individuals, and above $250,000 for married couples who file jointly (note the hefty marriage penalty). It is important to understand two key elements of this surtax. First, the thresholds are based on *earnings*, not on Adjusted Gross Income (AGI) or taxable income. The fact that it is based on earnings, rather than on AGI or taxable income, can result in a significantly higher total tax. Second, for those who have self-employment income, this surtax is *not* deductible as part of the usual deduction of one half of the self-employment tax, which will result in higher *income* taxes as well.

𝄃 **Note**   The $200,000 and $250,000 thresholds are not indexed for inflation. Each year, this new tax will affect significantly more people, simply because of inflation over of time.

The 3.8% surtax of *unearned* income can be even more significant than the tax on earned income. One reason is that this tax on unearned income is a very significant shift in the tax rules because it applies "employment" taxes to income that doesn't come from employment. Before the health care reform bill was enacted, Medicare and Social Security taxes (of which these two new surtaxes are a part) applied only to earned income. This change may signal a significant shift in the thinking of lawmakers: they are showing a willingness to apply employment taxes to income that does not come from employment, in order to gather more revenue.

> **Note** This new surtax will apply to unearned income such as interest, dividends, capital gains, rental income, royalties, and nonqualified annuities. However, it will not apply to income from retirement plan distributions (IRAs, 401(k)s, and so on) or to tax-exempt interest.

This tax on unearned income will be levied on taxpayers who have a Modified AGI (MAGI) greater than $200,000 for single individuals, or $250,000 for married individuals. The 3.8% tax is applied to the smaller of their investment income, or the amount by which their AGI exceeds the threshold.

> ⮑ **Example** Doug and Maxine have an AGI of $280,000 and an investment income of $35,000. The 3.8% surtax will be applied to $30,000 of their income ($280,000 AGI − $250,000 threshold = $30,000, which is smaller than the $35,000 of investment income).
>
> Scott has an AGI of $230,000 and an investment income of $10,000. The surtax will apply to the $10,000 of investment income because it is a smaller number than the amount by which his total AGI exceeds the threshold ($30,000).

This new 3.8% tax will have an especially heavy impact on capital gains income, and even more so on dividend income. With the maximum capital gains tax at 20% and this 3.8% surtax on top of these other tax increases, the maximum taxes on capital gains is be 23.8%—a 60% increase over the previous 15% maximum rates applied to these income sources.

As you can see, if your AGI is above $200,000 or $250,000, this new tax will noticeably affect your marginal income. Keep these changes in mind during your long-term tax planning, giving special attention to the portions of income you'll expect to get from dividends, self-employment income, and tax-exempt interest.

Reduction in Medical Expense Deductions

Beginning in 2013, allowable itemized deductions for medical expenses will be reduced for those under 65 years old—effectively increasing taxes for those who deduct medical expenses. Previously, if you itemized deductions on Schedule A, you were allowed to deduct all medical expenses in excess of 7.5% of your AGI, as long as you were not subject to the Alternative Minimum Tax (AMT). Beginning in 2013, only medical expenses that exceed 10% of AGI will be deductible.

↪ **Example**   Mary and Jon have an AGI of $80,000. Their total medical expenses for the year add up to $7,800. Under previous law, they could take an itemized deduction of $1,800, the amount of expenses that exceed the 7.5% floor, which in their case is $6,000 ($80,000 × 0.075 = $6,000). Beginning in 2013, under the same circumstances, Mary and Jon could deduct no medical expenses because their new floor would be $8,000 (10% of AGI), which is greater than their $7,800 of expenses. If their combined federal and state marginal tax brackets equaled 35%, they would end up paying an additional $540 in taxes (0.30 × $1,800 that they could no longer deduct = $540).

Penalty Tax for the Uninsured

All insurance programs need a mix of healthy individuals along with the sick ones in order to spread out the cost of coverage over more people. For this reason, the creators of this bill needed a way to encourage those who don't need insurance to buy it anyway—or at least to pay into the system if they refuse.

Beginning in 2014, if you're not insured at the minimum level of coverage dictated by the government, you will pay a penalty tax. In 2014 the penalty equals 1% of all income in excess of the filing thresholds (which in 2012 were $9,750 for single individuals, $19,500 for married couples). The uninsured pay a minimum penalty of $95 per adult and $47.50 per child younger than age 18, if the 1%-of-income calculation comes out to be less than those amounts. The maximum penalty is $285 per person, no matter how high their income.

The penalty increases dramatically over the following two years (2015 and 2016). In 2015 the penalty is 2% of income, with a minimum penalty of $325 and a maximum penalty of $975. In 2016 the maximum penalty increases to $2,085, and it is indexed to increase with inflation each year thereafter.

Insurers will send 1099 forms to the IRS to prove coverage of those with individually purchased plans. If your insurance is provided by an employer, the value of your insurance will be reported on your W-2. Using these two methods the IRS can verify that each person is covered by a qualifying health insurance plan so that they can in turn charge the penalty to those who are not.

○ **Tip**   If the penalty goes unpaid, the IRS cannot charge additional penalties or interest on the original penalty. Nor can the IRS file a levy or lien to collect the penalty. Their only means of collection is to withhold the amounts owed from future refunds. This nuance will make for some interesting tax planning for a few people out there, I am sure.

Increased Penalty on Health Savings Account (HSA) and Flexible Spending Account (FSA) Withdrawals

If you have an HSA or an FSA, you'll want to understand two important changes the new bill makes in those accounts. First, as of January 1, 2011, the cost of over-the-counter medicines and drugs are not allowable expenses for HSAs and FSAs, *unless you have a prescription*. For example, if your doctor writes a prescription for fish oil, though that prescription is not required to purchase the supplement, it makes it okay to purchase the fish oil with your HSA or FSA funds without penalty.

○ **Tip**   Save a copy of your prescription with your tax records in case of an audit. And of course, keep in mind that your doctor could write a prescription for many things that wouldn't qualify as a medical expense, regardless of the prescription (such as a prescription to buy a big-screen TV to help you alleviate stress).

The health care reform bill does not require a prescription for deductible medical expenses such as medical devices, glasses, contact lenses, and so on. The rules regarding those items remain the same as they have been in previous years.

The second major change is that if you spend funds from your HSA on non-allowable expenses, you will pay a 20% penalty (in addition to income taxes)—twice as much as the former penalty. These changes began as of January 1, 2011.

Refundable Credit for Low-Income Households to Purchase Insurance

The bill includes a refundable credit to low-income households to help them fund the purchase of insurance through the government "health exchanges." The value of the credit will be based on a percentage of the household's income. The credit will be sent directly from the Treasury to the Exchange, so it will not come in the form of money to the individual.

To qualify for the credit, your income will need to be between 100% and 400% of the federal poverty level. In 2012, a family of four would qualify for the credit if their income fell between $23,550 and $94,200 (between $11,490 and $45,960 for a single individual). Families with incomes *below* these levels do not qualify for the credit because they would qualify for other government assistance for their health care needs.

The Effect on Businesses

Many provisions in this bill will affect employers to varying degrees, based on the size of their company. I here focus only on the effects this bill will have on businesses that employ 50 or fewer people.

Health Exchanges

By 2014, each state is required to have a health insurance exchange—a place for individuals and businesses to buy insurance. These exchanges will be government regulated and will offer four plans. The major difference between plans will be the co-pay percentage: 60%, 70%, 80%, and 90% for each plan, respectively. Each plan will provide an out-of-pocket maximum equal to the out-of-pocket maximum for HSAs (which in 2013 is $6,250 for individuals and $12,500 for families). Exchanges can also offer a fifth plan, which would be a "catastrophic coverage" plan for young adults. It would offer a bare-bones coverage at a lower cost (perhaps "bare-bones coverage" is a poor choice of words in this context).

Penalties and Limitations

Companies that offer plans with benefits that are too generous will pay a heavy excise tax. Beginning in 2018, a 40% tax will be levied on "excess" benefits offered by the business (unions excluded). A company's benefits are "excessive" when individual benefits exceed $6,580 and family benefits exceed $17,750 (these are estimates of the 2010 inflation-adjusted numbers that will go into effect). The benefits used in this calculation include the cost of premiums, reimbursements from HRAs and FSAs (even when funded by employee contributions), and employer contributions to HSAs. The dollar amounts of the excess benefit thresholds are indexed for inflation.

Beginning in 2013, FSAs will be a capped at $2,500 per year, indexed for inflation thereafter.

Tax Credit

To help cover the cost of insurance coverage, a credit is available to small businesses during the first five years of the new bill. For businesses with 10 or fewer employees and an average employee salary of less than $25,000, the credit is 50% of the cost of premiums (or of the average cost in the state, if lower) for the coverage of employees (but not for the cost of covering the owners). The credit is only available for those companies that purchase their insurance through the government exchanges. It is quickly reduced for companies that have more than 10 employees, as well as for businesses that pay their employees better wages. The credit completely disappears if the average employee wages are higher than $50,000 or if the company employs more than 25 people. The owners and family members of owners are not counted in the employee number or in the average wages.

To qualify for the credit, the employer must pay at least 50% of employee premiums. The credit can be used against the AMT, but it is nonrefundable, so the employer will receive no help in paying for the insurance if he owes no taxes.

○ **Tip**   This credit is not as beneficial as other credits. This is because the credit takes the place of the health insurance costs the business could have deducted if it had claimed no credit. This increases the company's taxable income and thus reduces some of the credit's benefit—at times making it not worth taking the credit at all.

Wellness Programs

The bill will provide some kind of incentive, through grants, for small businesses to establish workplace wellness plans. The details are still to be determined, but the grants will be available for up to five years to businesses that have 100 or fewer employees who had no such plan before the bill was signed.

The Effect on Health Insurance Plans

In addition to the changes that were mentioned in the "Health Exchanges" section earlier in this chapter, the bill makes a few other significant changes to all health insurance plans. First, all children of employees must be offered coverage up to age 26, even if they are not dependents or students, and even if they are married. The only exception to this rule is if they have coverage through another employer plan—but beginning in 2014 even that won't matter.

Next, the health insurance plans cannot exclude anyone because of pre-existing conditions. This is the case for children younger than age 19 right now, and the rule will be applied to adults beginning in 2014. Adult children (ages 19–26) may face a waiting period for certain pre-existing conditions.

Finally, maximum lifetime benefit limits will be prohibited for nearly all services. This new rule is currently in effect for essential services, and it will be in effect for other services beginning in 2014.

I

Index

Get the eBook for only $10!

> Now you can take the weightless companion with you anywhere, anytime. Your purchase of this book entitles you to 3 electronic versions for only $10.

This Apress title will prove so indispensible that you'll want to carry it with you everywhere, which is why we are offering the eBook in 3 formats for only $10 if you have already purchased the print book.

Convenient and fully searchable, the PDF version enables you to easily find and copy code—or perform examples by quickly toggling between instructions and applications. The MOBI format is ideal for your Kindle, while the ePUB can be utilized on a variety of mobile devices.

Go to www.apress.com/promo/tendollars to purchase your companion eBook.

Apress®
THE EXPERT'S VOICE™

Other Apress Business Titles You Will Find Useful

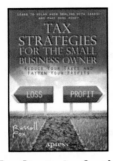

Tax Strategies for the Small Business Owner
Fox
978-1-4302-4842-2

Control Your Retirement Destiny
Anspach
978-1-4302-5022-7

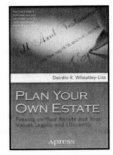

Plan Your Own Estate
Wheatley-Liss
978-1-4302-4494-3

Know and Grow the Value of Your Business
McDaniel
978-1-4302-4785-2

Fixing and Flipping Real Estate
Boardman
978-1-4302-4644-2

Startup
Ready
978-1-4302-4218-5

Getting a Business Loan
Kiisel
978-1-4302-4998-6

It's Splitsville
Gross
978-1-4302-5716-5

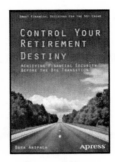

Healthcare, Insurance, and You
Zamosky
978-1-4302-4953-5

Available at www.apress.com

CPSIA information can be obtained at www.ICGtesting.com
Printed in the USA

9 781430 263104